the
good
little
girl

She stayed quiet for a very long time...

the
good
little
girl

She stayed quiet for a very long time...

BIG SKY PUBLISHING
www.bigskypublishing.com.au

Annette Stephens

Big Sky Publishing Pty Ltd
PO Box 303, Newport, NSW 2106, Australia
Phone: 1300 364 611
Fax: (61 2) 9918 2396
Email: info@bigskypublishing.com.au
Web: www.bigskypublishing.com.au

Cover design and typesetting: Think Productions

National Library of Australia Cataloguing-in-Publication entry (pbk.)
Author: Stephens, Annette.
Title: The good little girl : she stayed quiet for a very long time- / Annette Stephens.
ISBN: 9781922132024 (pbk.)
Subjects: Stephens, Annette--Childhood and youth.
          Child abuse--Australia--Biography.
          Abused children--Australia--Biography.
          Cult members--Australia--Biography.
Dewey Number: 362.76092

National Library of Australia Cataloguing-in-Publication entry (ebook)
Author: Stephens, Annette.
Title: The good little girl : she stayed quiet for a very long time- / Annette Stephens.
ISBN: 9781922132031 (ebook)
Subjects: Stephens, Annette--Childhood and youth.
          Child abuse--Australia--Biography.
          Abused children--Australia--Biography.
          Cult members--Australia--Biography.
Dewey Number: 362.76092

To Nina and Stefan.

contents

acknowledgements

I would like to thank all of the people who have supported this book: Margot Holden for generously donating her time and expertise to this project. Lynk Manuscript Assessment Service, especially Sean Doyle, whose advice and support has been invaluable. Big Sky Publishing for their willingness to take on a complex project. Thank you also to all those people who have shared their stories with me.

I wish to acknowledge my late mother, Gladys Stephens, for allowing me to publish her letters. A big thank you especially to my husband, Darcisio Bianchi, for his advice and loving support, and my children, Nina and Stefan, who have supported this project for a very long time.

prologue

It was an ordinary-looking photo, me in my cowgirl outfit, barely warranting the fact that it was enlarged, coloured and framed. Yet Mum thought it did. Perhaps that was her marker, the one she never quite recognised, the one that pointed to the time before she often said, 'I don't know what's wrong with Annette, she never listens anymore.' Before my father called me his dreamer, and said I would forget my head if it wasn't screwed on. Before chunks of my life began to go missing from my mind. Before I began giving up friends.

We lived opposite the Heidelberg Station in Melbourne, Victoria. On either side of the entrance, land slopes steeply down from the tracks. One side was my secret place. I once described it as somewhere 'no one can hear you, with open drains big enough for a small girl to hide in, fairies never go there, they stay put, sipping hot tea in a sunlit messy place safe in our backyard'. In this place, darkened and shadowless, eucalypts and peppercorns glowed after rain.

On the other side of the entrance to the station, the land also falls down from the tracks and flattens. A line of palm trees, intermittent and placid, stands among scatterings of agapanthus. I often ran up this slope and rolled down, dust and grass tagging my clothes. Mum would always shake her head.

Mum took the cowgirl photos near the path in the small park that separated my playing and rolling slope from the other, glowing and beckoning, side.

❧

Smooth clouds filled the sky, the light was flat. It was a perfect day for perfect prints. Mum and Dad gave me the cowgirl outfit for my 11th birthday. On the day of my birthday, Mum couldn't wait to see me all dressed up. I wanted to play, but Mum insisted the photos came first – while my outfit was brand new. Spit and polish helped my shoes, and I was centred for posterity.

Arms straight, fingers pointed to grass, tummy out, I stood smiling at my mother.

'Annette, stand still.'

Mum drew back, squinted at Dad. 'John! There's something wrong with this camera.'

'No, girlie, there's not.'

Mum looked doubtful.

With her attention back on me, her dismay mounted; my proper, photographic, stance had lapsed.

'Annette, keep your hands by your side ... look ... here!'

'But Mum, Mrs Jones is coming.'

A sprightly Mrs Jones charged along the path, nodded to us and kept walking. The park resumed its stillness, apart from the three of us and our dog. Mum looked at me, and harrumphed; I resumed my pose. She re-aimed her camera, stepped back and peered intently at her framing. I remained impatiently in place.

My girlfriend arrived and sat, cross-legged, on the grass. I shuffled, embarrassed by the cowgirl outfit. It had a red, long-sleeved shirt, separate black-and-white leather bands extended from wrist to mid-forearm. The black vest had white piping and the matching skirt had a white leather fringe. A scarf, tied around my neck, hung halfway to my waist. The hat was black and too big for my head; the holster held a pretend gun that dangled on my body.

Mum was proud of it and had tucked my hair under the hat and tied the scarf.

One last photo.

My girlfriend and I.

Then ... oh no, not the sun. Oh yes, and brighter by the minute.

More fussing from Mum.

My dog, Terry, pawed at my legs.

The afternoon beckoned; the park now astir; a crunch here, a rustle there.

'Stand still, Annette, like a big girl now ... John! Will you tell that girl to stand still!'

'It's not me, it's Terry's fault, Mum.'

Terry, an Australian terrier and the tiniest dog I'd ever seen, and I were inseparable. He licked my hand. I smothered him in cuddles and always hauled him up to my cubby house. This private place was on the roof of our rusty tin shed, its walls the hanging, swaying boughs of the weeping willow. Once an Alsatian attacked Terry in a park and he fought back, snapping at the big dog's heels until the owner dragged it away. Watching Terry that day, I vowed to be exactly like my dog: if I were attacked, I would be brave in the face of danger.

'John! Call Terry away from Annette.'

Finally, Mum was happy; the day and my new outfit would, through these photos, live on.

My girlfriend and her parents lived behind their flower shop. My parents and I lived in the dwelling behind a milk bar. She returned to her place. I didn't.

Out of sight of Mum, I tipped my hat off my head; it hung by the straps. Terry and I lingered, dawdled, traipsed, wandered … well I assume that is what I did, I certainly didn't go straight back over the road with my parents to our place.

It was nearly dinner time when I arrived home. Mum was cross.

Not only was I late, my cowgirl outfit was wrecked.

Torn.

Dirty.

I had lost some of it: the vest, hat, and holster with its toy gun.

'See John,' she said, 'she never looks after anything. That girl's only had it for a day. Annette, what have you been doing?'

My words spurted out.

'I've been rolling down my hill.'

An intense, startled ripple of sensation surged through my belly, then abruptly ceased. In different circumstances I might have dwelled on this, but not then and there. Before me stood my very angry mother.

'Ruined!' she said and silently fumed.

In between the dash to play and fronting my furious mum, I said I rolled down my hill. I was insistent.

I should know.

My photo was taken.
I rushed to play. I came home. Dirty.
If anything else had happened I would surely know.
I *was* there – present in the day that changed everything.

chapter 1

Seen and Not Heard

After her second miscarriage, my mother Gladys, spent her pregnancies in bed. I was her sixth attempt at motherhood; another child only survived the time required for burial.

I am an only child, a war baby born in 1943, child of the silent generation; seen and not heard. When I was born, I was declared a miracle.

Dad had 'picked up' Mum on one of St Kilda's questionable streets – to her eternal pride. When they married, Mum shook in anxious enthusiasm for the entire ceremony. When it finished, she bolted down the aisle, her bouquet disintegrating. Dad followed, trampling the remains. This was Mum's favourite story and encapsulates their difference.

Tall with dark, wavy hair, a long face and thin lips, Dad moved his body with languid ease and had the most beautiful, slow, sweeping smile. Dad was an office-bearer of the Melbourne Cricket Club, a Freemason, and a clerk at the Melbourne Metropolitan Board of Works, the then water authority. Rejected by the armed forces due to a health issue, Dad struggled to reconcile his lost sense of place.

Mum lived on her nerves, vacillated between hapless and breakneck, and was happiest when socialising. She twisted, plaited or curled her hair into the latest fashion and adored clothes – the fabrics, buttons, belts, the cottons and zips. A tailoress, her penchant for fashion showed and, with that, nothing was too much trouble; if a shirt didn't fit, Mum took it apart and restitched; if she needed a hat she bought one, and if the gloves didn't match, she dyed them. All dressed up, awkwardness slipped from within like the silks she loved, and Mum's enthusiasm for her outings lit up our days.

I stood one night, a small blonde girl, watching Mum dress for a ball. I can still hear the swish of her pale grey gown, see the shine of her fur jacket and see Mum at her dressing table, powder puff in hand, air imbued with the heavy scent of compacted face powder. Another day as Mum ran down the stairs, the red and white spotted lining of her cape swayed with her step. She arrived at the bottom, expectant, but only I was there to see. Mum passed, her perfume lingered. It was a fleeting moment, which captured the woman and her sensuality, all pegged in time. The poetry of this went straight over my head.

Mum couldn't cope with her emotions; they struggled to erupt, she fought to keep them contained and civil. She did as she was taught, not with words but the example of her family and her generation. 'Grin and bear it'. Nowadays my mother would be diagnosed as suffering post-natal depression but I think sadness crept through her from way back, pressurised and impetuous. She was meant to adapt to her changed circumstances (me) with its restrictions and resultant internal, and failing, battle. Mum fought against it all the way, aiming for the impossible – perfection.

Once, when Mum's temper got the better of her, she was severely repentant. 'I nearly shook the living daylights out of you when you were two years old. You did a poo in your cot and played with it. It was everywhere, all over the blankets and you drew all over the wall! Oh, I was harsh on you that day.'

'Oh, I was harsh on you that day', became Mum's most frequent 'oft-repeateds': those brief comments Mum regularly made about her life that seemed to validate her very existence.

Perhaps Mum drank to calm herself, although she would never have entertained that possibility. Both my parents drank. Drinking was as socially acceptable as smoking cigarettes and, for my father, tied up with his concept of mateship. Mum always said, 'I never touch a drop before five o'clock,' and Dad nodded. Our meal was served late at night after my parents consumed their quota; my mother always planned an earlier dinner, the result being our vegetables boiled to a pulp. My parents didn't behave badly or yell at me. Each night simply faded away.

We moved to Heidelberg in 1950. Wanting to prove his independence, my father resigned from his job and leased the milk bar opposite the Heidelberg Station. We settled in behind the shop in that suburb of flickering leaves, solid houses, hilly streets and blue flowering agapanthus. Our backyard was brown, apart from one green willow and a bountiful blue wisteria, both at odds with our starved garden.

I was seven and still had plaits when the games with a visitor, a man much older than my father, began. Brian and his wife, Norma, were customers. He was sarcastic and she was subdued, torn between what she had and what she wanted – Brian made her laugh but earned little money. In our untidy, brown backyard Brian whizzed me round in dizzying circles with one hand between my legs, then in my pants.

It tickled. I liked our game. Once, he nearly dropped me as someone called his name.

My parents reciprocated with the occasional visit to Brian's house. One day, as I played in his backyard, he joined me. He took me by the hand and led me to his outside toilet. I stood facing him, my legs cold against the bowl. He blocked the door and hogged the space. He seemed so big. I had never seen a penis before. Fumbling and urgent, he pulled my hand towards it. Afraid, I pulled my hand away. Brian turned and walked out of the toilet. He never, directly, approached me again.

I kept our secret from my parents. In some way I was aware of Brian's scorn. It was the 1950s. In my life there was only a formless hint of sex, and none of sexual abuse. My sexual response was not unusual but it was private. No one spoke of sex in my family, apart from awkward references to sex education. That a jovial family man might furtively abuse a child was hidden in the 'too hard' basket. The possibility that children might be sexually responsive was taboo. As I grew up I understood, and guilt set in. I had responded, enjoyed the earlier games. Naughty girl.

I never told anyone about another incident with the same man. It was some years later, in 1956, the year television began in Australia in time to televise the Melbourne Olympic Games. I was 13 years old. Mum had taken me to Brian and Norma's house so I could watch the

Games. Brian and Norma sat on a couch. I stood at the door, facing them. As Norma watched television his hand crept up her skirt, high up her inner thigh, and her legs slightly parted. She closed her eyes and smiled and, on opening them, saw me and flicked his hand away. All the while, Brian never took his eyes off me. I stood, rooted to the spot, held firm by an old man's contempt.

I must have been 18 when I stood next to my mother as she and a friend discussed the news that Brian had approached another young girl, and the police had been notified. Their attitude, 'not him, he's such a nice chap,' riled. The conversation paved the way, opened up the topic and when we arrived home, I told my mother about Brian and me. It was the wrong time … or the wrong subject.

'It happened to me,' I said, 'with Brian.'

I tried to explain.

'Oh, we haven't seen them for years!' Mum said.

Tears stung. 'I am not lying. It really happened, Mum.'

Mum responded with a stifled yes, so it continued to drift.

⌒∽

Downstairs, our rooms behind the shop were small, piggybacking each other. But upstairs, two large bedrooms stretched from the front of the building to the back. In the kitchen, the stove blithely shed its lining, grease gathered in implacable patches on the floor and nothing bigger than a bread and butter plate fitted in the sink. The bathroom walls were stained brown from fumes emitted by the gas hot-water system that, one day, went up in smoke, taking half the bathroom with it.

Inside the shop, glasses and sundae plates glinted on the wall behind the refrigerator counter. The counter was high-topped and stainless steel; the gentlest touch left fingerprints and dirty cloths left smears. Under the bench sat rows of stainless steel containers: chocolate, passionfruit, strawberry, lime and vanilla. The chocolate container dripped brown, and the lime dribbled green.

Regular customers rushed in and out; some dallied and spoke of lost cats, sick parents, weddings, of small woes and bright spots. Parades of men, wearing check jackets, came from the Returned Services League building on the opposite corner. Late afternoon, workers fled the railway station seeking sustenance in the form of malted milks, sarsaparillas, packets of cigarettes and newspapers. On weekends, kids hassled for something bigger than a threepenny ice-cream. One nasty girl said I wasn't as good as her; I wasn't Catholic. And each day a strikingly attractive, raven-haired woman with red, dishevelled lipstick sipped her spider at the tables and chairs recessed into the front window.

Every morning, my father dragged bundles of newspapers from the pavement, picking up money left in exchange for newspapers taken from the pile, drove to factories collecting sweets, stacked milk crates on the stairs leading to our upstairs bedrooms and littered the landing with more boxes.

While Dad fronted his shop, Mum cleaned her sphere of influence – with a resolve like hell in a fury. In the bathroom she vehemently scrubbed; in the kitchen she boiled our handkerchiefs clean in an old saucepan. If she couldn't match others' middle-class homes, she could match their gleam. Her female friends wrung their hands in woeful anticipation of the worst: the collapse of Mum's dubious nervous system. 'How Glad manages to serve in the shop, with her nerves, is a mystery.'

At ten, I was old enough to serve in the shop and loved making drinks and sundaes. To make Banana Splits, I placed three scoops of ice-cream in a line in a rectangular glass bowl, then peeled a banana, sliced it lengthwise and placed each piece on either side of the ice-cream. Chocolate was the most popular flavour and I poured it from one end of the bowl to the other, sprinkled crushed nuts on top, added a wafer and long-handled spoon and then stretched, on tiptoes, to the top of the counter.

To make lemonade spiders, I placed vanilla ice-cream in a thick curved glass and filled the glass with lemonade. It fizzed to a miracle of ice-cream-muted colour and froth. Making sundaes, mixing drinks and measuring contents for milkshakes, hearing the lunatic clatter of the milkshake mixer, knowing the exact moment to hook the container out, the unending surprise as each milkshake rose to three times its original height, was thrilling.

Our shop was next door to the Heidelberg picture theatre. Dad also leased the shop inside it. Patrons overflowed the tiny space and streamed down the street to our bigger premises. Saturday mornings, my job was to fill lolly bags for the day's matinee. I made penny and threepenny bags, four lollies for a penny, and sometimes two for a halfpenny. When the small, white, paper bags were filled, I lined them up on the other, timber, counter.

I was given free tickets to the pictures, and proudly bragged. 'Oh, *I* don't need a ticket,' I'd shout to the usher. And to my friends, 'I've seen that film, and that one – and that!' During the matinee interval, kids thronged round the counter in rows five or six deep.

Money was kept in a wooden till under the timber counter. Before each interval, Dad grabbed sixpences, shillings, pennies, halfpennies, pound notes and the odd 'fiver' (five-pound note) and placed them in piles on the ice-cream counter, ready for the pandemonium. We were lucky that everyone came to the rescue – neighbours or friends helped Mum and Dad each week. When the servers behind the ice-cream counter ran out of change, they made a mad dash for cash, squeezing between each other to reach the till, or shouted across it. Mum was wonderful; she tossed shyness to the wind and yelled. 'John! I need a sixpence!' and 'John! I'm still waiting for that fiver!' After each madcap interval, Dad beamed. Mum said, 'Thank God, that's over!' and headed to safety. As Dad carted his till into our lounge, notes floated to the floor and, for days afterwards, we discovered stray coins in odd places.

In our lounge room behind our bustling milk bar, Mum looked to her motherly tasks. Sex education was the responsibility of parents, and some were diligent and some were not. Mum tried, instigating chats with the hopeful words, 'It's perfectly natural.' I squirmed. Crushed (and/or relieved) she activated plan B: bail out. I knew that kissing was relevant and sex nice – and natural. Not that it mattered. When I was older and had my period, serious talks loomed.

I'd heard about kissing games played behind the school shelter shed but had never tried them.

My girlfriend and I played another game in her damp-smelling basement. Holding a toy stethoscope, she seriously examined my slight, flat, naked body and found nothing wrong. Then it was my turn. She took off her clothes and lay on the bench. I stood before her, still naked. As my face neared her body and approached her genitals, I said, 'That smells nice.' She ran. I held my crushed, hurt innocence.

My innocence was removed from comprehension and beyond words. There was no love, erotica, crudity, exploitation, no desperateness of the human condition or cognition of its continuance, only a self-contained sweetness.

✌

In 1953, Shirley Collins was murdered. Her murder has never been solved. Fourteen-year-old Shirley was off to her first adult party and planned to travel by train to Richmond where a young man, a workmate, would meet her. Her mother drove her to the Reservoir Station, where she caught the train, but she alighted at the wrong station, at West Richmond. It is believed she accepted a lift. Her body was found, 70 kilometres away, at Mount Martha. She had been viciously battered but, although her clothes were scattered, she had not been 'raped'.

I read the headlines behind the counter in our shop. Mum snatched the newspaper from my hand. 'John, don't let her see that!'

At night I snuck into our moonlit shop and riffled through newspapers; her murder remained unsolved. The facts got lost in my mind, but one point remained fixed. Shirley was on her way to a party. Everyone knew about them; people got drunk at parties. Perhaps she hadn't been a good little girl? I was. I wrote a letter to my father and my mother kept it.

'Dear Daddy, I am a good little girl. Love from Annette.'

As Mum and Dad relaxed with a beer each night, a customer setting off the shop bell invariably interrupted their drinking. With his white apron tied in front of him, Dad entered his shop, sold his goods, chatted, and found someone else to invite inside for a drink.

When visitors crowded in, I sometimes slipped away to the stairs or to my bedroom, wondering if anyone noticed me after the clock had struck five. At night, a single globe cast shadows and the lounge room seemed smaller, meaner. The fireplace sat angled in the corner and an open passage led from the shop, past the stairs, through the lounge to the kitchen. One unused half of the lounge housed the pianola and crystal cabinet; in the other, chairs clustered around the fireplace. There were always beer glasses left abandoned on the mantelpiece, on side tables and on the floor. The smell of beer drifted from bottles and prowled the room.

Many new visitors were men. These new friends of my father sat or stood at the fire, beer in hand. They were unlike my father's known and loved old friends, like Pat, who drove his car, with me on the running board, round his backyard; or Fred, with the quick tears. That changed once Dad leased the shop I now had to be nice and polite to strangers with red noses, and one with parched eyes who lived nearby. This man had a child, and a wife; neither came with him to visit my parents. Nice-looking with black hair and a moustache, he drank my parents' beer, sat in their chair and warmed himself by their fire. He entered our home, genial, and engaged my parents in conversation. When my mother went into the kitchen and my father to his shop, he sipped his beer and silently observed me. As Mum or Dad returned, our silent gulf opened up to the welcoming buzz of my parents' hospitality.

When the man with parched eyes abruptly stopped visiting us, after my 11th birthday, Mum was indignant.

'Just like that! No explanation at all!' she said.

The fact that my birthday present, the cowgirl outfit, had been ruined slipped aside. Mementos of the day, the photos, were tossed into a box in memory of a special, spoiled, gift.

'Mum,' I asked, not long after she had taken the cowgirl photos, 'what happened to the child who was murdered near here?'

'I haven't heard of a child being murdered roundabout here, Annette.'

I knew differently.

'Nothing to be frightened of,' said Mum, with loud asides to my father, 'what is wrong with that girl?'

There *had* been a murder nearby.

I *knew* it.

For months after the cowgirl photos, my dog, Terry, barked at our strange-eyed neighbour. Then, Terry ate baited meat and died. It was weeks before I noticed that my dog was not by my side. That I had not missed his barking and licks was inconceivable. Remorse and confusion smeared into one and set hard. It was rumoured that the man with parched eyes had tossed poisoned meat over our fence. But, barring an explanation that made sense to anyone, the story died.

The debacle of that birthday was replaced with the excitement of Christmas, then Easter. Mum and Dad went about their daily chores. Life continued as before but I had changed. At bedtimes I would take a flying leap onto my bed in my upstairs bedroom, kneel on my bed praying to a smiling Jesus, then hunch up, wide awake, scared of shifting shadows. Our unlit outside toilet, its clanking chain and pitch-blackness, became formidable.

My teacher saw the change in me and told Mum and Dad. I had loved my schoolwork. I tried to concentrate as I used to, but I idled and lost focus. The prizes stopped. It was baffling and my teacher said, 'I can only do so much.' Her words became another of Mum's 'oft-repeateds'.

Another day I changed my writing. It had resembled Mum's, determined and correctly slanting; however, I then copied a friend's small, round and upright letters.

My first kiss, in front of the entire primary school, was delivered by a bespectacled, school friend. Petrified, my response bizarrely exaggerated, emotion flooded my body, and stopped with the speed of a guillotine. My school day resumed, as if nothing had happened.

I refused to go near my secret place. I also stopped going to the park where Terry had fought off an Alsatian, where I had vowed to be as brave as him. In this park, pebble paths lined with blue-flowering agapanthus meander through peppercorn and eucalyptus trees; there are quiet places here, in which trees stand like sentinels and grass covers hollows. It is here that I believed a child had been murdered. I deeply missed this park. I missed running with grass tickling my legs. I missed the annoyance of stopping to remove burrs from my socks. Most of all, I missed the uncluttered ground of the sports oval, where I ran with Terry yapping at my heels.

∾

One day I sat on our toilet seat and cried, 'I can't do a wee. It hurts me.' The pain persisted and x-rays were taken. I was rushed to a hospital where nuns were nurses. Waking from the anaesthetic, I took myself to the toilet where a nun found me sitting, surrounded by vomit and crying. 'Oh dear, we can't have this,' she said and gathered me to her habit and beads.

The diagnosis was three kidneys and a blocked ureter. The doctor said my hymen was broken, and asked if I had been 'interfered with'. 'Of course not!' replied Mum. At home, Mum reiterated, 'Of course not. The doctor said that, well, sometimes girls are born without a hymen.'

Perhaps the thought sat on the tears in Mum's handkerchief?

That hurt stopped but the inexplicable ache I felt continued. I couldn't call it pain. It was a reluctance, a shoring-up, an unease, and I bypassed it.

My interest in Shirley Collins grew. Her murder clipped itself to me. A newspaper photograph of her sat in frightened corners of my heart. Her photo stalked my mind.

I stopped playing with my old school friends and took to inviting as many different kids from school as possible to our shop at lunchtime and implored my father to give them icy poles.

It was 1954. There was nothing to be afraid of. Children weren't locked up. Adults didn't watch every move, eyeing strangers, on the lookout for bad men with lollies.

Although, look what happened to Shirley Collins. Murdered.

And if anything had happened to me ... sometimes ignorance is bliss.

chapter 2

Nana

The paddocks behind my grandparents' house stretched fenceless, and almost treeless, for as far as the eye could see. Had she wished, my grandmother Ada could step out her back door and not stop for ages, relishing the changing smell of grass, the languid flowing of paddocks to sky; but she didn't. Nana never ventured beyond the distance required by her daily chores in the backyard, a rectangle defined by the house itself, picking vegetables, feeding chooks and hanging clothes; marooned in the calm raggedness of her flat and stretching land.

In her mid-sixties, Nana's slight body had stiffened. She drew her tightly-waved grey hair into a bun at the nape of her neck; her hearing aid was tucked in the bodice of her dress, its wire rumpled from its hiding place to her ear. She had grown up in the city. Sounds recognised before her deafness had no place in Nana's paddocks. Perhaps she was hemmed in by silence?

When Nana was young, she was beautiful. The young Ada cooked for a wealthy household and had been destined, by her mother, to rule an abundant one. Instead, she married Roberto, a saddletree maker whose trade became redundant; the saddletree is the frame of a saddle, and it became superfluous with the coming of cars.

His claim to fame is his solution to the problem of the outdoor toilet – an archetypal spider-ridden, piss-echoing, stinking outhouse. In a flash of inspiration he uprooted it, and plonked it above the underground stream running, previously pure and conveniently mute, behind the house.

No claim-to-fame stories exist of Nana, who spent her time cleaning, crocheting, mending and cooking. Her clotted cream was to die for, her sheets were starched, her pots were scoured but when it came to her floors pragmatism reigned. Broom in hand, she swished everything out the back door and slammed it shut.

In their enclosed lives, Grandpa dug his garden and Nana cooked. He cracked jokes and Nana dissolved into giggles, and when Nana fretted, Grandpa comforted. This juxtaposition, the tacit understanding of needs, sums up their days.

∽

Once, I spent two weeks with them in Springvale. My parents holidayed in Sydney, and my mother kept in touch with Nana by mail. I was five years old.

Mum and I caught the train from Melbourne's Flinders Street Station. Swooping under rows of clocks showing the train departure times, she glanced up, and continued her swooping. Under the high corrugated-iron roof her hand gripped mine, and we were small and clean.

On the ramp, I broke free from her hand and ran its length, fast enough to live the thrill of nearly tripping. Catching up, the hand restrained. I urged toward the platform edge, it tightened. We waited. Underfoot, the asphalt softened and the smell of age intensified with the heat. Then we sat in the carriage, in dark brown seats, in the dark red rattler that reeked of grime and screeched metal.

Stepping from the train, Mum removed her glasses, fogged them with her breath, wiped them, and then seized my suitcase and hand. In Springvale, over 20 kilometres out of Melbourne and still rural, the enticing smell of summer was all about us. Walking the three kilometres of flat straight road past a straggle of houses and hunched-up sheds, my young eyes played with the world, my feet followed a lackadaisical rhythm. Mum adhered to her own particular determination, never relaxing her resolve to grip my hand, keep her shoulders straight and hat on.

With a glimpse of Nana and Grandpa's house I, and it, tingled. Freed from Mum's hand my plaits flapped as I ran, 'Nana, Nana, we're here.' Gatecrashing the stillness, I ran into the only holiday I remember spending with my grandparents and, as I ran, that house leaned to me. Inside, it waited with a pride undiminished by poverty.

Nana opened her front door. Sunlight swamped the hall until Mum closed it and pushed me forward. I resisted, dallying, arm-in-arm with the house. I peeped into one room with a dark red brocade chair, a fireplace and a ticking grandfather clock. Mum pulled my arm. I glanced towards Nana's bedroom where light goaded scratches in the mirror. Mum tugged harder. Kisses and Nana's hugs over, I scooted down the hallway, out the back door to the sun and Grandpa's chained-up dog. A lean, black Kelpie-cross, Digger was as ferocious as a wolf in my grandparents' absence but in their presence he was a tail-wagging mutt.

The table, shades of lavender polish, dominated the kitchen. The black wood-fired stove licked and spat and hummed. The blind was down, the aspidistra gasped: there was not a breath of air. Here, melding into the oppressive heat and in her silence, Nana wrote her letters.

Blinking as I left the bright light, I joined my mother and grandmother in that intimate ritual, tea in the kitchen. The few spoken words trailed off. The sound of water pouring, the clink of cups and the almost imperceptible rustle of clothing were quietly determined. Two generations of women looked to each other and glanced at me. Smiles flashed, lit their faces, their eyes met again.

Late afternoon, carefully staying her hat with a hatpin and with one last, 'Be good for Nana', Mum waved and marched back to the station.

Our rituals then began. They were simple and repetitive yet each day was magical. Rising, playing, watching, learning, full of smells and satisfactions: the crumble of earth on fingers, the snap of strawberries from their stem, the clink and yank as Digger strained on his chain, Nana's voice melting with fondness as I offered the morning's harvest to Digger, 'No pet, they're for you, not the dog.'

One sun swept morning, Nana and I entered the tin shed, long and flat and hiding mayhem. I squealed with delight at dozens of rustling chickens. With her sleeves rolled up, Nana caught one, carried it to the chopping block outside, and then chopped its head off. Digger snarled, jerking at his chain. The smell of innards mingled with that of dry grass. I stared at her; the mess and the death were awful. 'Are you alright, dear?' Nana reached inside her dress, adjusted her hearing aid and repeated, 'Are you alright, dear?' Eye wide, I looked at the chopping block, and said nothing.

For dinner, starched white tablecloth and serviettes – old sheets – were placed on the table. The napkin rings gleamed. Butter was placed neatly in its dish, the cheese sat in the cheese dish and jam in the jam dish. Everything was in its proper place. We ate with, and in, dignity. At the head of the table, my grandfather carved the departed chicken and said grace. 'For what we are about to receive may the Lord make us truly grateful.'

On Sunday we went to church. My grandparents were members of the Plymouth Brethren, a religious sect established in the late 1820s when men, opposed to the idea of church membership, believed that when people gathered together to worship they met in the presence of God and stood in unison with Him. They refused ordained leadership and assembled in halls or homes, referring to themselves as the Brethren; as the Centre in Plymouth, England, grew they became known as the Plymouth Brethren.

For the first 25 years the Brethren had lived in peace with their Bibles but, despite their rejection of leadership, the conflicting opinions of men claiming to have the correct interpretation of the Bible led them, in 1848, to divide into two groups. They were then referred to as the Open and Closed/Exclusive brethren. However, my grandparents still called themselves Plymouth Brethren. Their congregation welcomed new flock and pinned notices of their services on the doors of the halls they gathered in.

For church, Nana ignored her floral dresses and chose a dark one with a handmade lace collar, and a soft black hat. Crushed between her and my suited grandfather, arms pinned to sides, I sat as good and quiet as my grandmother. In this church one dress seemed indistinguishable from another. Men rose, as did my grandfather, and spoke words unintelligible to me. Women sat, shrouded and irrelevant. After church, I watched these dolefully dressed women chat, heads inclined, dark garbs in relief against a shabby hall and hanging sky. I never went there again.

My parents mailed their news and Nana wrote back. My mother kept that letter.

Each day of the fortnight tumbled into the next. My grandmother went about her chores, my grandfather went to work, and soon it was over.

Mum then arrived, looked at me and asked sternly, 'Have you been a good girl for Nana and Grandpa?'

'Oh Gladys, she's been a darling.'

No high-jinx or high drama, or visits, apart from church. It was wonderful.

In those two weeks, Nana taught me her values: good and kind, insignificant and harmless. I was her good little girl. She is seared to me and indelible. In the future, when love would stretch and shred, Nana would pray for me.

⁓

Mum was the proud black sheep of the family. Millie, her sister, was Nana's taller double, with the same narrow face, compact body, skinny legs and hair worn in a bun at the nape of the neck. Neither wore make-up, bright clothes, or shouted – unlike Mum who had been known to yell. All had the skinny legs inherent of the family and all loved floral dresses.

The girls were brought up to believe in God. There might have been a big world somewhere outside Nana's boundaries but God oversaw everything within. Only Millie shared her parents' beliefs. Mum had no interest whatsoever; whatever God provided for Nana and Grandpa, Mum could do without. To her, religion kept people off the streets and the Ten Commandments could be, expediently, cherry-picked.

At 29, three years before I was born, Mum was given a family Bible. It was passed on to me but not before I was old enough (and perhaps respectful enough) to keep it safe. Several sections are thumbed, stained, annotated and underlined, especially those referring to the virtues of believing and the perils facing non-believers. Revelations 22:13-15:

I am Alpha and Omega, the beginning and the end, the first and the last.

Blessed are they that do his commandments, that they may have right to the tree of life, and may enter in through the gates of the city.

For without are dogs, and sorcerers, and whoremongers, and murderers, and idolaters, and whosever loveth and maketh a lie.

Centred in a blank page at the front of our book, are pencilled the words, 'Be faithful and you will be useful.' Despite the religious undercurrents that pushed, urged and divided, the sisters were close.

While Millie stood, maybe wistfully, at the top of life's water slide, Mum spluttered and splashed its length.

༄

I must have been nine when Millie, her husband Dan, and son Noah moved into my grandparents' Springvale house. Millie and Dan were poor. The house was extended to accommodate them. Between my grandparents and Millie and Dan, enough money was scrounged for a proper roof and floor. The new walls were canvas.

Millie seemed tired and Dan God-fearing; it was whispered he was the most God-fearing in the family. Millie and Dan had met through Nana and Grandpa's church. Thin, dark-haired, sharp-featured, Dan stands starkly disquiet against Springvale's jonquil-soaked, cold paddocks. Millie leans to his hard body as he reads his Bible, and trains Noah to recite, revere and fear God. Millie would remain in her rightful place, dictated by Dan's austere and literal interpretation of his faith. She would not drive, or work, or go anywhere except shopping, without her husband and children.

Millie's subsequent children were born into that house. But to me, there was only Noah. We were the same age; he was serious, with his grandfather's stiff hair. Noah was my make-believe brother, the one I had always wanted. When I stayed overnight, I slept in Noah's room. Moonlight entered by stealth; the sheets were coarse. Noah and I talked at night as the wind cracked the canvas and the shadows danced.

One day, about two years after the cowgirl photos, Dan stood in the rust-infused utilities shed in Springvale when I blundered in. He turned to face me. I turned and ran. Dan had neither touched nor hurt me but something about him scared me. Dan would, in my future, become a symbol of evil.

By the time Noah and I were 14, Millie and her family no longer visited us in Heidelberg. We only occasionally talked in that quietly flapping house in Springvale, but not at night; I no longer stayed with them.

By then, God was nearly everywhere in Nana's house. His word drizzled and leached from the Bible, to adult, to child, from chair to chair – but not to Grandpa. From his red brocade chair, my grandfather asserted his tolerance, and resolutely and silently countered the intrusion of a harsh and inflexible God into his house.

Then, the house in Springvale wandered off and sat on the sidelines. The seasons changed, rain fell on the tin roof. The sun baked the ground where the vegetable patch had once been abundant. I was growing up and became more interested in my girlfriends than my increasingly confusing family. Nana grew old, body unbent, as gentle and accommodating as ever. Grandpa died a silent and lost death. Dan took over at the head of that humble table, and the house slid imperceptibly to the ground, sighing at its canvas seams.

We still visited, spasmodically, for Sunday lunch.

Mum was 51, and I was 17, when Nana sent Mum a letter that would change their relationship forever. It was postmarked 1961:

Dear Gladys and all,

I have been trying to write to you for some time but hadn't the heart to tell you what I am going to. You said you might be up this weekend and I'm writing to say not to come as I find I cannot ask you in again because I have felt that I have to give up all natural feeling for Christ's sake and

He is all in all to me and we have nothing in common now. I cannot give Him up for anything in the world as He gave His life for all. I know dear you will think I'm mad but I would rather that than give up the love of God. I do pray for you all, that you will know him as your Saviour. The time will come when it will be too late and then what? It just breaks my heart to say this but you do reject God and want nothing to do with anyone that loves Him so how can I be a party to that as I would be if I had fellowship with those that do not love Him? I still love you all and will always pray for you and hope you will not think too hardly of me. I need not say that Millie is of the same mind ...

Your loving mother.

Mum, Dad and I didn't visit that Sunday. We never stepped foot inside the house in Springvale again. Being not of the faith – like the murderers and lie makers – we were doomed, and separated from. My Springvale family were weaving new lives, tangled up in the dictates of the newly formed Exclusive Brethren.

When the Brethren had split into Open and Closed/Exclusive Brethren in 1848, along doctrinal lines, a prominent leader of the breakaway Closed Brethren was Nelson Derby. Following Derby's 'reign', there were various groupings and several leading figures over the years. Between 1953 and 1959 there was a power struggle called the 'Interregnum'. In 1959, James Taylor Jnr became the leader of a splinter group that called itself the Exclusive Brethren, and adopted policies of rigid separation. There are about 43,000 of these Exclusive Brethren worldwide, currently (2010) led by an Australian, Bruce Hales. Approximately 15,000 of them are in Australia.

The Exclusive Brethren are enjoined to not eat or drink with others, attend university, listen to radio or television, go to the theatre or movies or take part in worldly entertainment, such as playing a musical instrument. They should not join professional associations. Nor should they vote. They should not live, or work, in buildings that share a wall with non-Exclusive Brethren, nor should they share a driveway. They should not marry non-Brethren and they should sever connection to their non-Brethren families. Women wear head coverings to show submission.

Dan followed the hard line of James Taylor Jnr. Nana and Millie, two seen-and-not-heard women, adapted to their place in life, and donned their scarves; their place being the kitchen, pregnancy and an insistent upholding of the faith. Perhaps Millie had become acclimatised through her years with Dan. Nana, Millie and her children obeyed, mute, but not without pain, as I discovered much, much later.

'Bloody religion', muttered Mum; this became her most touching oft-repeated comments. Perhaps Mum understood more than she indicated? The fallout of the Brethren had caused great and lasting pain among many Brethren families. Perhaps Mum had refused to read the reports – a protest? Perhaps it was too hard and Mum hurt as well?

My rare questions to Mum as to their wellbeing hung in mid-air then floated to that place of unanswered time. Mum couldn't reach beyond her pain, Dad was preoccupied with his finances and I was miles away in my head. However we might have individually described the religion of my grandparents; it had hitherto not been considered a threat to our unity. In the event, Mum, Dad and I were as mute as our severed family.

About six months after that fatal letter, I walked past Mum's bedroom door. She angrily shoved her handkerchief in her apron pocket.

She tried to avoid me but I got in quickly, 'What's wrong?'

'Nothing, I just got a letter from your grandmother and … I told you, we'll never see her again … bloody religion.'

Mum bottled her silent ache, squashing it wherever she could find the space in her tight body – the letter read:

Dear Gladys

I fear I have offended you beyond forgiveness and I'm nearly distracted at the thought of what I had to do. I don't want to live; I feel there is nothing to live for. I'm not apologising I do feel as I said, but it's like death to me to have to do it, and I do pray that some day you will realise I'm doing it for Christ's sake. If I gave all of that up what would I do here? They could not have anything to do with me; I've just had enough worry. I just had to write these few lines to explain a little.

May God bless you, your loving mother.

'That bloody religion', remained Mum's sole, intermittent reference to this poignant and underscored time. Now, I understand there was no incongruity between the message and Nana's words: love had not abated, just removed itself from reach. Mum's tears often fogged her glasses and she would take them off and clean them. She had no salve. No understanding. Her upbringing of 'grin and bear it' was sadly wanting.

Nana prayed to her God as her family trod insoluble paths. On depleted Sundays, Millie continued to cook for her devout husband Dan, and watched as he taught his children the disciplines of the Exclusive Brethren.

There was another, and final, letter from Nana. It is not dated; this grandchild was born in early 1962:

Dear Gladys,

I just thought I'd like to tell you that Millie has a son born the eighteenth. She had a big worry over him with jaundice but alright now. I don't suppose you will be interested but his name is Nicholas John, six pounds. Well dear I don't want you to think Millie and Dan influenced me in any way. I feel more deeply now than you will ever know. May God bless you all and I do pray that you will know, be blessed in His love and especially Annette, that she will know Him too.

Love, Mum.

I believe Nana did find a kind of peace, and that is the reason she, once again, could call herself 'Mum'. I don't believe her peace came easily. Awareness of Nicholas John, six pounds, is ensnared in the smell of the paper his name is written on. Nicholas John was the last of Millie and Dan's six children.

Nana's wish would eventually come true. I would find a Him.

And Noah? I would never forget him; I like to think that he sometimes thought of us – of me.

Nana died in her early eighties. She had a stroke and was found dead in the bath in Millie's spartan addition. It seemed appropriately like her simple life that revolved around the local shops, the house, my grandfather and, once upon a time, all her family.

Millie wrote a short note. Mum threw it away. The funeral was over. Mum hadn't been told of the death, or invited to the funeral. I think it was then that Mum's heart really broke. Nana's Will left practically everything to Millie and Dan, including the house. Mum received the tick-tocking grandfather clock that Grandpa managed to ignore as he sat in his red brocade chair, and one hundred dollars.

After Mum stopped crying she said, 'At least she left me something, that way I know my mother still loved me.'

Ten years after Nana's last letter, a slight ray of hope for Mum and Millie had shone briefly. The Exclusive Brethren leader, James Taylor Jnr, had reportedly been increasingly seen drunk and swearing, his behaviour erratic, and when he was caught out in 'immoral conduct' with a woman, all hell broke out. The Exclusive Brethren refer to these events as 'Aberdeen'. The group Taylor personally led was reduced to two Brethren families. The further away, the less impact this had on followers, especially those overseas who, in general, stuck with Taylor, convinced he was innocent. The fallen leader died shortly afterwards.

Mum never knew of the possibilities that had, briefly, existed. Had she, she might have hoped that Millie's beliefs were open to scrutiny and tried to contact her. As it was, Millie and Dan's faith did not waver.

Mum stored Nana's letters in another of her shoeboxes.

'One day,' she said, 'I'll give the letters to you.'

And one day she did, with the words, 'Oh, do what you want with them. No one's interested.'

chapter 3

Grown Up

My teenage friends were Jewish. It had been assumed by my girlfriends' community that I was too; after all, after school and on weekends I went everywhere they did. That I wasn't Jewish was never hidden. My friends knew, their parents tolerant.

Summer holidays consisted of the blearing sun, scorching sand and two-piece bathers at St Kilda beach. My darkly beautiful school friends, Laura and Lynne, and I tossed our heads and wriggled our bums through the summer spray, with sand between our toes and sticking to the oil we coated ourselves with. We waded to where sea salt lapped at our waists, squatted in the water, rose to rub the no longer existent sand off our bellies, splash shoulders, and glance at the boys.

And it was during those summer months that I met my first boyfriend. His parents suspected that our tender and clumsy relationship might be serious and asked questions about me. We were nearly 16; our innumerable glances had led to kissing in the picture theatre and holding awkwardly straying hands.

Arriving at the entrance to a dance held at a Jewish Centre, I was stopped with the implausible words, 'Annette, you can't go in!' My peers rubbed past. I shrugged a hand from my arm and pushed towards the door.

A melange of whispers, dark expressions and helplessness followed, and Laura said, 'Annette, you can't go in, his parents found out you're not Jewish.'

No more watching the boys playing soccer, no more holding hands with my boyfriend; our relationship had not gone beyond those passionate kisses. No more imagining myself as an emerging , almost, Jewish young woman. But there is always more life, and dreams – those teenage hopes that compensate so well for real-life.

Laura, Lynne and I maintained a relationship for some years, but I was excluded from the rest of the group. Their families spoke of suffering; the word 'Holocaust' shivered in my mind and numbers tattooed on limbs played hide and seek with images of suburban Melbourne. I read *The Diary of Anne Frank*, which eloquently conveyed the terrible things that happened somewhere else, things whispered in taut words, ordered through time into a painful sense. I sensed their pain, and somehow related to it. In a place unimaginable to me, I had sensed connection.

Laura's family took me to the *Family of Man* photography exhibition and one caption and accompanying photos seared themselves in my mind. 'I am alone with the beating of my heart.' They bought me the book. I lost it. Laura's parents once brought me, from Paris, a beautiful black velvet drawstring purse; I left it in a public toilet and then I moved on with my life.

This was not the first time that I had abandoned friendships. Although I missed them, the haziness in my head dulled my mysterious aching that, in fact, intensified with closeness.

⌒◯

By the late 1950s, Mum, Dad and I had left the milk bar in Heidelberg. My parents were exhausted and, despite its success, had no money. Perhaps they spent it all on me?

We moved twice, before shifting to a sparse house in an arid court in East Brighton. Dad leased another mixed business in Brighton on a bend in the main beach road, opposite the yacht club. This salt-rimmed shop was on its last legs.

The late teen years, past school and before responsibilities, were meant to be the best time in the life of a young woman, when hope still outclassed reality. Hurt found its hiding place, and my rebellious streak flourished. When good little girls rock boats it is glowering, wilful, avoiding the repercussions they cannot openly deal with. Life seemed increasingly remote but hope was still out there ... somewhere ... tailing the music of J. S. Bach, which I loved. No matter how far it soared, it always found its way back to a known place. To Mum's horror I took to walking the Brighton pier late at night. When the wind screamed, and I cranked up the music of Bach in my head, I looked to the dark and felt alive.

In my East Brighton bedroom, Mary, my new non-Jewish girlfriend, and I planned life as 'beatniks', and part of the Beat Generation, namely sitting on the floors of suitably grungy lofts, drinking cheap wine, quoting esoteric poetry, and dreaming of a life away from Australia.

Mary, classically pretty, had a big smile and auburn hair with a kink in it. Socially confident, she followed up on invitations whether they led to Melbourne's best or most dingy addresses. She wonderfully tossed her head and, hair swirling, found a place evocative of Bohemia, right in the heart of Melbourne. At the back of a derelict mansion, this loft was in Melbourne's St Kilda Road, a wide, treed streetscape lined with mansions. It was a credit to our forefathers but was soon to be mutilated in the name of progress.

This collapsing edifice represented my future; the last thing I wanted was suburbia, the humdrum life of the great silent majority, the predictable and stultifying routine of 'Hello dear, how was your day?' I would climb its rickety ladder with my hair hanging loose, my morals at odds with my hairstyle. I savoured the exchanges, the poetry and aspirations and ignored the flaws of the people that made them.

Mary and I were on our first adult-free holiday when, at 17, I had my first sexual encounter in a grey guesthouse in seaside Sorrento. The protagonist was the painter who lived in the loft. It was my first time; why, I wondered, did I not recall pain, or blood? The time between my lying on the bed with him and walking down the corridor after the sex was scrappy: my acquiescence, his weight on top of me. I had no recall of the actual sex. 'Sexual intercourse,' Mum called it. My experience was a little more basic than 'inter' anything. I never told Mary. Then, I side-stepped our friendship.

In need of cheaper accommodation, Mum, Dad and I moved again, this time to Middle Brighton, one of Melbourne's most expensive suburbs. Ironically, my parents had found a very cheap flat there. Financially down, aesthetically up. Classically shabby chic (before it became a 'style') with peeling paint, climbing ivy and cracked moss-filled concrete, I loved the ramshackle, old mansion from the moment I saw it. It consisted of four large apartments with rooms from gigantic to tiny. Amenities were unsightly but functional. Our lounge had large Victorian windows, a marble fireplace and an almost threadbare carpet square. On one wall sat the pianola and, neatly opposite, the crystal cabinet.

Upstairs, our entrance was on one side of the house; our garage with timber doors that somehow managed to stay together when scraped open, was on the other. The garden fell short of my yearning for an ordered and fertile retreat, but had a whimsical determination in the face of neglect.

My parents walked from our garage, I traipsed. They climbed the outside stairs; I loitered, fingering patterns left by dead ivy on the wall, little clinging tentacle tracks going nowhere in particular.

Dad sat daily in that windswept delicatessen, sandwich fillings in readiness, waiting in vain for someone to enter his shop. At the end of each desolate day, he shut his battered garage doors, walked through our back door and called out 'Hello girlie' to Mum as she gathered the glasses and bottle of beer.

One day, I caught sight of Mum fighting back tears in her cramped bedroom. I hesitated. Other people's bedrooms have, to me, a daunting quality, as if something preciously furtive hangs in mid-air. Her sewing machine had broken. Mum sat there, sewing a floral summer dress, stitch by single hand-made stitch. I stood gingerly, half visible, and asked why she was upset. Mum shouted at me, her face a hurt mix, 'Why do you think? We've got no money!' Mum brushed past me, steadied herself and walked down the hallway, her back as straight as ever.

Friends, family, even neighbours, seemed to think I ought to be 'something'; my ambition was singularly wanting. Through my Jewish friends I had discovered a world of art galleries, film festivals and classical music concerts so came to the decision that I would be an artist. How much further from suburbia, and my parents' woes, could I get? Short on talent, I chose photography; it was second cousin to art but, nonetheless, related. To support myself I found part-time work as a waitress. Enrolling as a photography student at Royal Melbourne Institute of Technology, I decided I had found my niche. I loved my camera, swooned over my light metre and sturdy, leather camera-bag, adored the twisting, rolling and clicking involved in using old cameras but all I seemed to photograph was statues, and bridges, and more statues. I longed to celebrate real life in beautiful black-and-white, eight-by-ten inch photographs that would hang on a white-walled gallery. I silently carped at my lecturers and fellow students, who aimed for perfect prints, but ... we were meant to be artists, weren't we? Give or take a definition or two.

Sue Ford, the only other women enrolled in the course, and I became friends. She had no doubt about her direction in life, photographer and artist, and fitted easily into Melbourne's alternative life. We both looked the part, with our long hair, black jumpers, fake leather coats, bare feet, cigarettes and attitudes of high intent. It was 1961. We were 18 and legal.

Ninkies was a café on the ground floor of a two-storeyed terrace house in Melbourne's Little Collins Street. Its owner envisaged a lively hub, a European Bohemia but unbeknown to Sue and me, it was limping to a defunct future. Its upstairs room became our studio. Sue's parents contributed to the rent. Our studio lights took up residence, along with our 2¼ square cameras, so-called because these cameras used 2¼ inch square negatives. Mum sewed approximately 25 metres of hessian into a room divider; its smell overpowered the room. Sue took hundreds of photos in that studio, some immortalised in a published book. Mum's curtain proudly features on the front cover.

I liked the darkly moody world of Melbourne's alleys until, one day a dirty, unshaven man flashed me as I hunted Melbourne's dim corners for real-life photographs. I emotionally froze. Strangely intimidated, my enthusiasm for becoming the world's best photographer palled.

My commitment to Bohemia was unravelling with its reality. Artists, as it turned out, were real people. In our studio, I stared through space; dejected and floating. Fleeting images of Shirley Collin's murder inexplicably haunted me. That I had not noticed my vanished dog, Terry, still unnerved me.

Sue spoke easily to people. I was lost between blinks. I'd find her in Ninkies, talking to the owner and his friend, hesitant, quiet Sam who smiled politely and, equally politely and unobtrusively, committed suicide. Ninkies closed. She went on to establish a fine reputation as photographer and filmmaker, while I went on and on in my head. Sue and I remained friends for some years, but it had already begun – my pulling away.

I disliked the randomness of parties, the clamour of pubs and the Beatles. Nor would I rally to hippy fashion, or Flower Power, or smoking marihuana, or making love not war. I liked one-on-one; intimate and quiet. The rebelliousness of my early teens had not dramatically manifested itself; it had morphed into an unpredictable, internal umbrage. The women of my family 'grinned and bore' – and I was my mother's daughter.

Contact with my girlfriends continued to dwindle. In conversation, we were equals. In deeds, we were not. Mary, Laura and Lynne were pursuing professional careers. Sue was planning her first solo exhibition. I had dropped out of school and photography, and had discarded each job I so easily found.

Unable to say no to the men who approached me confidently, those I acquiesced to were mostly one-night-stands. They were the nights I barely remembered. Although I was pretty, men were not attracted to me. Perhaps they saw what I didn't, my blankness, and passed me over. Mum had informed me that sex was nice – and natural. So far, she was wrong.

By 1965, Mary and I were back in touch. The black outfits and beatnik ambitions were, for Mary, a thing of the past. I had begun to feel empty. Like a chameleon, I merged into 'Mary' and became a prospective wife and mother.

I remember when it happened; it was at the Melbourne Cup, Australia's famous horse race that is equally famous for the fashionable women, and their hats, that make the day sparkle and sway. Mary, dressed in a frothy dress that continually snagged and I, tastefully dressed by Mum, are giggling, straightening our dresses, and hats. In the evening, at the Hilton hotel, Mary and I shimmer our porcelain bests, eyes roving, on the lookout for handsome strangers. Mid shrimp cocktail, Mary nudges, 'He's still watching you.' I flutter. He asks me to dance.

My future husband had done a stint of male modelling; I have photos of Josef wearing a suit, head tilted, his square Eastern European face and jaw jutting handsomely from beneath a hat as he leans, casually, on an umbrella. In real life, he was diametrically opposite to the poseur in the photograph.

Born in Poland, in 1925, he was 18 years older than I. One of four children, his father died when he was very young and he was sent to live in a Catholic convent, cut off from his family. By 14, he was living on the streets of wartime Warsaw, separated from his mother, sister and two brothers, surviving on his wits until taken by German soldiers and sent to a labour camp in Norway. Six escaped on furtively handmade skis; they had one small gun. Not all survived. Josef made it to Sweden, his family eternally lost to him. He joined the Swedish merchant navy, jumped ship in Sydney and then moved to Melbourne.

This is all I ever knew. I could dwell on how he had been abused, his fears and the unadulterated horror of being a lone, young teenager in the bombsite that was Warsaw; there were no government handouts of food, clothing or shelter, no counselling or charitable collections. Josef found food wherever he could, tins in burning buildings and crumbs of black bread; he never spoke of the inhumanity etched into the soul by wearing clothes torn and soiled by vomit and urine. In the camp guarded by soldiers, he found, in the midst of despair, some hope. The soldiers treated him civilly; he had somewhere to sleep and food to eat. I don't dwell on it, because he didn't.

Josef arrived in Australia with nothing of his past except a few photographs. There is a very old one, of a young woman. She is beautiful and grave. He mumbled something about a relative. I felt otherwise, and sensed his loss.

I saw the nobility of suffering, and believed my heart was so full with compassion as to render his pain healed. What was love? I thought the compassion I felt for Josef's life was love; however, I rejected that and learned much later, it is indeed part of love.

We were married at the Melbourne Registry Office. Josef wore a suit. I wore a pink, self-striped, satin dress and matching coat made by

Mum. 'Are you sure you know what you are doing?' Mum had asked, crawling on the floor, her mouth full of pins while I stood on a coffee table trying not to shuffle and wreck the hem. I don't know how, or when, I told my parents I was pregnant.

Constant anxiety had made me thin, I seemed breakable; a hundred-tiny-pieces-fragile. What happened, I wondered while waiting for my wedding day, to the girl who inaudibly raged against authority, roamed Collins Street wearing all black, on her way to being the best photojournalist ever?

Mum and Dad and Josef and I traipsed to the ceremony and then to our small reception, held in a multi-mirrored room, our guests a kaleidoscope of flashing, bevelled images. My father proposed a toast with tears in his eyes, and Mum grabbed a sherry to hide hers. Josef promised to look after me. Outside the sky was blue, the air still. We made not a dint in either.

I didn't marry because I was pregnant. I had already had an abortion. Mary, who knew about these things, had taken control. 'Annette, shave your pubic hair off or risk infection, or worse!' The nurse looked at my exposed, shaved, self with some amusement, 'Oh, we don't do *that* anymore,' she said. The 'worse' was my wounded dignity. Now another abortion held no fear.

Laura and Lynne had married. Even Sue, my strong-minded, feminist friend was married. Mary had met that special someone. If marriage was good enough for them, then it would be for me. With my decision to marry Josef, I did what I thought was the best thing to do at the time. I wanted someone to love; being with child meant that I would have two 'someones', and love would grow.

On a deeper level, I had linked Josef's pain to my inexplicable aching. Instinctively, I hoped he might understand, that his infinitely greater pain would allow the release, or perhaps comfort, of mine. As it was, mine remained inaccessible. Josef kept his hurt to himself. Our connection was inadmissible.

Married life began in a small flat compacted into a backyard in Elwood, and later extended to a first-floor, two-bedroom box in East St Kilda, surrounded by concrete, in a sterile street, lined with similar buildings.

During my pregnancy, carting shopping bags, I looked at the asphalt road lined with cars, watching the light flashing off rows of identical windows. My world shrank to the size of the farthest glimmering window. Self-pity rose in abundance blooming into tears. I looked at Josef with hangdog reproach. In public I smiled my waxen smile. In my internal world, my daughter growing in my belly sustained me.

Her birth came on quickly and four weeks early. Lying on my side, I burrowed into the pain, wondering and alive. Fathers, generally, did not attend births. Seemingly alone in this deeply personal moment, attended by strangers, I breathed deep and looked forward.

'Lie on your back,' said a nurse.

I wouldn't.

'You'll be much better if you turn over,' soothed another.

My resistance hardened.

'Lie on your back!' snapped another.

'No,' I whimpered.

Hands reached out, forcing me on my back.

'Please, no.'

My legs were dragged open and pulled to shackles. Terrified, I panicked. I sobbed. I fought to stay on my side. Faces loomed, large and grotesque. Arms grabbed roughly at me. I lay shaking, jerking at moves towards me. Reinforcements were rushed to the birthing theatre, one growled, 'For God's sake, you're only having a baby!'

But I wasn't. I was reliving something shut away.

I was given an epidural. Its warmth coursed through my body. My memory of this birth stops there. After the trauma, a baby slipped out between my legs, unnoticed.

My newborn child was whisked away to the premature ward – a lovely little girl, I was told. I returned to the multi-bed ward, a pink crocheted bed jacket over my shoulders, receiving visitors, flipping through magazines, looking at other mothers, and shell-shocked.

'What will you call her?' a nurse asked.

'Anta, after Josef's mother. Nina for short.'

With few hours of her birth, my tiny, four pound, 12-ounce baby had cerebral haemorrhage. Nina lay isolated in a humidicrib. Her head popped to one side and she was naked, with tubes attached to her tiny body. I pressed against the glass wall of the premature ward. Other babies were being taken home.

'Annet you have to leave,' a nurse said.

What he died and I wasn't there? I stamped myself to the glass.

'Annet Go back to the ward!'

I had rely touched her.

Ten days after her birth I went home without her. My hand-expressed milk was warm and sweet smelling and dried in patches on my breasts. Every morning, I took it to Nina and hoped that the smell of my milk would be easy to her.

Concerned about possible brain damage after the haemorrhage, the doctors planned to assess it later. Unexpectedly, they rang. Nina had meningitis and little hope of living.

I thought I would never get to her. Josef was at work. I didn't drive. Mum and Dad worked. My neighbours were out. I had no money for a taxi. The train's slow clacking departure and constant stopping, the delay as the conductor waited for passengers, the rustle and turn of newspaper pages, the catch of breath as standing passengers jerked to the train's momentum, were interminable.

When I arrived at the hospital, breath bated, I looked at Nina; so still and small.

'You can't do anything, go home, we'll call you,' the hospital staff said, and that was true but I should have been there, constant and next to her.

Every afternoon, for weeks, I watched Nina fighting for her life through the premature ward window. When told she had survived, her doctor said they couldn't explain some things. Some babies have the will to live, he said, because nothing else explained her survival.

Josef came home from work late one night and found me sittin the toilet seat in our bathroom. A mass of clotted blood sat in towl. I had sat there for hours, mourning the whoosh of life rushingdeath. The acceptance of bereavement for a miscarriage, or abortio as still some time away and I pushed it aside, but sometimes I thou of this formless child that, had it lived, would be a year younger t Nina.

One year after my miscarriage, my son, Stefan – named a Josef's father – was born. He rushed into this world. If I could, I wouescribe my son's birth at length. A mother should remember these ngs. Yet, I can't. Nor did I wonder why I couldn't. I had learnt to liwith my vagueness, to tuck it in and pat it down.

Unable to hold my son for four weeks, I waited. Stefawas also premature but not ill; he was too tiny to come home. Ce again, warm milk ran down my breasts and stained my clothes. Wi Nina in her pusher, I made the daily tram trip delivering breast milkn a jar to the hospital. This time, an adult and a toddler pressed up ainst the glass. On his back and naked, Stefan cooed to the ceiling; w knew he recognised us! Nina giggled and tore away from me. I smild. Stean would be fine.

Nina and Stefan were the first people I loved, and knew that I lovd.

Walking around Elwood one day, I pounced on an old-fashioned blok of flats. Feeling like the spy I was, I peered through the front windovs into two large, empty rooms linked by double doors; one had a fireplae and was linked to the room behind it by another set of double doos. Enchanted, I determined to live in that flat of allied rooms and in tht street of enormous trees. Miracles do happen. The owner pulled up.

Josef and I shared the desire to fix up our new home. He got in firs. I looked aghast as heavy antique furniture was dragged in, Russian tea urns placed on elaborately carved tables; my magnificent lounge suite sidelined by Eastern European clutter.

The flat, despite Josef's efforts, was warm. The front of the flat that had so enchanted me was light. The rest, alas, was dark. In our huge kitchen, the fridge was raucous, the stove green, the lino dilapidated.

Outside the backdoor there sat an old gully trap and I cleaned it until its brown, pottery walls gleamed.

Mum always said that clothes hide a multitude of sins but I think trees do. Big and green and swaying, encompassing overhead and underground, forcing asphalt to rise and crack, touching walls, imbuing rain with scent. If there are trees there is comfort. Giant trees lined our street, solidly in front of our flat, and every day I walked under them and I'm sure they sighed and looked, and sometimes moaned. One day, Nina and Stefan would walk, ramble and run along tree-lined streets. Josef grumbled at bird shit on the car and I praised the shade. Once more a mother swooped, as Mum and I had once swooped along footpaths and under soaring roofs, holding hands with my children, small and clean under the trees.

Sadness has a way of swathing, congealing and nurturing itself. Nina, Stefan and I went to the movies, to the beach, visited friends, walked through the Botanic Gardens to feed the swans, but when all was quiet, my tears resumed. I thought my melancholy must have been my marriage. What else could it be?

I took to walking Elwood streets seeking dilapidated houses I could mentally renovate to gleaming realms of 'really beautiful'. In the country I did the same, converting dull streetscapes to magnificent order. Each and every house I revamped had my family and I happily in it.

❧

Nina and Stefan had started school when I met Farida.

'Good-morning,' said a loud, distinct voice, 'my-name-is-Fa-ri-da.'

'Hi, how are you?' said I, stunned by her precision.

'Oh! … I thought with your name you probably couldn't speak English!'

She was tiny and slim, with short, dark, fly-away hair; I self-consciously towered over her and she was not at all perturbed by constantly looking up at me. We had been in conversation for five minutes, when Farida went through a routine that was second nature to her. She reached into her handbag, drew out a tube of hand lotion, moisturised her hands and offered the tube to me.

With Farida, I found my consoling friend. She was Jewish but had married a non-Jew and they had two children. Independent and brave she was, but she paid a price and had virtually no contact with her family. As Farida looked up at me and I looked down at her, our marriages floundered. Farida and I trudged, children in tow, from her square flat to my rambling one where we endlessly commiserated. 'He said *what*?' And supported, 'Well, if I were you!' We were torn between the old values of eternal marriage, come what may, and a new sense of entitlement.

Farida returned to the work force, which limited our confiding, but she inspired me. Shortly after Nina's birth, I had decided to complete my schooling. Too apprehensive to attend classes, I studied by correspondence. To compensate for my poor marks in the subjects that relied on memory, I passed additional ones. I had fantasised myself into the best teacher imaginable, long before I made any concrete moves towards teaching. I stayed at home until Stefan started school and chose teaching because of the hours, and something to do with saving the world.

Training for mature-age students was encouraged in the early 1970s. I only had to complete a form and, without a debilitating interview, was accepted into primary teacher training at the Melbourne State College, in one of the last years to offer paid studentships.

Assessment for the course was predominantly through multiple-choice questions or essays; my memory was bypassed. To my surprise I excelled.

Josef feared that if I became independent I would leave him but I hoped teaching would make me happy enough to stay. When confusion threatened to overwhelm I reached down to Farida, and she reached up to me.

Teaching would be wonderful and terrible. The terrible part was being called on to participate in role-playing games when stress ruled and I shunted to a robotic halt. The wonderful was a new world opening. The chalk-and-talk approach to teaching was being replaced with an emphasis on teacher development and child participation.

At South Melbourne Primary School, I painted the cupboards, kids' worktables and blackboard frame in vivid pink and navy blue and set up my classroom, my blackboard a multi-coloured grapevine. In this wonderful old school building, ceilings rose high, corridors were lined with school bags, some hanging neatly and others tossed haphazardly, and scraps of whatever lay everywhere. Voices rang and barked and shimmied. Walking through, I dodged the lot, and puffed up at the sight of my classroom.

The parents of my Year Ones were mainly from the towering Housing Commission block nearby or children of Greek migrants. They were amazing. Greek mums carted their children to class with the words, 'Greek school last night. He's still asleep. Sorry.' Kids from the Commission flats had to be dragged from a spectacle; it seemed each day some bright spark put dishwashing liquid or red dye – or both – into the fountain and pink suds bubbled and oozed to the gutter. The parents were kind and generous. I had expected maybe one or two would be slapdash, or worse.

Mornings were Maths and Language. How many wheels on a car? How many cars? How many cars with four wheels? Three cars with four wheels. Gold star! Fill the gap. Put the sentence in the right order. Find the hidden words. Who hasn't read yet? And in the afternoon we had activities. Grass seed men. Food dye in dirt, flour, water, clag. Houses, suburbs, whole wondrous cities were fashioned from trash. Paintings ran out of space to be displayed from. Piles of everything were scavenged from the grounds. Why? How? What? And words, words, words.

And then came Jack – screaming, riotous Jack. Jumping from table to table, skittering as he landed on papers, his classmates cowered in his wake. I was warned. 'Be careful of this one. There were problems with him at his previous school. Lock up your purse.' In a teaching moment of which I remain proud, I gave Jack my purse to mind and, on a pretext, stepped out into the corridor. On re-entering the room, Jack rushed to me waving my purse, 'Look Miss, I looked after it for you.' From then on, Jack kept popping up in front of me, his face grimy, 'I love you, Miss.' I loved him back. Not many people, in Jack's young life, did.

But, each year I had another Jack. Each year I seemed less able to cope with the Jacks of this world. The daily grind, the conflict between the needs of the Jacks and their impact on the other children in the class escalated. There were days I despaired, when I wanted to just throw them out of the room and to hell with the consequences. My migraines increased. I began to dream of ways out.

Immersed in books, I tried to find answers; I couldn't find the questions. If I had more money, saw more plays, took Nina and Stefan out even more, spent less time at night preparing lessons, went back to study, had at least one Persian rug ... if I left Josef?

Then my father died. As a boy, he had played Two-Up to his father's (Victorian Police Superintendent, Alfred Stephens) horror. As a young man he took a chance on a girl he picked up on a St Kilda street. As a father he staked his all on a milk bar in Heidelberg. In Brighton he hoped to recoup his losses by moonlighting, from home, as an illegal bookie. Only one in four chances had turned out well – Mum.

Dad's body had long been on its introverted journey; a shoulder drooped, an arm slumped. His aging physique was at odds with his intentions. He had been diagnosed with lymphoma not long after Stefan was born. My parents' life changed to a routine of hospitals and doctors, and rising grief.

In hospital, my father lay in a bed too large for him, his face receding, his pain recoiling from living. Mum and I sat tentatively on the side of his bed, careful not to squash his deserting life. He died in 1980, at 69 years of age.

He was the most decent man I had known, but I had kept him at arm's length. All I have, in memory of his funeral, are a few minutes of standing in a kitchen at his wake; the cream space was undulating and fading. I had missed out. No longer trusting my own judgment, I had listened to others and misjudged him. Dad had tried and failed, made a small comeback and finally regained his self-respect. Some considered him weak, but in his hopes there was a touch of Don Quixote.

Stress is a windswept thing, whipping differences together, slowly screwing their jangling in place until locked tight and invincible. Had I looked squarely at myself, I might have understood that my mothering was not the disaster I had come to believe it was. Late at night I cried. Emotional pain ballooned, with no hint of the source. I wafted far and wide and reeled between my dreamy floating and an internal and resentful railing. It was one thing to not remember the date of an historical battle or name of a mountain range at school but to forget my first sexual experience, to look back and not know which men I had sex with and who I had not, my actual marriage ceremony, the entire birth of my son and only those traumatic moments of my daughter's is another matter. Aware of the minutiae of the daily doings as they happened, when they passed, many were lost. In the absence of memory, I blamed myself. If something upset someone I loved then it was my fault. It must be. My child cried, and only I was there with her.

༄

Josef worked hard, leaving home by lunchtime six days a week. Nina, Stefan and I went to school before he woke up, and to bed before he came home.

Sometimes differences dovetail; Josef's and mine didn't. We were a girl and a man, divided by our personal entrapments. Behind the disintegration of most marriages is a tale of hope and despair, and mine is no different.

We were together for 15 years. I wish to write more of Josef but cannot; however, not through bitterness. I still hold a quiet sadness for him.

༄

When I first left Josef, I stayed in Elwood, but soon made the important move symbolising change. My rented single-fronted Victorian terrace in Carlton boasted a pillar-box red hallway that extended into the lounge. The pianola dwarfed one wall, the couch poked out of another.

In this cacophonous room, I listened to Marianne Faithfull singing '… at the age of 37, she realised she'd never ride through Paris, in a sports car, with the real wind in her hair …' with a gut-wrenching desire.

Nina and Stefan had loved Elwood and enjoyed school there. Stefan coped in Carlton, but Nina? She kept disappearing. I hoped it wasn't to a dangerous place; that the independence she had learnt would protect, and not hurt, her.

In Carlton, I completed a Graduate Diploma of Media Studies and had enrolled at Melbourne University in an Arts degree. No amount of activity penetrated my sheer and taffeta self. Mostly, I lived enclosed in a quiet yearning.

Oh, if only I could leave teaching and find a new job. If I found my white knight, fixed up my migraines and sinuses, learnt to relax, made my children smile … I wanted to feel something, to connect, to stop living life at my God-awful silent remove from everything. Bleakness, inferiority, limpid thoughts of suicide, the failed and dreaded calls to memory, my silent obsessions and emotional flips threatened to overwhelm me and I sought solace in my floating. This isn't normal, I told myself.

If only I could live in Sydney, with the smell and sight of water and boats and hot dusty streets and big tired trees. And preferably in the crumbling room I had briefly stayed in, nestled in the water under the harbour bridge. At night the sea lapped against my wall and during the day, conversations bounced off the skylight. Inside was cool and inhabited by penniless people who minded their own business in a building removed from, but within earshot of, a bustling city.

Mum always said that the grass isn't greener on the other side. I thought she had never sought it.

If only …

&

'Lee, it's not really me,' I muttered, sitting in the beautiful house of a stunning, dark-haired woman who had her life together, laughed easily, made friends, had a prestigious job, travelled overseas *and* tried new things.

'You're miserable Annette, if you want to change your life you have to do something. These people are experts. They regularly give weekend personal-development workshops, usually in Sydney. It's only one weekend. How do you know if you'll like it unless you try it? I did one in Queensland. It was great; we got to know ourselves a bit better. It's at Melbourne University, and is the first one here. If you don't like it, you can always leave.'

I'd never been to a workshop before. Lee was right, if I wanted to change my life, I'd better do something. A workshop wasn't really *me* but ... why not?

If only I had thought otherwise ...

chapter 4

Bring on the Clowns

If only the day had signified itself: a black cat crossing my path, a mirror smashed to smithereens, ominous claps of thunder. If only dangerous men looked bad and decent women stayed that way.

It was March 1982.

'Dress casually,' Lee had said. I chose a black jumper, jeans, long boots and a dazzling cape, a look I liked regardless of the weather; it was still warm. Short hair suitably unkempt, I disregarded Mum's frequent exhortations to walk proudly and with a straight back, and slouched out my door.

The early-morning walk from my car to my future was a beautiful one; under lacework shade, past big elm trees, across newly mown grass, along a well-trodden footpath, to the heavy doors of an old hall in the grounds of Melbourne University.

Inside was darker, cooler. The drab hall had a high ceiling and splintered floorboards. It was a room for swaggering orators who thumped lecterns to a handful of people; it was a room for anxious strangers.

Well, I'm here now … I dumped my bag and cape, paid my fee and tagged myself to the group.

A woman stood before us. Lee had thought she was captivating. She had long, brown hair and wore a cream jumper with cream trousers tucked into knee-high, brown boots. Her features were neither stunning nor plain, but when she spoke her face mobilised and transformed to vital. In her thirties, her face had begun its deepening. As tiny as she was, her voice was loud, counterbalancing her slightness. Fists bunched up inside her baggy sleeves, she wrapped her arms round her body and, sleeves dangling, waited.

On edge, I waited for who knows what. Finally ... but no ... someone ambled back to their bag. We watched, and waited until this man returned to the fold. The cream woman had no intention of starting until we were garnered and quiet.

'Well, brave people, thank you for being at this first ever "Communication with Time, Space and Energy" workshop with myself, Jan Hamilton, and Mr Ken Dyers.'

He must be the man in the shadows.

'Are you ready? Stand up!'

Exercises. She can't be serious! She was. Jan jumped and stretched to the count of eight and an assortment of bodies and fitness levels limbered up. None could limber like her; the scene was set.

Jan asked each of the 30 or so attendees to say why they were there, and what they hoped for. Early responses were polite but, with each individual, the emotion ramped up. By the time a woman called Nadine gave her reasons, sorrow and apprehension drained from one to another. Nadine cried as she explained why she wanted to change the direction of her life. Startled, I said that I'm here for the same reason as Nadine, hoping the worst was over.

Nadine's tears had touched me. Tall, well-built but not overweight, she had short, dark, curly hair and eyes that effortlessly linked to others. Nadine was a rescuer of the sad; she was also a chatterbox. I like chatterboxes, forming bonds with my mouth shut.

I glanced to the shadows. The man called Ken had come out of them and was watching us so intently it was unnerving. Jan snatched my attention back.

'Welcome to clowning. Inside each of us we have a clown. The part we are frightened to bring out, because it has been hurt, betrayed or misunderstood. The clown represents human naivety and trust. To find our clown we remove our identity of John or Mandy. We change into clothes our clown likes and wear that symbol of the clown, the red nose. If your clown likes baggy pants and a gold hat, so be it.'

Holding a box of red, clown noses, Jan continued, and as she spoke of clowns a gaggle of bridesmaids and flying bouquets came to mind.

'Today, your clown will stand alone in front of everyone. When it is your turn to do the exercise, don the red nose; while wearing it, you are "in-clown". When you have finished your turn, take it off. This is to respect your clown and to let your clown know that, in-clown, it is safe to come out of hiding, in all its funny-sad glory.'

That this concept of clowning was both unique and important was demonstrated by the spelling Jan referred to: 'klowning.'

In this first exercise, each clown would say hello.

A confident me just might emerge, via a clown born from clothes scrunched in cardboard boxes. I chose clothes that represented my hopes; flamboyant, brave and destined. Grabbing a plastic nose, I clasped it firmly in my hand and joined my fellows on the floor in a semi-circle.

With a shrug of his shoulders and wooden wave, the first volunteer stood in front of us and said hello, only to be reprimanded by Jan. His clown had failed. Real clowns are natural; they don't pretend to look hurt, or silly; they allow themselves to be vulnerable, and find their child-like ability to trust the audience; they, too, have clowns in hiding.

My turn. The intensity of the strangers sitting on the floor before me fostered crying, not confidence. Apprehension had elbowed my tears ever since I walked through the door. I stood rigidly before the group. No plucky and appealing clown blossomed from within.

As ambivalent as I was towards Jan, her words were seeping through my barricades to this grown-up, good, little girl.

Sooner or later, the man of the shadows had to make his presence felt; Jan constantly deferred to him, and he patently wasn't there for the watching. We had changed; clowning clothes were strictly for clowning. As Ken emerged to stand with Jan, those who knew him responded with a ripple of appreciation. Ken wasn't good looking but who noticed? Wearing a cream top and matching pants, straight, slicked-back hair, edgy and cocksure, he commanded attention. Combining nonchalant sexuality with business-like efficiency, he silently appraised us. And then he began. Before I knew it, two hours had vanished.

'Aren't you clever?' Ken said, 'You know how to listen. For this exercise, find a partner. Tell them something. It could be what you did yesterday, but not in English, in gobbledygook. Find out you don't need words in order to communicate. When I say "start" talk to your partner until I tell you to stop.'

My partner shouted me down, so I yelled back, bolder and louder by the minute. This was not acceptable. Everyone repeated the exercise.

'Most people accept the status quo; their loss is our gain. If everyone thought they could reach the top there wouldn't be room there for us. Think kindly of those who have given up, they let us find out who we are and why we're here. Isn't that what everyone wants?'

Not noticing the condescension, I sat, a small bird, puffed up and pecking.

'This next exercise will help you take a position outside of yourselves.'

Whatever that meant, Ken did not make clear. These people are experts, Lee had said. She should know.

'Imagine you are sitting in a matchbox,' said Ken. 'Expand your box to include the person nearest to you.'

Ken steered us as we progressively expanded our awareness of space. We moved from one tiny box, to the room, to the grounds of the university, to the skyscrapers and lanes of the city, to the sprawling suburbs of Melbourne. 'Look at its muddy Yarra River,' he laughed.

He took us wider and further afield. 'Ah, the Queensland beaches. Take a little time, look at the kids on the sand, feel your toes in the water; you don't need to be there to experience that ... How far can you go? Look down on the Earth, its snow-capped peaks, its deserts, gullies and rivers. A quivering pendant of liquid can be sublime; a torrent of water can kill a man ... Well done.'

Our collective silence settled in that great, international space.

'Shrink your box ... say goodbye to those countries you visited.' Ken guided us back from the Acropolis, the Statue of Liberty and the Amazon jungle to Australia's Kimberleys and, like Spiderman's perfect landings, we arrived back where we started from.

Our stretched silence surged to applause. Clapping Ken, the feeling that my head was being snapped into a clamp dismayed me. This sensation was not new; the exercise had nudged my unrecognised detachment, set it slightly aloft, a zeppelin straining at its moorings.

Ken continued, 'We'll explore communication without words. Look at your partner's eyes. Don't speak; be completely still, mind and body. If you do this exercise properly you will see your partner in all their potential, and they will see you in yours.'

Staring at my partner's eyes, I found it remarkably easy to still my mind and banish thought but, as I did, my vision blurred and I blinked to refocus. Ken told me not to waste my time and, eyes straining, I continued. With my eyes wide open, I experienced the room as fading to blackness. There were no people, no Ken, or Jan, or partner or even Lee. The room hadn't literally gone black. It was dull daylight for everyone else, but I experienced it as moving to black. Many responded positively to Ken's call for feedback. I had nothing to say. I sensed my experience was different.

With each repeat, we stood opposite different partners for a longer time. And the same thing always happened; the room went black.

By day's end, sweat had flattened my hair and faded my lipstick. I could smell my crotch. Walking back over the grass and under the trees I wondered why Ken said not to drink alcohol that night or listen to heavy rock 'n' roll music, but it hardly seemed important.

On the Saturday night of that first weekend, Stefan stayed with his father and Nina with her friends – the ones she hoped would feel comfortable with the poor state of our house. I hoped she wasn't at a disco that accommodated underage teenagers while the music vibrated – grunt-grunt-thump-thump, again and again.

In bed and sweating, my legs touched and stuck together. Spread-eagled and restless, head awash with half-formed intentions, I chewed over the day. I liked the strength of Ken. If only I could be as brave and forge a new life for myself, Nina and Stefan.

Day two began with clowning. Jan slowly turned, eyes resting on me in a garish and garbled costume. She stood petite, too slight to fear, and as Ken pushed through our quiet boundary he almost broke the magic. Jan waited, apparently used to Ken's interruptions. She seemed a strident feminist yet accepted his disruption and listened reverently to him.

Expressing renewed admiration of our outfits, Jan continued, 'Let your clown stand in front of the group and silently be there, nothing else.'

A young woman wearing outlandish clothes peeped past a red nose and engaged her audience with mute sincerity. The following clown was leaden. Encouraged by this miserable performance, I ventured forth.

'No,' shouted Jan, 'don't look at me, look at them. They won't bite. Next!'

I told myself it's easy for the others, but I'd watched and knew it wasn't. A thin thread of communication, like fluff stuck to clothing, was opening up with Jan.

'A clown has a name, one that is perfect for you. As you stand before everyone this time, let your clown name simply come out.'

One by one, participants chose names representing their non-clown desires. Jan was not impressed. I watched as men and women in crushed, incompatible clothes repeated this exercise. This time, clowns responded with elation, or sobs, as their unforeseen clown names sprang forth and surprised them. I sensed something delightful.

My turn. Juggling 'Natasha' and 'Naomi' in my head, it happened. Standing in front of this costumed crowd, my clown's name toppled out. I stood trembling with disbelief. 'Clarence.' What? That's a boy's name.

'Fantastic, give yourself a clap, hug the person next to you. Congratulations!'

Jan sat cross-legged on the floor. 'I love my absolutely preposterous clown who thinks she's so clever. She has a blue belt in karate. A blue belt! She couldn't defend herself in a fit, but she thinks she can.' She shared her clown name with us. 'Gladys'. As Jan said my mother's name, Gladys, I thawed a little; enough to further erode my resistance to her.

Head listing towards painful, I sensed my flailing. Ken cut across Jan. 'We all have destructive identities that have been impinged, usually by parents. Happened to you, hasn't it Annette? You have a picture on you that screams failure. Teachers like Annette stand alongside parents as the most repressive people. Isn't she a sad example of both? Look at her, determined she's not going to let go and allow herself to be vulnerable. Not her! Do you like that identity? Has it worked for you?'

My hard-held reserve slipped. Ken was right, and being pretty failed to mask it. His eyes bore into mine, my throat hardened. A long eyeballing exercise followed and, in my blackness, blind tension gripped me. My head clamped tight.

The weekend was drawing to a close.

Jan spoke softly, her every word validating the path of Ken as we prepared to finish this day with a clowning exercise. With fermenting mind I joined the semi-circle. There had been a fight over clowning clothes. A clown was told to get a hat. A clown always wears a hat. We should know that by now.

It was late; we should have finished some time ago.

The simplicity of the exercise would move us all. Look at the other clowns and let your human through.

One by one we stood before our peers. Men trembled, women cried. Watching them, I swallowed. Our applause approached feral.

I was the last clown.

In front of a rag-tag group.

All eyes on me, all eyes compassionate … candid … clown eyes … and time slowed.

Tears formed, my lips quivered.

I would not cry.

I moved to run. Ken took my arm holding me, centred in a semi-circle. He moved away and I was alone, exposed and bewildered before bonding strangers.

Tears formed. I tried to flee. Again, Ken stopped me.

My self-control vanished. I stood wretched and abandoned, fearing rejection.

'Help her. Help her!' said Ken.

Pent-up feelings gushed, the torrent unstoppable. I cried. I screamed and, in time, my heaving body stilled.

In that quiet moment there was only Ken.

The semi-circle fused.

Quietly he said, 'Thank you, Annette.'

One by one, my peers hugged me.

This empty body responded to their touch and was grateful, inchoate.

'Would you like another workshop next month?'
Hands and arms rose in the air.
'I thought you might,' said Ken.

〜

With that seminal recognition of my aching self, my mind had cantilevered. No floundering with a detonated mind, called a nervous breakdown, for me. I seized Ken's solution, its promise for Nina, Stefan and I.

As tempting as it was to call Lee that Sunday night, something stopped me. Either I was brave enough to take this chance and follow Ken's instructions – or I was not.

Sleep was ragged in a room alive with the casting of shadows. In that darkest, hidden core of night I woke, jerked upright by a thunderous sound like a giant eagle swooping, its wings heavy, struggling in a turbulent room. I sat erect and rigid in the middle of my bed. Air pitched around me as a voice boomed, '42 people.' My children must have heard.

It must be related to the power of the workshop, and an omen, I thought. This had no explanation unless … I attributed it to Ken and his mystifying psychic powers. He spoke to me. Me. I deemed myself chosen.

〜

Ten people from that destined semi-circle met to organise the next workshop. They did not include Lee; she preferred to revisit an ashram in India. To be part of a group was new and not entirely welcome, but I liked Nadine. She couldn't find which bow to tug at to escape her religious heritage, a quest her family disagreed with.

Spurred on and already charred, in the weeks before the next workshop, Nadine and I encouraged and visited each other. She and her partner, David, a fellow attendee, lived in a tree-splattered house strewn with leaves that failed to understand the difference between inside and outside. She taught me to make homemade yogurt, I weeded her tumble-down garden and all the while we chatted about Ken.

Workshop arrangements included hiring the hall. I had, wrongly, assumed they were held under the auspices of Melbourne University. To boot, our bonding clutch of enthusiasts had to find people for the next one by handing out pamphlets to colleagues, friends and family – anyone, actually.

Wearing his trademark cream casuals, with slicked-back hair, Ken stole the show in our next workshop. With too many words to grasp their hidden mutilation and, lost in the warm fuzziness of expectation, Ken's camaraderie and his casual exposure of individual frailty, judgment slept. Ken pranced and cooed and preened and raged and gave us his thoughts on life.

According to Ken, we could locate the hidden thoughts that unconsciously control us, become flexible with identities, and utilise the right personality for the job at hand. Most people, he explained, have rigid personalities and see themselves in limited ways;

A woman might call herself a nurse and for as long as she is with patients that persona is appropriate. But when she wants to dance with abandon, her inflexible, careful nurse identity holds her back. We would learn to slip from one identity to another; from nurse to mother or lover, or spy.

Ken turned to David.

'You're hiding behind your beard and long hair. You don't want anyone to see you. An old hippie living in the past! David, do you want to be like that?'

Ken called him up in front of everyone and suddenly mock-punched him. A shocked David struggled. He looked at Ken with muzzled eyes and when Ken pounced to his balls, David crumbled. Ken handed David his masculinity back on an expertly decorated plate.

'Those in the hot seat have the courage to stand and cop it for everyone here. Everyone here has learnt something from David. Give him a clap.'

This individual acceptance of problems that should and could be fixed, for a combined personal and common good, was the basis on which Ken predicated his intentions.

'A group is far more powerful than any individual,' said Ken, 'and we are forming one. We call it Kenja. Jan and I began working together a few years ago and Kenja is a combination of our names. It means "wise man" in Japanese. Most people are frightened of a group but here, in Kenja, we learn to understand one and find our individual strength within it.'

'Everyone slots into an energy scale, called a "Tone Scale". It ranges from high to low. You can't see it but you can feel it, it is emotion. Freeing up the energy centres in your body will enable you to choose the level you want. Communicating with a high-tone and a light level of energy is far more persuasive than a low-tone, heavy, near-death one.'

The format of this workshop was changing. Ken's talk was followed by an eyeballing exercise. This format was repeated throughout the day. Subsequent talks were much shorter than his opening address; each exercise lasted longer than the previous one. With each exercise, partners were to silently focus on the energy flowing from a particular energy centre.

My eyes gripped those of my partner, and soon lost their focus. I could blink clarity back but I didn't want to. The blur before my eyes moved like slow clouds, gathering force and darkness. With my eyes open and linked to those of my partner, the light in the room waned, turned dark, then surged to blackness; the room disappeared and I stood in the middle, troubled.

Forcing a hole through my fears, I asked Ken, 'Why does everything go black around me?'

'The blackness is due to the extent of the dishonesty and lies you have around you.'

Ken had hit on a truth. All my daydreaming of impossible dreams, and hiding in the music of Bach ... something about me *was* very dishonest. I sensed it – always had.

Jan was surprisingly quiet that day. Her clowning class had been relegated to the Saturday evening. She began it with profuse praise of Ken. I rolled my eyes; her 'humble Jan' attitude was hard to believe. That night, 'Clarence' and I were awkward and gentle, and frequently cried. I took us both home, vowing to be really impressive the next day.

I passed another restless night thinking of Nina and Stefan ... mothers and teachers had the most repressive control over others, said Ken. I was both. If I learnt Ken's way, I could drag myself from the bottom of the heap. Nina and Stefan would recognise the new me that Ken promised, and rush to embrace me.

Next morning, the eyeballing exercises became formal sessions. Ken called them 'processing sessions' and told us that he had invented, and continually fine-tuned, them. The person running the session was called 'the processor', the person receiving it, 'the processee'. Sessions were the same, whether they were run, as they soon would be, between individuals in a private room, or between pairs in workshops, or in the classes I would later attend.

The format of workshops was being established. Ken talked for up to three hours before we had our first session. Two more sessions were preceded by short talks. There were tea and lunch breaks, but these were never between Ken's talks and the sessions. Jan's clowning class was, from then on, given on Saturday night.

Each session was preceded by verbal agreements to have it, followed by the 'session command' and up to two hours of the silent, non-verbal eyeballing that Ken now called 'processing'. Each session was concluded with a formal set of instructions that stopped the actual processing. A brief feedback, from processee to processor, followed.

Sessions are based on the assumption that human beings are, unconsciously, governed by the pain of experiences that they have not understood and, therefore, have not let go of. A session is a safe environment to understand and eliminate this unwitting control.

The session command gave the session its focus but was, overall, general rather than specific. If the command focused on, for example, why one lacked love in one's life, or on problems with our parents, the assumption was that we would find problems relating to these; but the specific problems were personal.

The wording of session commands was complex and difficult to remember, and had to be given precisely. Surreptitiously listening to the person next to us, trying to grasp Ken's words, or loudly pondering them, was unacceptable. Delving into unknown areas, where mistakes of the past rear up and banshees moan, was dangerous. The commands, Ken said, kept participants focused and out of uncharted territory. As Ken elaborated, a fear of personal gods and demons, latent and portentous, stole through our embryonic group. A whiteboard was found so each processor could read Ken's commands, word for exact word.

The confrontational delivery of Ken's pre-session talks was thrilling, but disturbing. He prodded participants to question their identities, stressing the benefits of change. This opened up cracks in one's identity and provided an entry point for his ideas. As a prod became a battering ram, he reinforced these ideas. This emotional breaking-down allowed for access to, and manipulation of, previously controlled emotions like jealousy, rage and ambition. Ken paddled in the lot, offering them up as something individuals needed to confront in session before these devious feelings controlled us.

By the time the session began, Ken had stoked us up and damaged our defences. Many cried while he was still talking. For me, the emergence of my missing, presumed-dead emotion was, in itself, remarkable.

In workshops, sessions began with a scramble of finding partners and lining chairs up in rows. Processors always sat on the same side of the row and ensured that both waited quietly. Jan sometimes sat in our rows opposite someone in session; she was always the processor.

Ken gave the order to begin. The room snuck to life as processors softly ran through the verbal agreements to have this session, followed by the session command. As the session commenced the room stilled; a sigh and a shush extended to walls, floor and ceiling. From the silence, pain rose.

'Go into the eye of the pain.' said Ken.

Ken observed us, often walking the length of the aisles separating the rows of processing pairs. He said that images might form in our minds, perhaps relating to events in our past, and to watch them like one watches a movie.

In session, Nadine sobbed loudly. A newly beardless and short-haired David moaned. Ken moved to him, touched his body, and David released scraps of his pent-up life. My mind went blank. The flickering room dimmed to sludge and merged to black and, without knowing why, I cried. Tears hauled themselves from deep within and

I gasped for breath. When the session finished, Ken talked and smiled and understood, and warmth and hope flared.

Processing is not hypnosis, said Ken. Hypnosis is a man in a white coat swinging a watch on a chain, telling people to do things they later regret. Hypnosis, he knowledgably asserted, takes control away from an individual; he taught the exact opposite, returning control to people through releasing the pain that, in fact, controls them.

Much later, I would learn that processing sessions are actually regressive hypnosis, dangerous in the hands of unqualified people and an unknown factor in a group. Hypnosis is difficult against one's will, but when knowledge and consent are bypassed it is relatively easy. Participants not susceptible to hypnosis, dismissed sessions as a non-event and didn't come back.

As the last session of this second workshop finished, Jan beamed with love for all. Ken sat calm, benevolent, stoking embers, reminding us of our potential, and quietly thanking us for our contribution to the workshop. Leaving the stage, Ken hesitated, returned to it, and faced his audience.

'Imagine a toy wind-up rabbit that totters for minutes then sits dead and waiting.'

Clacketty, happy, tin, wind-up toys of my childhood flooded my mind.

'Now imagine a little wild rabbit running, frisking its ears and on the ball. Which would you rather be?'

Everyone, bar me, chose the wild rabbit. I liked my show of individuality. Ken said that in Kenja everyone (bar me) could find their dormant, wild rabbits.

'Next time ... I'm assuming you want another workshop. Do you?'

Of course, we did.

'Next time, book in for a session with Jan. It'll blow your mind.'

Not mine. I had no intention of spending $40 on a session with her.

'In our Sydney headquarters, I train people called "professionals" who are paid to run processing sessions. Their clients are also called processees. Kenja professionals offer sessions to the general public, and many of these people decide to become Kenjans. I will, if you wish, train you to professional standards by giving a monthly workshop, in Melbourne, for the next 12 months.'

If only memory served me better, I could have seen my actual life, instead of the one Ken lambasted me with. If only I had stuck with my usual resistance to potentially confronting things. If only Lee wasn't my friend. If I hadn't cried so much at workshops, I might not have linked Ken to my tears.

Or felt my heart stop in wonder at 'Clarence', my clown.

David's arm teetered in air. Nadine's punched it. Mine flew up.

Ken's expression said it all. Aren't we clever?

We were – and very brave.

chapter 5

Not Yet, Not Quite

As dreams go, the beginning was humdrum. The reality was our hatching, organising committee. I had winced as Claudia, Jan's sister, removed the large black and white photos of Ken and Jan from the workshop walls; they *were* gauche, but when in Rome ... One might even ask what, exactly, did we have to organise? The single most important item on our agenda was the number of people attending the next workshop.

My fellow aficionados were nice people. But inspiring? If Ken hadn't been larger than life ...

'Not another meeting!' I complained to Nadine as these escalated.

'Well, we have to, we need to set goals.'

'Ask Claudia to ask Jan to ask Ken ... would that be alright? Why do we need so many people – and meetings, for that matter.'

'It's all about commitment to yourself, Annette.'

To that I had nothing to say.

The recruitment of strangers began in earnest. We divvied up suburban Melbourne and plastered shop walls with posters advertising Ken Dyer's 'Time, Space and Energy' workshops. Every weekend we ventured further afield, to newer and sparser suburbs. Recruitment was hard. This increased our resolve and annoyed everyone we repeatedly invited but ... no people, no workshops.

Ken had begun to talk about a strange new, psychic world, in which the power of thought would be ours; simply being a Kenjan and striving for the good of the world would be rewarded from on high. Recruitment would, one day, be easy: one incisive thought would see a rush of new people to Kenja.

Ken's rules were slowly introduced. They weren't called rules, but barriers for our protection. No jeans or black or red or orange should be worn, these were associated with evil, devils and horrible energy. Split-second punctuality was a vital show of respect. Details of a session were strictly confidential. Drugs, including alcohol, were forbidden. There was a qualified acceptance of medication. One could not have a session for 48 hours after medication, except for antibiotics.

When Ken suggested that living with people who take drugs was not in our best interests, I ignored this. I lived with Nina and Stefan, who used medication when they needed it and headache tablets didn't, to me, count. Nadine was late for everything. And we both wore our usual clothes.

By ignoring Ken's instructions, Nadine and I braved his wrath. We loved processing and vowed to stick rigorously to its rules. Did the rest really matter? The doing of multiple things together, the breaking of clothing and strict time rules, and the shared failure of finding new people for workshops drew us closer and gave us some courage of the Dutch, and dicey, variety. But then, Ken rewarded us all for being good girls and boys and sticking to his instructions, and we hadn't. Guilt kicked in. Nadine opted for dull clothes. I abandoned my black.

Our reward was 'co-processing'. This involved having two sessions a week, one as processor and one as processee, in our homes. These sessions followed the same format as professional sessions; a half-hour talk was followed by an hour-long session. These were structured around an imagined circle. Within one week, Nadine would process David who processed me and so forth until the last of our circle processed Nadine. When we opted for a second co-processing circle, four sessions in a week, the rule relating to medication (the 48 hour rule) impacted. I stopped taking Panadol.

Nadine and I still bucked some of Ken's dictates, and ran our private sessions in the bedroom of her leaf-stained house. However, Ken put a stop to that. Bedrooms were bogged down with energies of decayed dreams and leftover sex.

'Processing will take you to a level in your life you cannot imagine. The barriers are not sloppy. They are not for fun. Processing in rooms with stale energies only makes it hard for you. Isn't that right, Jan? Find appropriate premises or don't process. No hard feelings. It's your choice.'

So find premises we did, and on a wintry Saturday, Nadine and I had our first processing session in our rented room. It was draughty, the floor creaked and the blind barely covered the window.

Nadine was the first person to stand, naked for this session, in that grumbling cupboard of a room. She undressed awkwardly and stood in front of me, like a bird with a broken wing. I had wondered why? Ken said nudity has no significance other than what you give it. Processing was a release of energy and nudity allowed for an uninterrupted flow.

I was fully dressed, except for the standard removal of shoes and belts. There was no heating and Nadine shivered. I moved my chair closer to her, grateful for my jumper. In one flowing movement she unbent her body and rolled her shoulders. We were ready. Nadine for her traumatic unearthing of repressed pain and I, for the almost motionless dedication I would give to her. Tilting forward, I began the session.

Ken had put aside the usual hour for individual sessions. I would process Nadine until she had gone through her cycle of emotion. Nadine could ask, even beg me to stop the session, but *I* decided when it was over, not her.

Of course, she could simply walk out. But then she may no longer be involved. It wasn't safe to leave our silent ritual mid-way, in the midst of distress. I would ensure that Nadine was safe; I would hold her in place. Jan had already called processing 'Our Excalibur' – it was *that* important.

Our room darkened. A chill descended. Tears ran down Nadine's face. By the time her silent howling ceased, two-and-a-half-hours had passed.

By then I had stopped painting my classrooms and carving out nooks. Kenja had co-opted my spare time. The four weekly co-processing sessions, the regular cleaning of our rented room, workshop meetings and (useless) hours of recruiting workshop attendees were fitted in. The more we gave to this new venture, the more we would get out of it, said Ken.

Too busy to visit Mum, I became impatient in her visits to me. My girlfriends' reluctance to become involved in Kenja puzzled me. Lee was no longer interested; she considered Ken bombastic. Sue, in the reddish glow of her darkroom, said unequivocally, 'No, no, no.' Sue tried hard to stay in touch and often rang for coffee in Carlton, but I was busy. Farida invited Nina, Stefan and I for dinner. Ditto. Still I plagued my friends; sooner or later someone would give Kenja a go.

And Farida did.

She found Ken angry, controlling; his beliefs bothered her. She even said he was dangerous. I tried to explain that Ken was a wonderful, unique human being. At a lecture long ago, promoting some bizarre group, I had smirked at those stupid enough to be conned. Our group was different, my misgivings proven wrong. I had seen the light and she, poor thing, had not. Farida, her children, her timber house that rattled with passing trains, and her haphazard ex-husband slithered away. At our last dinner, I looked dispassionately at her. We had shared our worldly wisdom but I was learning otherwise. As Ken said, 'Kenja is not for everyone.'

A few months into Melbourne's 12-month course, I bought a house, a renovator's opportunity, the deposit was a loan courtesy of an aunt. A dream had come true. I cried to Ken that he was right: if not for Kenja …

Having been rewarded by this intriguing, psychic world with my house, I figured this would continue, and the house would be fixed. Nina, Stefan and I would live happily ever after in it. In my own house, dreams would come true. My unconscious escape from Kenja lay in this house. I would be nailed to place.

Impatient to have my home beautiful, renovations were commenced by a friend of a friend who called himself a builder; he *had* done a nice, cheap job converting Sue's garage into a studio. We lived in a house that had lost its entire back section, had a hole in its side and a profusion of wires. The misnamed builder took out a wall. It was a structural wall. I have no recollection of the ceiling collapsing, but am assured it narrowly missed me.

At first I resisted Sydney workshops. Two a month was doubly expensive. But then, everyone from Melbourne went and that meant they would change faster than me. They were held at the Woolloomooloo State Primary School. My mouth set in a cartoon zigzag and my throat constricted as Jan and Ken strode into the hall. A topsy-turvey clan of men and women rushed to sit. Ken and Jan mounted the dais. Tumultuous applause filled the walls, the air stilled and doors closed.

I looked at Jan and felt her pride. All those people were standing and cheering her. She was our example, an ordinary woman on a world-changing journey. She must lead us with elation and humility, and never falter. Ken had already made it and had nothing to prove.

At least 100 people were present; we couldn't lasso 30 in Melbourne. There were far more women than men, and many were beautiful. I hardly noticed the few men. I judged them needy.

With the mass of Kenjans in their muted clothes and Ken in his cream, workshops attested to an ancient ritual. As sessions finished, we sat and stretched and lay, chins in hands, on the floor before him. Surrounded by his inseminated beauties, Ken looked like a pagan god.

That was the first time I met Nicholas. Tall, angular, brick-jawed like a cartoon hero, Nicholas, with his thick, honey-blond hair and bright enthusiasm, seemed a tower of strength. But we all have the straw that finally breaks our camel's back, and hidden away – especially from himself – his heart could fall like dominoes. Each of us in Kenja had an Achilles heel – being too, too human was Nicholas's. An aspiring writer, he had been involved with Kenja since pre-formal days. Nicholas was a Sydney professional, the one Ken anointed as having beaten everyone and healed first. When he met Ken, he was a casual drug user. Ken insisted he attend Narconen, a drug rehabilitation centre associated with Scientology. Nicholas gave the credit for his rehabilitation entirely to Ken and, in return, devoted his life to promoting Ken and Kenja.

After Jan's clowning class, I hugged into his back as his motorbike roared and weaved across Sydney's Harbour Bridge This attention, showered on me by Nicholas, was not entirely spontaneous. He was doing what was expected of him and making a newcomer feel special. Had I known, I wouldn't have cared.

The next time I saw Nicholas was at a seminar in Queensland. One after another Kenjan was put in Ken's traumatic hot seat. Men stood proud of their ability to cop it on the chin and women sobbed in the knowledge that, this time, tears were not in vain. Nicholas was the next to be singled out; he had, apparently, broken a Kenjan rule and had sex with a married Kenjan woman. Ken screamed at him, chain-smoking, his ashtray full, and as he angrily stubbed out another cigarette the ashtray overflowed. Watching Nicholas repeat the words, 'Yes Ken, yes Ken, you are right Ken,' was terrifying; galvanising.

Ken maintained that he could smoke and swear because he was superior to others and acted entirely by choice; lesser mortals smoked due to addiction and swore in unfettered frustration. As Nicholas, Ken's most praised devotee, stood tall and resolute, proud of his capacity to submit to, and learn from, a higher authority, Ken's power was palpable.

It was at this seminar that Ken raised the possibility of a Melbourne Seminar alongside those of Sydney, Noosa and Brisbane.

He looked at me, and started. 'How do you expect to run a new Melbourne Centre when you think you can show up here for only one day of this weekend!'

Noosa was a long way from Melbourne, a day-and-a-half bus trip away! I considered it noteworthy that I had made a big effort to get there at all.

'I know you want Melbourne. But you've never been to a class or lecture in Sydney. How do you plan to run it, sweetheart?'

Alive with the hope of leading a new Kenja Centre, I feared this chance in a lifetime might disappear before it had begun. I shook my head. One didn't make excuses to Ken, or lie; he could see straight through you. My body turned in on itself. Ken, before my peers, acknowledged my pain, hopes and potential. I said nothing; no one answered Ken back. I rose to his expectations.

I vowed to visit the Noosa Centre. But not Sydney. Not yet. Perhaps I sensed that involvement in the Sydney Centre represented a commitment to Kenja that was total.

Before my involvement, Kenjans performed a show called *Noosa Magic*. As an extension of clowning, Jan created musicals and the public performance of *Noosa Magic* had been met with some popular approval – hardly earth-shattering, on the way to Hollywood praise, but enough. After 26 hours on three buses, I fell out into a wall of Queensland heat. Sitting under an umbrella, in front of a five-star hotel, tiredness evaporated. I sipped coffee with my fellow aficionados, immersed in the most delectable expectancy that shimmered in tune with the haze: Noosa magic.

The Centre's décor reflected its tropical location. Marilyn, the director, was self-assuredly and gorgeously 'ocker' and she greeted me warmly.

That night, the heat was stifling. Overhead fans hummed. The blinds were open, windows sparked to outside lights; we had nothing to hide.

Marilyn shone. 'Welcome, Annette.' And to the assembled, 'What do you want me to talk about tonight?'

'Money.'

'Who hasn't got enough?'

Many hands answered.

I had heard the money lecture from Ken and, as Marilyn spoke, I censored my half-formed words: she does it better than Ken.

'You need to have affinity for money, respect it, understand its language. I don't have a problem with money, do I?'

Not with the number of paid sessions you give each week, I thought.

'Don't treat notes and coins as if they are filthy lucre. Money is a communication, like any other. I don't have crushed and damaged notes. I iron them. Fold them. Some of you may smile, but I have the money. It comes to me because I understand it.'

Ken called his ideas on life and his research into processing, his 'data', coming up with new data on a regular basis. Marilyn passed the latest on to us. Soon it was session time. She waited as the whisk of belts slipping from trousers, and the thud of shoes dropping, subsided. My processor and I sat close enough to reach out and touch, knees against opposite knees. The swell of whispers would soon abate, our ideal of perfect stillness sought. As a lone voice unsettled our silence, a collective intolerance blazed.

Mid-session and sweating, I fumbled for the top button of my shirt. Marilyn's voice, sharp and fierce, lashed out. 'Annette, don't touch your clothes!' The heat of anger swarmed through my body. I knew the rules. My discomfort should be ignored.

In that room I felt safe and responded to Marilyn's voice by delving deeper. I seized my processor's eyes, disappeared to my blackness and unashamedly sobbed.

'Wow. Ken says, freedom from the chains that keep us stuck in our damaged minds is our natural right and this is the path we follow to find that. Thank you everybody, that was a fantastic session.'

We applauded. Marilyn smiled the biggest smile.

Her house, where I stayed overnight, reminded me of something pristine and innocent. It had an outside shower nestled in the surrounding rain forest. Next morning, I stood naked under icy water as the bush huddled round, then I sipped coffee with Marilyn and listened to the tweet-tweet of birds and the sway of that forest.

I fell in love with Noosa. Light swept across the floor as the Centre doors swung open ... that wonderful hotel where we sat, feeling very fashionable, sipping coffee, looking out to sea ... the sun warmed our bodies as we sauntered along, our collective and sweet secret guiding our steps.

Emulating Ken seemed a long way off, but, perhaps I could become like Marilyn?

The months passed, changing from balmy to chilly. Leaves crunched underfoot, blew away and gave way to bare trees, dormant and waiting, enclosing budding Kenjans and their indiscernibly moulting lives. A year had almost passed.

One cramped day, the smell of burning invaded my slow senses, the room was acrid and the radio crackled news of the toll taken by bushfires in Victoria and South Australia. Seventy-five men, women and children were burnt to death in the firestorm that was Ash Wednesday. I gazed out my window, remotely guilty for my insipid response. Why do I not feel anything much, outside of workshops, I asked myself?

In every workshop, Ken's eyes twisted my very soul, unearthed pain, rustled it, shook it out and then he smiled at me – pain isn't that bad, is it? In a state akin to the disarray of love at first sight, I gave myself away. I had not fallen head over heels in love with Ken. Spellbound yes, but Ken held no sexual attraction for me. Jan could have him. That made him safe.

I believed that, after the course, life would continue as before, only vastly improved. I thought Ken was creating a group to support each other; he was creating Kenjans. After 'graduating' from our one-year course, our fledgling group rented a small partitioned office in central Melbourne, with me as the magnificently titled Director of Processing. I had no idea how to run a business, but Kenja was about taking chances and trusting myself.

The front half of the tiny, partitioned Centre boasted a dark, donated, desk. The back half saw ten kitchen chairs pushed against the wall for our class processing sessions, and a further sanguine six (we *would* get more people). We called it a Centre, the designation optimistic. It was legally ours, not Ken's. Nor did we, officially, use the Kenja name.

Income I earned from sessions was ploughed back into the Centre. At first Ken took no money, except from workshops. Regulars contributed from their pay packets.

My school principal urged me to take leave instead of resigning from the Education Department. That implied I might fail. I resigned, and spent some more of my meagre savings on a nice cream suit. One day, I would parade it before an excited audience in a sophisticated Kenja space. In the meantime, I gave a weekly, informal chat to the odd, curious soul. During our Thursday gathering, euphemistically called a 'class', I imparted Ken's latest words of wisdom to my counterparts. Then, ten people lined up opposite their partners for the session, nine in their blandest clothes. However, one was a former devotee of the Bhagwan Shree Rashneesh, who was still wearing dangerous red and lurid orange.

The first workshop sponsored by the Melbourne Centre was held at that leaf-rippling, floor-creaking hall in the grounds of Melbourne University. Melbourne Kenja would, cross my fingers, excel.

'Are you sure everything is ready?' I queried my collaborators at our pre-workshop meeting.

No response. I tried again.

'What about Jan and Ken's meal?'

David stopped shuffling papers. 'Well, I thought that egg and lettuce sand ...'

'Sandwiches!' I screeched. 'You can't give Jan and Ken sandwiches! They're not exactly *anybody*. Can someone cook *real* food, not brown rice and cabbage?'

Egg and lettuce salad would have to do.

I locked eyes with David. 'You're still picking J and K up from the airport?'

No, David couldn't. His car had broken down.

'Can someone else do it?'

I might as well have been talking to myself.

'Well, David, you're still driving Jan and Ken to Jan's mother's house, where they are staying Saturday night?'

No, he wasn't. He had no car, remember? He suggested Nadine.

'Oh, no!' I gasped. Not with her heavy energies.

Nadine suggested I wash my car and *I* drive them.

That was the last straw. 'It's not appropriate I do it. I'm the bloody director!'

On the day of the workshop, my hopes rose with each arrival. Many Sydney Kenjans were expected in Melbourne. Forty-two deposits had been collected. It was more than a year since Ken thundered '42 people' to me in the middle of the night in the bedroom of my cacophonous cottage in Carlton. Nadine, in a flurry of efficiency, was collecting money and ticking off names. Disappointed, I waited as Ken took his place on the rostrum with 41 present. The doors closed. I thought I heard knocking. It persisted. Ken looked annoyed but, as the 42nd person took their place, jubilation rinsed my flagging energies.

༄

There were two kinds of 'wall-walking', one with a partner and the other carried out alone. In partnered 'four-hour wall-walking' the usual rules of silence, no leaving the room and no non-vital disruption to the process applied. Buckets were available to be used as a toilet and for vomiting in. No food was eaten for several hours before the session. The doors were locked.

My first four-hour wall-walk took place in Melbourne, with a Sydney Kenjan, Kathryn, in charge. She was the processor and I, the processee. By submitting to a senseless set of repeated instructions for a minimum of four hours, I would experience my resistance to control. Only those able to submit to control could benevolently control, and therefore help, others.

Kathryn was tired, her shirt un-ironed; she had better things to do than spend four hours with me.

She gave the first command. 'You walk that body over to that wall.'

I looked coldly at this pretty, young woman, and then walked to the wall opposite. My eyes flashed but I stood motionless, hands by my side, facing the wall.

'With that body's hand you touch that wall.'

Raising my arm, I slowly and deliberately touched the wall, dropped my arm and stood still, determined not to falter. If I jumped the gun, Kathryn would rerun the command.

With my back to her I sensed her every move.

'Thank you,' she said, 'you turn that body around.'

I turned to inspect Kathryn standing at the other end of the room. She thanked me, then repeated the first of the three commands.

'You walk that body over to that wall.'

I returned to my starting point. She said, 'Thank you.'

Kathryn hooked into the corner.

'With that body's hand you touch that wall.'

As my arm returned to my side, Kathryn thanked me.

The only sounds were Kathryn's voice and my bare-footed pacing.

Standing in the same position for four hours, I saw her small body slowly bend then jerk, while her eyes drooped. Her voice ranged from drowsy and resentful, to bored and impatient as she went through her own cycle of emotion; several times she confused the commands.

After two hours I was on automatic: listen and walk, listen and walk. Unlike normal sessions, I never cried as I wall-walked – it didn't take much for this good little girl to be obedient.

Later, when I ran four-hour wall-walks, I observed turbulent emotion from my processees, especially men; my sense of power over them probably added fuel to the fire – as Ken probably intended.

⌁

'Solo wall-walking' consisted of a person privately walking from wall to opposite wall, touching it, then turning and repeating this for half-an-hour. Ken taught us that people are unconsciously loaded with snivelling and glum emotions that they do not want.

Have you ever felt like someone else? Ken explained that this is an ability we have, to acutely sense another. Sometimes, you know who it is you feel like. People like their own nice feelings, but not their depressing ones and off-load their rubbish onto Kenjans because we have a way of ridding ourselves of these: solo wall-walking.

As Ken demonstrated this, his body warped and spasmed. The secret, he said, was in one's ability to banish thought. I was good at that.

As I walked from wall to wall, my face and body twisted, my head shuddered to a degree I could not consciously emulate. This powerful emotion grabbed my head, as if it were clamped, and then seemed to drain quietly through my skull. Following this squeezing out, I felt light as a feather, until another grim sliver of someone's life came up for inspection. It was not unlike exorcism, when an evil spirit is supposedly dragged from a person; at least, according to Hollywood movies.

I solo wall-walked daily. Swooping blackness surrounded me as it did in session. One wall-walking session was different: I wasn't being purged of the baggage of others; I saw a small movie in my mind. I had longed for this moment, something tangible to understand. Midway through walking back and forth, a black and white image exploded through my eddying, grey mush.

A young child, perhaps five-years-old, with fine, blonde curls stood looking to the horizon, wearing a white, summer dress buttoned down the back from neckline to hemline. She stood in the middle of an asphalt path. One side of the path was flat with short, dry grass. On the other side of the path a treeless slope stretched upwards; the grass here was longer, and golden.

I recognised her. She was me. Something didn't add up. This image seemed to exist before I was born. The image in my mind was black and white, yet I knew the colours of the child and the landscape. Something moved to her right and the child turned to look. The upper half of a man's body was silhouetted against the ridge; a man with greasy, shoulder-length hair. I knew him. He was Uncle Dan, the man who took my grandfather's place at the head of that lavender table; he wore a dirty, ill-fitting suit and carried an axe. A look of wild ferocity was fixed on me. He approached me, silently and with intent … The picture abruptly finished. I was as wild-eyed as my Uncle Dan.

∽

Walking through the open door of the Sydney Centre for the first time, my heart sank. I stood in a wide corridor with dull, flaked walls and, walking, my image reflected in the linoleum. As I waited for the lift, the linoleum continued gleaming as it disappeared around the corner. Jan gave me the standard welcome: how clever I was by being there. Sitting opposite Jan in session that Thursday night class, I understood her passion for sessions. Our small bond firmed.

A session with Ken was arranged for me.

When I arrived at Ken's, I immediately thought this had to be the wrong address. I paced Ken's street past a drab block of flats. Even the weeds struggled; hardly a demonstration of the financial success Ken claimed. At 9.00 in the morning, I knocked on the front door and looked through the old-fashioned keyhole, in time to see Ken rushing to get dressed. Another surprise. He claimed to be up every morning at seven, at his age, nearly sixty. Entering the bathroom, desperate to pee, I came face to face with a naked, wet Jan hastily donning a white towel. Her eyes and her black pubic hair stared me out of that room. Turning around, I found myself facing a huge mess; papers and clothes were piled all over the place. I stood, stunned. For a couple whose energy level was at the top of the Tone-Scale, this was a disgrace.

Ken made coffee and approached me confidently. My confusion faded.

An enclosed balcony was set up as his session room; two armchairs laden with cushions faced each other. Ken closed the window and blinds. Doing a session in those huge chairs seemed privileged.

'Do you mind taking your clothes off?'

Of course I took them off. Why not, in front of Ken? As processee, I had sometimes undressed. It would benefit the session; energy could flow unimpeded.

'Are you comfortable?'

Ken gathered more cushions, plumping and moving them. Here or there? He was laughing and personal. He hardly noticed my nakedness; he was fully dressed.

Sitting opposite me, he bypassed the formalities of a session and just said the word 'start'.

After those dramatic wall-walking images of poor Uncle Dan, I had hoped for clarification in subsequent sessions; so far no luck. As I looked into Ken's bone-still eyes, I feared I might disappear into my still surging mists. My neck was tense and I sank into the cushions.

The session finished; to me it had barely begun. Two-and-a-half-hours had passed.

Ken lay on top of me with his trousers and underpants hanging down around his ankles. Uncertainty flooded my senses.

Ken stood. Dressed. Smiled. 'That was a great session, Annette.'

He asked for feedback. I stumbled.

I had failed to see any pictures, let alone another movie in my head. I noted the colour of Ken's penis.

I wondered, the question brief, did we? If Ken had touched me, let alone had sex with me, I would surely have known.

How could a woman have sex and not know it?

If nothing else, I would have noticed the smell of semen. I liked its sticky pungency.

From the depths of my unconscious mind, something had involuntarily asserted its authority. I shut my uncertainty down and closed it off. Nothing had happened, I concluded. In session, Ken had released my unpleasant energies. That was it. I should know. I *was* there with Ken in the session.

'It was,' I said, 'a fabulous session; years of pain just flew away.'

'That was an important session, Annette. Take a little time, pamper your human, fluff it up a little and walk along the beach.'

I had no time for a beach walk; unease shivered and I disobeyed Ken.

A dribble of new participants saw the numbers in Melbourne slowly rise. It only took a few for us to require more space than our cubby-house office provided. The new Centre in Carlton, close to trendy cafés, great boutiques, superb cake shops, the university and alternative theatre, was every Kenjan's dream; Kenja was on the move and growing.

Within our four walls we built an administrative office, joint lecture/class/workshop space plus the individual processing cubicles, secured internally. (That the cubicle doors were locked was never questioned by me; processing was Kenja's gift to mankind, hence protected.) These, plus a food preparation area and bathroom, preferably with showers, were the basic requirements for Kenja Centres; all embellished with the Kenja logo in the Kenja colours: pink and blue.

At lectures, suit buttoned and shoes polished, body rigid with strain, the information I was meant to impress with went missing from my mind. I fumbled to represent Kenja with some dignity. Daytime was lonely, my recruitment unproductive and demoralising. Melbourne finances went from bad to worse.

Nadine contemplated moving to Sydney; David would follow. Sydney was where those struggling to let go of intractable identities stood the best chance of succeeding. Sydney had Ken. Claudia had already left and fled to her sister, Jan's, side. Others intended to. I counted the small number of Melbourne Kenjans, and calculated the sums that didn't add up.

But as Ken said, the more you give, the harder you must try; I gave everything and even though Ken hovered large in my mind, I still gave for Nina, Stefan and myself.

Kathryn was Ken's pet for no apparent reason – apart from being petite, dark, curly-haired and pretty. Two things singled her out: Ken's consistent slating of her mother and Kathryn's constant falling asleep in session.

She had swept into Melbourne, ostensibly to help us out, in fact to snoop. Kathryn had recently gained nursing qualifications but instead of nursing she devoted her life to Ken, nearly 40 years her senior.

Ken said Kathryn would become director of our new Melbourne Centre.

Over my dead body!

Why Kathryn? In Ken's talks, when she wasn't asleep, she fell apart, wringing her hands, her tiny body clenched to rigid, her prettiness filched by tension.

The omnipresent Kathryn was soon living in Melbourne. She usurped my position of director – courtesy of Ken – and most of my faithful clients. I remained a professional with three clients. My income was subsistence level. Ken's financial largesse had finished.

Thrown together with little in common, Kathryn and I were obliged to respect each other and overcome our joint hindering. When I walked to the city to recruit, Kathryn sanctimoniously announced that I wasted time, and when I caught the tram and she walked, she insisted that exercise was so much better for a Kenjan. Killing time in our bathed-in-stardust Centre, Kathryn frowned at me for obviously dragging her down the energy scale. I held the view that I was the rightful director of Melbourne and she was an upstart.

The world was out to stop Kenjans, the 'tall poppy syndrome' we thought. Resistance appeared in strange ways. Ken told us that once, he had stood outside a building used by evil businessmen and conjured, in his mind, a picture of an enormous, evil, black and breathy spider that would scare people away. He 'flipped' the picture onto the building. People, he said, were influenced by its invisible sway. Some glanced at their watches, others put hand to head. All turned tail and left. Scary picture. No clientele. The business closed.

Ken suggested that invisible, gruesome, psychic pictures had accumulated on the walls outside our building, and this explained our forlorn recruitment. Kathryn suggested we remove them. After class when all was dark and quiet, with Kathryn leading, out went the devotees of Melbourne.

Eliminating the unconscious control of these pictures was another aspect of processing; purge the power of the pictures by experiencing the pain contained in them. One person could eliminate the pictures on the walls, but that took time. Working together was like sharing a plate of cupcakes, and devouring the lot.

We stood outside our moonlit, two-storeyed building and looked straight in the eye of the pictures on our walls. I saw giant eagles loom towards me, toxic waste ready to flash to an exterminating whiteness, and an abundance of evil terminators flexing their haunches. My body distorted and emotions quaked until the power of these pictures settled and, convinced nothing nasty graced our walls, we all went home.

Alas, for poor Kathryn, the exercise wasn't successful. Few new people showed up to lectures and most of those never returned. We consoled each other for our inexcusable recruitment, then remembered Ken.

Desperation set in, the failure of the Centre a possibility. We couldn't ask Melbourne Kenjans to give more than they were. Ken said that Kenja Centres should be financially viable from income raised from sessions, classes and seminars, in the process demonstrating the success of processing. How could we make money, short of the miracle of more people?

Selling flowers was a popular income earner for some Sydney Kenjans; at the time, I thought Kathryn had come up with the idea. In a rundown, city building, Kathryn and I lugged heavy buckets of flowers up flights of stairs to a room she had rented. Kenja premises were strictly for Kenja activities. We were desperate and figured Ken wouldn't find out what we had done; Kathryn and I were professionals – the elite. I plodded along the streets of Melbourne, loitered over coffee and returned with an almost full basket. Dearest Kathryn returned with an empty one.

The following Saturday night, Kathryn and I were in Carlton's Lygon Street, carrying a frayed shopping basket full of roses wrapped in green cellophne that shrank and wrinkled when sprayed with water. Ten others went out and sold out. Unfortunately, Kathryn was so proud of herself, and her cohorts, that she told Ken. He let us know that this was not in the spirit of Kenja's successful game and that was that – and Kenja was called a game because life is a game, and Kenja the greatest game of all.

⟅⟆

One night a new person came to our lecture; panic clotted our space. In our midst sat a doctor called Alex. Mental health and medical specialists were rejected. That we had another doctor involved in Sydney was overlooked; his dedication to Kenja had been demonstrated. Incapable of understanding, these professionals labelled people and, if that failed, took the easy option: drugs. Yet there was Alex, tall and slightly stooped, a bear of a man with hurt, sharp eyes. Despite his many years studying he was soon diligently introverted; too busy looking inwards to notice the real world. Instead, Alex admired what he saw as his newfound capacity to cop the flak and confront his deepest fears.

It wasn't long before Alex was one of us, a Kenjan having regular weekly professional sessions, involved in everything, including co-processing. Alex, with his endearing giggle, would be Kenja's public face, but not before he had a hard look at his nice guy identity. It was difficult to look, dispassionately, at the things we liked about ourselves, but we had to do that too. We, his friends, would help him by acknowledging change and cold-shouldering its resistance. There was no pity; we were in it together but we were playing a tough game.

Processing sessions were infinitely superior to anything the professions had to offer, Ken bragged, and in any other country he would be paid thousands of dollars per session. Alex, anxious to demonstrate his dedication, complied and paid up.

He left his life in Melbourne and moved to Kenja Sydney to undergo Kenja's professional training, intending to return to Melbourne and use it in his practice. In class, Ken challenged Alex to stop riding someone else's tiger, especially Ken's sleek and dangerous one. 'Ride your own tiger,' said Ken.

Alex wanted Ken's. Ken shrugged his shoulders. No contest.

⁓

Not long before he died, Dad gave me some money, but now Mum was widowed, she wanted it back. Then my bank rang. The insurance company had inspected my house and given an ultimatum: repair it or they would no longer insure my dilapidated dream.

Standing on a ladder, clutching a sanding machine, I stared at endless shedding paint. Different levels of disrepair, from merely peeling to outright rotten, glowered at me and seemed impossible. I despaired and cried and gave up.

The excitement of Ken stood in contrast to my increasing separation from family and friends. As the thought, 'this is for Nina and Stefan', lost its placebo effect, I replaced it with the harmony of minimum thought.

The longer I was involved in Kenja the more remote I became, the more difficult it was for my children to reach me. My extended family shook their heads and said, corroboratively, 'Well, you know what she's like, she's always been a bit odd.'

Nina and Stefan were growing up. At home they waited, seeing less of me, sensing change, unable to define it. With respect for their privacy I limit their presence here. Despite my passionate belief I was motivated through love of them, they were moving to the mists.

I sneaked out of the house for sessions, classes, meetings and the trappings of my professional duties, guilty for the short time I spent at home, on another plane, obsessed with Ken's self-lauded success.

'I'm just going out,' I mumbled to Nina and Stefan.

'Where to?'

'I've left you dinner.'

At night, I lay awake trying to remember Ken's words that would transform me to a fabled parent.

What we put our attention on grows, said Ken, and the dismay of my mothering grew.

My finances didn't.

When money ran out, I sold my car, then my house, keeping some basic furniture: beds, table and chairs. My children and I would camp there for as long as possible, until the new owners took possession. My books, hundreds of them, were tossed into my garage and left to mulch on the sodden floor. My antique furniture was sold for next to nothing. Patchwork remnants, half-finished quilts and dozens of fabric-covered templates, were tossed into the shed. Maybe time would fuse the paper and fabric together, waylay the destruction of memory?

Nina and Stefan were locked tightly in my former lost mind, with the daily chores of the life we had lived together: washing on the leaning Hills hoist, gully trap stuffed with tea-leaves, childhood toys packed with a prayer for the future … maybe grandchildren, a second chance, an opportunity to remedy the mess of my mothering. My children became a pale yearning, guilt too great to comprehend, muffled in a house with holes in the walls.

❧

Ken said he would give me one last chance. I wasn't sure if he wanted to revive the Melbourne Centre or to save me. He arranged for his son, Matt, to give me a session. Ken said Matt was almost as good a processor as Ken himself.

Matt bore little resemblance to Ken, apart from his single-minded, stiff hair. With his clear, fine-tuned face he looked at Ken with a mixture of affection and … now I would say pain, but then I thought it was conviction.

Sessions had a routine. The person receiving the session always made the pre-session cup of tea. In that way, deference was shown to the person giving the session and, for me, contained a hidden prayer – this session would be the best of all.

Holding chocolate biscuits and cups of tea on the least dented tray, I stood aside, Matt first, before entering our session cubicle. Two upright chairs faced each other, a shelf held three knick-knacks, a plant sat on the floor and a picture hung from a wall. The room was narrow; stretched arms almost touched the walls. Outside voices intruded.

So much had been promised through sessions; I could relinquish sad and wanting Annette and find the new me. I tried but … maybe I didn't try hard enough? With no miracles to confide, I sat in front of Matt and wondered why I hadn't changed. Others had. Ken said so.

Looking into the eyes of this compellingly gentle man, I think I understood how easily, painlessly, life should ease and change. Particles of our lives might seamlessly merge and Matt's stillness would seep to me. I think it was my definition of trust.

The chairs were close; our breath merged. Ten minutes into the session, the grey swirling that had always surrounded me in session finally ceased. What I saw and experienced was startling in its rapidity.

I lay in my secret place, the one that had fascinated me since I was a young girl living behind the milk bar opposite the Heidelberg Station; where trains rumbled past; that glowed and beckoned; where the smell of peppercorn berries haunted an enclosed wildness; where a small, pearly girl could hide in drains. Where no one could hear you.

A man who had befriended my parents, who had visited our rooms behind the milk bar and drank their beer, was on top of me with his face in agony. He wore a bright blue jumper, had dark hair and a moustache. The picture was static; a man and a child frozen in time. I wore my cowgirl outfit, my 11th birthday present.

As the picture foisted itself into my mind, so did the terror. The picture lasted only for seconds. I sobbed hysterically for the rest of the session. When it ended, I told Matt. He said he knew, and was crying.

Matt offered tissues, held my hands in his, as this image clambered through my mind. If something had happened to me as a child I would know, and remember. I looked imploringly at Matt. He watched me attentively until my pain ebbed. We reached for our cups. The tea was cold.

Leaving the Centre, I wondered about this unexpected and deeply painful session. Had something happened to me as a child? I tried to recapture this image in my next session with Kathryn and couldn't. I remembered its few seconds of vivid horror, but could not locate it again with the emotions that had shocked and hurt. I tried to embellish these seconds into a story that made sense, but I knew that the embroidery existed only in my imagination. There was no flashing of light bulbs, or connecting of the dots: my oddly fragmented recall of sexual encounters, my confusion at a semi-naked Ken, my unexplained and savage cutting off of emotion when it threatened to overwhelm, my memory of Mum's pride turning to anger at my torn cowgirl outfit, the doctor's concern about the state of my hymen, my unexplained change as a child. No. I brooded over this appalling image as an entirely separate event, with nothing at all to support it, and then did what I do so well; I locked it away and hid the key. What I had seen in session with Matt was, I concluded, nothing more than my fertile and lonely imagination. After all, if anything had happened to me as a child, I would know. I *was* there that day.

The swiftness of what happened next floored my mind. I lost my professional position in Kenja. I had failed. Finding another job in my shaky state was, I feared, more than I could manage. The new owners were ready to move into my house. Where would Nina, Stefan and I live and how would I support them? An aspiring Kenjan did not pray but I did: the next workshop in Sydney would be my breakthrough; it was my very last chance. Ken had said that miracles could be ours for the asking.

Ken began this workshop in a foul mood and didn't let up on us. He looked derogatively at me. Ken said that I had imagined that I had been raped, and saw those pictures because I was degraded. 'Look at Annette,' he said to the mass of people sitting in front of him, 'so far she's shown no intention of changing.'

As Ken spoke, the image of the man in the blue jumper tore through my defences.

Ken watched me cry; his eyes softened. Like jelly crystals in hot water, I dissolved and set to someone different, more determined, more in need, and maybe more degraded.

The image of a man and his blue jumper slipped back to its secret hell.

The remaining slit of my eyes closed. I crossed a line of no easy return, and became a fully committed Kenjan.

chapter 6

Alpha and Omega

At my first encounters with Ken, he spoke of energy flows, the blocked energy centres that his processing sessions could clear and the psychological problems they would mend. Before long, this expanded to the real business of Kenja, the concept of two universes: the spiritual universe, the natural habitat of spirits, and the physical universe, which was the bustling here and now on planet Earth.

Ken explained that a window of opportunity had opened up to the psychic world, for the first time in a thousand years. And he had been chosen to lead a few to Enlightenment, to the very top of the Tone-Scale (measuring emotion or energy from apathetic to enthusiastic). This is where self-aware spirits reign supreme, high above the range of human energies to the mastery of all energy, to a level where Kenjans would know themselves to be 'pan-determined' spirits; wholly self-aware, self-determined powerful spirits who will reign supreme and who are ethical, indestructible and incorruptible.

According to Ken's data, there is a spiritual hierarchy consisting of alien spirits, the human spirit, rogue spirits (also called attached spirits) and entities. Alien spirits came to this universe from another galaxy, via an explosion. These ruthless alien overlords, having experienced countless malevolent lives throughout the history of the universe, were punished by entrapment here on Earth. Alien spirits do not belong here and desperately want to return home. Home, an unspecified far-away constellation, is a ruthless, lawless place where there are space controllers, whose job it is to keep alien spirits honest and who can create other spirits with doll or robot bodies. Implant stations bombard spirits with thought control, trapping them. Ken, who was aware of his spiritual nature and his personal spiritual history, was once an intergalactic space controller with a formidable task: keeping the lot in check.

The alien spirit is the supreme intelligence, separate from human bodies, but it needs a body to control, one that will do its bidding. Their phenomenal awareness lost, spirits became so deluded as to believe they were merely a human body, and controlled them blindly. Instead of freely creating the appropriate identities for its human body, it has become a narrow identity – I am not Annette; Annette is the current, small-time identity I, the spirit, am trapped in. They are doomed to stay here until they right the mess they have created; it is their responsibility to give human bodies back to the human spirit.

The human spirit is the native spirit of Earth. It knows all about Earth and is a natural builder, hunter and nurturer. It is attached to human bodies and, regardless of invasion by alien spirits, has never abandoned its body but, after aeons of alien spirit control, they cling loyally to a body having long lost their rightful place as spiritual partner to humans.

Rogue, or attached, spirits are next in the spiritual pecking order; they are inferior to alien spirits. They have lost the ability to claim a body for themselves; instead they attach to the alien controlled bodies of humans. The alien spirit is not able to fend off these attached spirits, nor can it defend itself against 'entities'.

Entities are at the bottom of this ladder. Tormented entities nest on people and can be complex or simple. They materialise as images, thought and emotion and can be from the past or present. Ken told of the difficulties facing a child of the 20th century who is unconsciously stuck with an entity of an old man masturbating in the street in the 16th century. He also told of a woman unintentionally trapped in the entity of a young girl, 200 years ago, in fear of being crushed by a runaway wagon; both, involuntarily, will re-experience the terror of despair and catastrophe. Being trapped in anything is painful. When it has been experienced in a processing session, the pain will go and understanding will ensue; a child's smile will brighten, that wheel will be fixed.

Ken followed his instinctive calling: fixing up the unbelievable mess on planet Earth by healing the rebellious spirits seeking redemption, freeing the millions of heavy-duty rogue spirits that attach to bodies, eliminating the entities that confuse and hurt and jostle for position, healing the wasting human spirits and, along the way, helping the human bodies stuck in the middle. This adds up to a rather big personal battle, one that Ken had mastered.

Kenjans did not use the term 'alien' and referred to themselves simply as spirits. When free, the spirit will be 'clear', literally translucent and 'cleared' of everything that stops it from exercising its natural abilities. A spirit does not exist in time or space, but has the power to control thought, and through a 'postulate' (a simple but powerful resolution) can alter the course of a life. When clear, a spirit will view emotion as simply energy. All emotion, anger, ruthlessness, determination or compassion, will be available to use as it wishes. A clear spirit can simply note and understand everything. If a spirit holds a picture still, through time, its power is inescapable. For Kenja to succeed, Kenjans only had to hold still a picture of Ken communicating to millions worldwide and opposition would, in the end, whittle away. When clear, Kenjans would postulate a new reign of peace on Earth; a clear spirit can command universes.

According to Ken, everything that individuals do and experience is by spiritual choice, consciously or not. Ken told me I was a 'suppressive' and had chosen a low role because I wanted to understand what that role felt like.

Deep meanings abounded but Kenjans would not be fooled. If a woman lost her engagement ring, it was no accident; she wanted to end the relationship. Police wanted to experience power, but legally. When the Sudden Infant Death Syndrome society took the red clown nose as its logo, Kenjans were convinced this demonstrated their importance; they had psychically copied Kenja's clowns. When people said no to involvement in Kenja, it wasn't due to their stated reasons, such as 'uninterested', 'too busy', 'it sounds crazy' or 'Ken sounds like a con'; they were simply not ready to make their journey to clarity.

While in the process of 'clearing', Kenjans had to make do with the muddle of their human minds. Ken had the solution to one problem. Why should Kenjan's thoughts be answered and not others? Kenjans were clearing spirits, hence the leaders of the pack. Their thoughts would be recognised by the spiritual universe because they were in its service. Kenjans worked their way up the energy scale; by virtue of thinking with lighter and lighter energies, they had more hope than the majority stuck in heavy grief and apathy, regardless of their good intent. And they did it tough, earning the right to be at the top. Further, the whole world supported Kenjans. Not consciously. Everyone is a spirit and the natural drive of a spirit is to be cleared, therefore everyone was on Kenja's side.

If Kenjans plunged into the journey with hope and trust, then happiness, self-determinism and love would be theirs at the flick of a metaphysical switch. Everything that stops the spirit from awareness of its true being can, through processing, be eliminated – hence Ken and Kenja.

Ken told these stories like a father telling bedtime stories. It is amazing that anyone accepted them. The truth is that many treated some parts of them as science fiction, but the pre-eminence of the spirit and the quest to free it was sacrosanct. The Kenjan quest was the birthright of every man, woman and child.

Ken claimed that Kenja was not a religion and had no belief system or philosophy. However, there was a belief system. It played an important role and provided Ken with the option to proclaim Kenja a religion, were that necessary.

Life experiences might predispose individuals to accept this particular Kenjan one (I had a nascent interest in the New Age.) For a contemporary audience, it was useful to claim it as scientific. Failing proof, it will certainly prove to be scientific in the future. One might note discrepancies. Kenjans didn't. Some claim it is unintelligible. Kenjans didn't.

For example, Ken explained the difference between attention and consciousness by claiming that, although related, they are separate features of awareness. One could be aware of being aware. Ken explained that although one may not understand this concept, the real me, the spirit, did; our minds would catch up sooner or later. This went beyond understanding the difference between being aware of, as in glancing at, and focussing on something. One could detach attention and apply it across one's 'time-track', lifetimes of the past, present and future, an added bonus being increased human intelligence. Many years later, I would ask myself what was this strange concept trying to understand and explain?

It was many years before I understood that the role of Kenja's belief system was to act as a framework for manipulation; it was the template that minds could be moulded to. It incorporated Ken's spiritual beliefs, his 'research' into processing (demonstrated, he claimed, by the frequently changing focus of sessions and their growing range and depth), his thoughts on success based on his own life, pop psychology and the unacknowledged, borrowed belief systems of others: Scientology, Buddhism and the New Age. Kenjans gave it the same reverence as religious people give to their sacred books.

Kenja's belief system is used to isolate its believers and to keep minds focused by constantly referring to it. Ken knew when to deflect dissent, understanding the subtleties of incorporating information that is blatantly at odds with the belief, such as praising the love of humanity while at the same time encouraging the rejection of uncooperative, non-Kenja family.

The details of Kenja's belief system are secondary to the role it plays in controlling its adherents. Once it has been accepted by an individual its details are the vital glue. To break free, it must be systematically dismantled, the lies uncovered and the control techniques understood. Resistance to anything that challenges it can be strong, not unlike the instinctive drive of a fight to the death. Confronting the lies is not nearly as easy to do as it sounds, and can involve great emotional and mental pain as the mind lurches and fights off the challenge to its stability.

The temptation of this belief system, especially to a mind in turmoil, can be powerful because of the sense of cohesion it can provide. Ken often said that he just 'keeps the mind happy'. His belief system maintained the Kenjan mindset within a harmonic framework. It may not have been sensible. It may not have been kind. It could be, at least to outsiders, quite evil. If, within the parameters of a flexible framework, it was harmonic then the Kenjan was, if not happy, then relatively focused and balanced for as long as that balance remained flexible, stayed within its limits and could be cut off from anything that might rock the boat.

∽

Aware that flogging a religion can be tricky, to say nothing of competitive, Ken declared processing to be a science and his research techniques unique.

Ken processed Jan but no one processed Ken. Following each weekly session Jan had with Ken, she validated him as our absolutely amazing, stupendous mentor and vowed that, for example, there is, as Ken had decreed, a difference between awareness and consciousness never before understood. The session provided scientific proof of the validity of this data. Jan and Ken processed selected professionals in their respective private processing rooms. They bowed to his brilliance. More proof. The professionals had sessions with each other during their weekly meeting with Jan and Ken and they invariably found this latest data phenomenal. This dizzying validation of scientific eminence spread through the remaining weekly classes. Then the whole process began anew.

I never questioned the validity of Ken's science, then. Why bother? I was experiencing its truth.

∽

Ken Dyers was born on the 14 July 1922. This is the 1983/4 outline of his life that I accepted wholeheartedly. The belief system, Ken's stories and maxims and the community of Kenja, formed the basis for what I believed would be a platonic 'love story'. One that, led by this remarkable man, would truly rise to rescue mankind from itself.

In describing Kenja and my experience of Jan and Ken in this period of time, I now have the benefit of hindsight and see the negatives for what they were. Then, I perceived them, but blinded by love, interpreted them through my Kenja mindset; one that, to the

Kenjan Annette, was simple in its 'rightness', reinforced constantly and comforted by my feeling that one person might be wrong, but not a whole group. People are individuals, are they not?

Ken always knew that he had a special mission. Why else would he have survived the Australian outback? As a three-year-old, he experienced that great Australian classic, lost in the bush. He was found by Aborigines and spent years living with them, where he learnt about a hidden, psychic world. In a later and more accurate version of this story, his father is the protagonist. His father, a boxer, pickled his hands in brine in preparation for a fight. Ken seemed in awe of the father who was in his early fifties when Ken was born. Ken called himself a boxer, giving the impression of him prancing in a gym, limbering and agile in silk shorts and satin dressing gowns. He later let slip that some fights were, more precisely, street fights. He rarely spoke of his mother, who gave birth to Ken in her forties. At 14, Ken was sent to live with a relative; his mother told him that there could only be one man in the house, and that was not Ken.

He said that he lied about his age to enlist in the army and claimed he was once court-martialed, then acquitted. He glorified his role as a soldier in World War II, at the raw edge of combat; indeed, a fellow soldier deliberately copped a grenade intended for him. Ken taught six of his troops his unique survival techniques and those six taught another six, and soon his unit was better equipped to survive than others. After the war, he claimed to have given his medals to his sons and refused contact with ex-servicemen, saying he had nothing in common with other returned soldiers.

He spoke of his involvement with British counter-intelligence and of the lethal techniques they taught. You only have to walk past someone in the street, Ken said with a small glint in his eye, as he showed us how to strike the vagus nerve. On buses he provoked passengers by standing on their toes, then profusely apologising and repeating the offending action, until the person whose feet he stood on gave up and accepted Ken's dominance.

After the war, Ken claimed to have sold surplus metals for the post-war housing market and bragged of smuggling gold. His résumé lists multiple business ventures between 1946 and 1973. Ken had no formal qualifications. His intelligence was so high, he said, that he tested 'outside the range' in IQ tests.

His first marriage, to the daughter of a wealthy grazier, lasted a few months. His second wife was the mother of his two sons. He claimed to have abandoned a successful business career, to the chagrin of his wife, to start Dependable Building. He went to his first job, fixing sash windows, carrying a building manual, hoping he could follow the instructions. The owner was worried, but reassured when Ken explained that the manual was so he, the owner, could read along with him and do it himself next time.

Ken often mentioned a little man in a white coat threatening to take him to Callan Park, an insane asylum in Sydney, and if Kenjans weren't careful, the things he taught them could be misunderstood and they could suffer the same fate. One early Kenjan, who knew him prior to the formation of Kenja, said that he was in a Repatriation hospital for two years, following his discharge from the army. Another uncorroborated story claims that after the war, Ken would 'hit the deck' on the sound of a car backfiring. That he was traumatised following his war experience is certainly credible.

Ken's mission was to go one further than his guru, the late L. Ron Hubbard. Ken would beat him at his own game. Not that he told us early Kenjans that he had been a devotee of Scientology; it was just something he happened to know a lot about. Ken claimed his sessions were infinitely superior to Scientology's 'auditing'; as it was, some of his earlier processing commands were exactly the same.

Perhaps the biggest difficulty for Ken, in relating his life story, was to keep Scientology out of it. I learned later that he was an Ethics Officer and long-term member and that, for many years, Ken has been listed by Scientology as a 'supressive'. The only man Ken called a friend, (Kenjans were all his 'best friends') was an ex-Scientologist who came to Ken's classes for some time, but he stopped coming and apparently returned to Scientology.

Ken said that at one point in his life he was completely friendless. There may have been other times but now I understand that the problems facing him when he left Scientology would not have helped him befriend other people. It is unlikely that he had, or realised the need for, psychological help. It appears that Ken remained attached to Scientology's belief system and adapted it. Perhaps, at one stage of his life, that was all he had?

By 1973, Ken was working from home. His mission was to research, develop and investigate the processing sessions that he later called 'Energy Conversion' – 'processing' sounded like something carried out in a cannery. His position in this one-man show was Principal. He had collected some clients for the sessions he ran from home, but despite his conviction that he had a mandate from the spiritual universe to implement his agenda, Ken did not seem poised to set the world on fire.

Ken met Jan Hamilton in 1978. Jan's background was conscientiously exact. Born in 1948, she moved to Melbourne following her parents' divorce, and attended an elite state high school; she became school captain before completing a science degree at Melbourne University, followed by a teaching diploma. She taught physics at high school for one year, hence her Kenja appellation 'our physicist'. She won a scholarship to study acting at the E15 Acting School in London, and on her return to Sydney ran clowning classes with her, then, business partner. Jan wrote and performed in her own musicals and plays, had a role in the television series *Water Under the Bridge* and seemed to have a future in theatre.

The minute Ken saw Jan perform, he knew she was it; the right woman had been presented to him to advance his creative game. Jan preferred to focus on the brilliance of Ken's work and the short time it took between meeting him and arriving unannounced on his doorstep, suitcase in hand.

Ken attended Jan's classes and, soon enough, Jan's students were given the ultimatum: have sessions with Ken, or leave those classes. One early Kenjan man ran a small commune in Queensland, until he and his small gathering were given a similar ultimatum.

Jan fell head over heels in love. Ken was passionate, but not always about Jan. She watched him like a hawk. He concentrated on himself and his impact on his followers. Just because I never saw Ken looking like a man in love with Jan doesn't mean that love didn't exist between them. They had a strong bond and would stay together.

Ken was flattered by the attention of the young (26-years his junior) attractive, determined, educated Jan. When I met them, Ken was in every respect head and shoulders above Jan. Over the years she inched up, but I never saw her recognised by Ken as fully equal to him. He never underestimated her or failed to acknowledge her position in Kenja; he never underestimated *any* threat to himself and Kenja. Even when Jan set up the most successful Centre outside of Sydney and recreated the physical Kenja based on her ideals, she still deferred to Ken because his data enabled her.

Jan often said she was one of us; I see her as his most important victim.

Once a feisty, funny feminist, Jan was genuine in her desire to transform Kenjans into a benevolent army. In her thirties when we first met, ambition had not yet consumed dedication. In the middle of one clowning class she declared Sigourney Weaver's character Ripley, in the movie *Aliens*, to be the quintessential heroine, fighting aliens against overwhelming odds and never, ever giving up. Kenjans would be like that.

When Jan talked about herself it grated on me but not on everyone, and some devotees came into Kenja on the strength of Jan and clowning. A robust ego was vital in pursuing her dream of a new culture based on her heart-beating, flag-waving ideal of perfection. She fought valiantly for Kenjans, including me, to achieve this on the premise that she and Ken could change the world and match Rambo and Ripley.

Jan had to learn like everyone else; her catch-cry, 'If I can, you can.' She took pride in confronting the myriad difficulties she encountered in following Ken. Ken challenged her with excitement, confidence and daring; he offered her a path to eminence. I have seen Jan's eyes glisten with tears at Ken's disregard for her feelings, seen her heart break and watched her respond; a good little girl.

Perhaps for Jan it was a double whammy. Love at first sight with a man who, I believe, knew that she had what he needed: ambition, talent, charisma and openness. With Jan jumbled up in love, Ken and his words, his careless sexuality, his raging dominance and slick empathy, slipped in to her mind and her heart.

She would be the first after Ken to 'clear', and our example. She would look squarely into the eye of pain. She would confront her human past: the sins of the mothers and fathers and sons and daughters before her. She would confront her spiritual past: aeons of debauchery, oppression, greed and cruelty, in which she was both victim and perpetrator. She would rid herself of the influence of seemingly endless congregations of rogue spirits and entities attached to her body. Empowered by the secret of the universe, risen above the emotional mire holding mortals back from their destinies, Jan would stand alongside Ken as his second-in-command.

⌒

Kenja grew from premises in Liverpool Street, Sydney and began officially in George Street in 1982, when workshops were still held in the school hall. As the George Street Centre physically expanded, workshops found a new home. By 1984, Kenja's timetables were well established.

Ken gave a Wednesday evening class, and spent most of Thursday at the Centre: running sessions, holding an afternoon class for the professionals, and giving his Thursday evening class. All his classes had the same format: his long talk preceding the processing session was followed by his concluding comments. He also gave a weekly promotional lecture.

Jan was the director of the Sydney Centre, ensuring that the Kenja machine ran smoothly. She gave her weekly evening clowning class and attended all of Ken's lectures and classes; he rarely attended her clowning class. The sole publication was a regular newsletter featuring articles by Jan and Ken.

Below Jan and Ken in the Kenja pyramid were the professionals, and below them the rank and file that Ken sometimes referred to as 'drones' or 'breeders'.

Over the years there were name changes: 'processing' became 'psychic osmosis' then 'energy conversion' and later 'energy conversion meditation'. 'Professionals' became 'energy converters' and then 'meditation consultants'. I stick to the original names of processing and professional.

As well as giving sessions, professionals should demonstrate their chosen status, set the example to the rank and file, effectively recruit (everyone recruited), attend everything and abstain from personal relationships. In addition, interstate professionals ran their Centres, attended the Sydney workshops and organised their own monthly one, gave the clowning and processing classes and the weekly lecture.

Ken and Jan ran sessions with selected professionals, and the most telling demonstration of their positions in Kenja is this: by 1989, Ken charged his professionals $100 for a session with him whereas Jan charged the same people $10 for a session with her – after all the work she had done and the tears she had shed, she was his ten-percent.

ᏯᎧ

Kenja poses as a personal development organisation, and is a personal development cult. At first, it was not seen as a cult but some visitors always sensed something was not quite right. Kenjans just believe that these people didn't understand the concepts. Kenjans *were* different from others due to their values, ethics and purpose in life. However, they were increasingly not different from each other. From the mid-1980s, public perception would begin to change; Kenja's leaders responded to criticism and denied that it was a cult.

Kenjans had no idea they were cult members and defended Kenja, sometimes desperately. And they knew the appropriate response to common criticisms, which included: cults have communes; Kenjans lived independently. Members work for cults and pay whole, or part, of their income to it; Kenjans paid for services. Cults have members;

Kenjans claimed there was no membership, as nothing was paid for in advance, but people *were* members of Kenja, and called Kenjans. Cults are religious; Kenja was presented as a personal development centre. Cults have strange belief systems; Kenja used an advanced technique, namely sessions.

Cult members look different; how could people who are nice and normal be cult members? Families disapprove of cults; families wrote testimonials in support of Kenja. Cults attract the uneducated; Kenja members were predominantly highly educated. Cult members are brainwashed; Kenja's techniques were scientific. Cults have gurus; Jan and Ken were invited to give classes and workshops.

And if that wasn't enough, Kenja had a printed set of ethics; therefore, *ipso facto* ('by that very fact'), it must be ethical.

In setting up the rules of engagement, or non-engagement, with the world outside of Kenja, there were problems to be countered. One was the separation of Kenjans from their non-Kenjan families. Ken's approach was two-pronged. He screamed his heart out, denigrating parents who should hang their heads in shame at the disasters that were their offspring, or he patronised them; Kenjans should have compassion for their parents, they did the best they could with what they had – it just wasn't good enough.

Parents were thoughtfully invited to Kenja shows and Ken's lectures and given the opportunity to join up; however, they overwhelmingly resisted. Some complied with requests to write testimonials. Through compliance and attendance at Kenja's major events they retained at least some connection to their children.

Apart from its professionals and Kenjan office assistants, Kenjans earned money outside of Kenja. They lived with other Kenjans, mostly renting units and houses; that flatmates were authorised as compatible by Jan and Ken was hidden from outsiders. The absence of a commune was good for Kenja's image but made controlling Kenjans more difficult.

Processing occurred not only in session but also across three aspects of life. The first covered member's personal lives and spiritual clearing; these were confronted in sessions. The second was through involvement in Kenja's many tasks; Kenjans experienced the pressures of these as they went about them and, in doing so, overcame them. The third level was the big, wide world in which they tested the validity of Ken's data on a daily basis – he effectively controlled his members' every waking moment.

Many levels of clearing lay ahead. Each had many steps and each step had sub-steps. In 1984, Ken was confident enough to proclaim the number of levels. This, now forgotten, number would slip into infinity.

Ken taught his Kenjans expressions that helped keep them united, and separate from others. Kenjans related by 'flowing', as opposed to giving and receiving, one either 'in-flowed' or 'out-flowed'. Members didn't make, or cook, or plan; they 'created'. The three aspects of life were called 'dynamics'. Kenjans called their minds their 'banks'; these 'banks' were 'reactive', namely uncontrolled and irresponsible. They didn't hug, they 'flugged' because only Kenjans understood 'flowing hugs'. When a Kenjan knowingly said, 'I', they referred to the real them, the spirit, and referred to their bodies as 'terminals'. And on it went.

Free time became increasingly structured to include Kenja functions and more and more meetings – where members talked about Kenja. They became isolated with little time to read newspapers, or watch television, read magazines, let alone books, or see movies, or eat at restaurants, or visit, or even phone friends. The 'no gossip' rule saw the most benign conversations as questionable and resisted for fear of breaking this rule. When attempting to engage in chitchat, Kenjans spoke in a jargon that confused others and, when faced with translating conversations into normal English, it was easier to limit them.

Members had no need for anything outside of Kenja; it provided everything that was important and what it couldn't provide was deemed to be either unimportant, worth giving up for the greater good and only a temporary loss; in the end the spiritual universe would reward sacrifices.

Ken considered that mental illness was caused by entities and that Kenja was better equipped to deal with psychological problems than psychologists and psychiatrists and that his techniques worked better than medication for mental illness. Early professionals, like me, had been instructed to refuse processing to anyone taking medication for mental illness. He believed processing could bring about substantial behavioural change, and when faced with the fact that this was not happening when he attempted to process one young man from homosexual to 'normal' – he blamed the young man.

The medication rule applied (no sessions for 48 hours following medication) however, there was no refusal of medical aid as, for example, in a prohibition of blood transfusions. In 1984, Ken claimed that his technique could heal illness, including cancer; examples to the contrary were explained away and blamed on individuals. His data was infallible; it was up to the individual to follow through.

I did not, at that time or later, witness or experience physical cruelty as in beatings, incarceration or deprivation of food. Nor were young women encouraged to produce baby Kenjans in lieu of their education. To the contrary, Kenjans were to be loving, hardworking, educated, well-fed, well-adjusted and athletic examples for future generations to admire. Verbal and emotional abuse, exclusion from Kenja, the long hours and many rules were seen as tough-love. It helped that everything done by Kenjans against the grain was done in the name of love. The end always justified the means and love is a powerful motive. Ken kept fear within tight boundaries; much better to talk about love as it drew far less attention to him and Kenja. Kenja might be seen by onlookers as wacky, but not dangerous. And love was the reward for responding like good little children to the fear.

Ken said that Kenja was 'wheels within wheels'. The public image was of a legitimate, open personal development group. Within its walls, members accepted the rules, rituals and punishments as being for their benefit. If further layers of mistreatment existed, in 1984 they were hidden from rank and file members like myself.

Then, Kenja was still Ken's construction. It was the brand of an electrifying, smoking, swearing, self-designated black magician. Ken played God; he and his data were infallible. He was not a holier-than-thou God but a vital, scornful, playful one who also shocked, overwhelmed and understood. He believed he had unique abilities, was before his time and had answers to the problems besetting mankind. His passion *was* genuine: for his bank balance, for the kick of power within Kenja, and the wider recognition he felt his due. He often said that the worst thing, for a man, is to look back over his life and see nothing. He wanted the thrill of beating his guru in the wisdom stakes; his reputation and good name were paramount and somewhere, in his own way, he had some caring, albeit conditional, for his poor, beached devotees who stood by him. Setting up Kenja possibly provided him with the chance to right wrongs, including the opportunity to establish a rebadged and reformed version of Scientology – perhaps Scientology as it was meant to be and not what it had, in his eyes, become.

The manipulation of the human, by Jan through clowning and Ken's nurturing them back to childhood, helped Kenjans revert to being good little girls and boys, nice and open to the dictates of their new mummy and daddy. Members were girls and boys thinking they were grown up, especially when daddy Ken peppered his talks with four-letter words, when he nurtured Kenjans with expletives and used terms of endearment as menace and, when he threatened to abandon Kenjans because they thwarted his game, Kenja's girls and boys sat bolt upright and begged.

Adapting to Ken's way of life, the old lives of Kenjans were seen as burdens: bleak impediments to future happiness caused by family, friends, life in general, and trillions of tiny problems made big. Everyone needed something in their lives that was more important than themselves and their immediate survival. For Kenjans, that was Kenja.

Member's paths would be difficult, said Ken, but Kenjans had the courage to weather storms. There are things they might resist and hence must concentrate on. Each had 'an old man of the mountain', their Achilles heel; the nemesis they do not want to confront. When it came along, they must own and love it and dive headlong into the pain associated with it. After the pain of clearing they could apply thought and wisdom. Pain and destruction are part of creativity and one cannot create more than one can destroy; as Ken said, to build a house one must first destroy a tree.

Ken created the conditions for an obsession with self, the constant diving into dim, destroyed recesses. Each individual could know the power of one. Kenjans looked inwards, becoming isolated and dependent, lost in the fog of Ken's inspiring words. Bugger psychiatry and the whole known body of human behaviour, said Ken. They were wrong and he, through his research into processing, could perform miracles.

With his charisma, his mastery of control techniques and his promise of redemption, Ken made each and everyone feel loved, understood and important. Sometimes I watched him as he wound someone up with love and hope and thought, he's faking it with them – but never with me. He was very good at separating his Kenjans from each other and ensuring their allegiance and affection went entirely to him. And did he play with that. Ken knew if he stirred people enough, he would find pain. Ken could look at the plainest women and lay her heart bare and watch her cry as he told her that, in order to love her neglected beauty, she must rid herself of all that stops her, and Ken would show her the way. Before one could say 'processing' she had begun the business of finding her limitations and she could, if she wished, join Kenjans in saving the world, be a wonderful human being, experience unsurpassed multi-orgasmic sex and get superbly rich, and everyone would be sublimely happy for her because Kenja is so creative to this poor planet.

A good cult leader has grunt and can demonstrate enough mongrel for his followers to feel safe – plus enough vulnerability for them to want to protect him. Ken knew what he was doing. In order to protect Kenja, someone had to be sufficiently outside of the game, and that was Ken. It was not Jan. She vigorously cosseted Kenja but, of course, had to work from within; however, this was a disadvantage. Ken used his prior experience of life to control and protect Kenja. In order to be good little Kenjans, his troops must do the opposite and forget what they once knew.

In forming his Kenjans into a group, Ken used one against the other. He sometimes pleaded that Kenja is a chance, a baby game in the world, one Kenjans must not destroy. Some of his maxims about the Kenja game included: the only way Kenjans would lose in the game of life is to leave Kenja; Kenja is always the main game and anything can be brought into it but not vice versa; the whole of life outside Kenja is a process of desensitising people so games can be played; to get out of a trap you first have to surrender to it; the war was not within Kenja but was between the physical and the spiritual universe. Attack Ken, said Ken, but not the game of Kenja.

He ruled his Kenjans like a top strutting cocky, unnerved them by planting dire thoughts and fears in splayed and churning minds. Terrible things would happen if anyone left Kenja; if they revealed the world's most important secret, processing, to the outside world; if they betrayed Kenja or broke its rules. Kenjans knew these fears, but didn't understand their depth. Ken warned them of the nasty games played by others – those dirty, desensitising games. Kenjans not only failed to notice him playing those games with them, they applauded his superior ability as a master player in the game of life; his willingness to be or do whatever was needed to forge his creative pathway. In physics, he said, particles in chaos will gravitate to the stable particle. He created the chaos and he was the stable particle. And he wove the lot around in circles and tied it up in knots and told Kenjans that the lies are hidden in the truth and that the truth is hidden in the lies.

Ken even told members that he controlled them – for as long as they couldn't control themselves. When clear, they would no longer need him; in the meantime, he played his dramatic game and lapped up the love.

Ken was arrogant, manipulative, above the law, egocentric, aggressive, controlling and he didn't hide this. He paraded these traits as something to be proud of, abilities at his disposal, his to use in the pursuit of truth and justice.

In 1984, Ken was a whirling, howling dancer with fire in his boots, slash-and-burn eyes and my leader, *par excellence* ('above all others'). I wanted the dream, and the fabulous promises of this baying black magician.

chapter 7

Dream City

House gone, job gone, money long gone, I left my children and moved to Sydney. I acknowledge the fact that I was in Melbourne then in Sydney. However, the actuality of leaving, telling Nina and Stefan, their response, the inflexion of their bodies, their hurt, all of these facts are hidden from me. I know only that I travelled by bus and cried. Nina and Stefan would live with their father. They refused to come with me, wouldn't leave their friends, father and nana. I knew then there was but one way to help my children – Ken's way.

❧

Inside Kenja, fluorescent lighting dulled the multi-purpose room, the odd ioniser substituted for fresh air. The high ceiling had a life of its own and drifted like cobwebs; Kenjan chatter did likewise. The centre of the room was empty; to one side clowning clothes sat in flimsy cardboard boxes. Diminished by the dimness I stared, disenchanted, at the few miserable garments left. How could my clown possibly look nice in those?

As we formed a circle someone muttered, 'This bloody hat is falling apart.' We waited as she found another.

'Welcome everyone,' said Jan, 'and a special welcome to Annette, who has burnt her bridges and come to Sydney.' Everyone clapped. I wished I didn't cry so much.

'Congratulations,' she continued, 'for having the courage to follow your purpose. When you cut off your escape routes there is no choice but to succeed, so watch her!'

Nadine smiled. She reminded me of my mother with her awkwardness but not her reticence. She, too, was only recently welcomed to Sydney.

Wearing a crushed pink ball gown, blue beanie on my head, holding tight the elastic of my clown nose, I stood before my fellow clowns. Jan's words rang in my ears. 'The more you give up for Kenja and the harder you try, then the quicker you will succeed.' I was nearly 40 years old. With the constant support of Jan and Ken, I would change quickly and, within a few months, return to Melbourne and my children. People go into hospital for longer than that.

Clowning was, like shopping or chocolates, our treat. We might have been saving the human spirits, but until we did, they had a limited place in our lives: 6.30 pm, the weekly time slot allocated to clowning. In this class we could be gentle or cute or zany, providing these sentiments were not feigned; we could also indulge in violence, as long as it stayed comic. In clowning, Kenjans developed the acting skills that were utilised in Kenja's public performances, the musicals devised and directed by Jan. These skills were equally vital for the development of our new flexible identities.

Despite my generally wooden clown and my questioning of Jan, I loved clowning. It was part of the reason I was a Kenjan: to have at my disposal the power and wisdom of the spirit and the sensitivity of the clown.

Jan's clowning classes *were* something else. Each week she seemed to have a never-ending source of ideas, and each week, as people donned red noses, they transformed to the magic of their clown. In one clowning class, each clown was to silently die. The first, his hands wrapped round his neck, melodramatically choked. The next one, holding an imaginary gun to his head, whimpered and writhed and finally died. Another hit the deck in a flash, followed by a slow and ceremonious clown regally keeling over. The next was hopeless. 'Oh no!' shrieked a laughing Jan, 'that was terrible. Do it again.'

Halfway through another class, Jan asked us to form groups of four. Each group would, in turn, create a non-verbal afternoon tea scene. Sitting on the floor in front of us, she ran her hand through her hair and nattered about the rituals of afternoon tea, from the proper English ceremony with finest china and ironed tablecloths, to tea and damper in the desert.

The groups were given five minutes to prepare and could build on the props of the previous group. My group mounted the stage; so far it had a table, four chairs, a messy arrangement of cups and saucers, sloshes of water and a bunch of daffodils. In line, we walked slowly, haughtily. Seated at the table, we lifted our noses higher and higher with disdain for the mess we were doomed to sit in. In unison we reached for our cups. Our little fingers crooked, our shoulders straightened, slowly our heads approached the clearly unclean cups. With puckered faces, soulful eyes peering over red noses, we silently pleaded to our audience to rescue us and Jan shouted, 'Okay!' and we received a riot of applause.

'Next!' Jan roared and the heroine of the next group merrily munched on the daffodil petals. My star-struck group might have handled that but, askance, we watched as she nibbled on the stalk; our ascendancy was over.

At the end of the night, Jan reined us in and gently reiterated Ken's data.

～⌒〇

Self-employment was encouraged, having no guaranteed income kept Kenjans on edge. Part of a cash economy, flower-selling provided the flexibility for sellers to maintain hours that suited Kenja. Flower-sellers were the forerunners of those giving up jobs for Kenja. The success, or otherwise, of selling provided a handy measure of progress; if I did everything Ken said, I would sail through the day and make heaps of money.

And so, in the backyard of a house in inner city Sydney, were my cohorts at sunrise … and flowers … and more flowers.

Deana introduced herself to me. With her young daughter Zoe holding her hand she squeezed me through the throng of her backyard. Deana was already exalted in Kenja; she was the mother of a small child and children would be our future. She would never lose her brown-haired, soft-eyed daughter; like mother, like daughter, they formed two sides of a heart.

A flower-seller herself, Deana's bunches were a delight of colour and style. She kept records of flower runs and allocated them to newcomers like me. Her partner, Rick, collected the flowers from the Sydney Flower Market. As she spoke, a truck reversed into the yard; a movie star of a man with a craggy, pitted face opened the rear door and crammed himself between the profusion of blooms.

In front of each flower-seller, a table held the tools of their trade – scissors, sellotape, silver wrap, secateurs and an implement that strips the thorns off roses. Beside the tables sat buckets of water, cane washing baskets and cardboard boxes lined with garbage bags; in the early morning light, silver wrap flashed.

Tucked among the mess was Nadine. I heard my name and received a bursting-at-the-seams hug from her. 'I'll look after you. I'll show you … look at these, oh … aren't these just gorgeous, I love carnations and alstroemeria together.'

Nadine cut string, stripped leaves, held flowers together, stood back, changed her mind, then tried another floral combination before wrapping them in silver paper.

'Oh, Annette, I'm glad you're here, you'll love it.'

I loved seeing Nadine again. I missed her big hugs and warm eyes, her tolerance of my troubles. She sighed at the divineness of her bunches, and my latent happiness. Finishing last, she placed her bunches in a large cane basket, a spray-pack heavy with water dangled from its side. Flowers toppled over and bunches were jammed between bunches. Ramming a recalcitrant bunch in place, she balanced the basket against her body and looked to me with pride – she would be my example. She headed to the bus stop. That crinkled backyard went back to sleep.

I had been in Sydney a few days, had somewhere to live (the floor in someone's spare room) and would soon have a flower run. At that moment I stood in a space, its early morning freshness hinting at the promise of another place in the past, my nana's house, that I had loved and would soon forget.

My first flower run had been Deana's. She had walked me through it, as happily and lightly as a petal. Shopkeepers waved, delighted to see her. When I walked the shopping strip shuffling my basket, the flowers wilted and my face knitted to a snarl. Not one sale. I only had two days of flower-selling. Financially, I was barely viable. My reluctant hostess had already suggested I move. I needed money for Ken's Thursday class.

Failure was not an option. No one had said it but I knew; a failed Centre director was the bottom of the Kenja heap. I knew people chose their fates. I hadn't experienced enough failure, and when I had I would let it go. In the meantime, I needed money. I lectured myself to use Ken's data – be a spirit, detach from mind and body, hold my image of success still, create a successful identity, use light energies. Be a real Kenjan!

Marshalling my brightest smile, I retraced my steps, charged into each shop and sold two bunches at half price. Soon I had only two left and returned to the Centre radiant but minus my expected profit.

I vowed to toe the line, enjoy the mandatory cold showers that dispersed entities and discipline myself to manage on four hours sleep – additional sleep was a luxury. I'd attend all classes, the workshop and Ken's lecture, have my professional and co-processing sessions, do my daily half-hour wall-walk, be on time for every little thing, join the teams that did all the work in Kenja and sell hundreds of glorious, chirpy flowers.

Ken said that 'after the potatoes comes the pudding'. And it was Jan who provided the treats. On an unruffled afternoon in a Sydney park, Easter bonnets big and small, sturdy and fragile, abundantly adorned with crepe paper twisted into curls and bows, and sparse hats adorned with a twig or a button, bounced through the greenery. A surprise wind swirled leaves, tousled hair and hats, and dozens of hands clutched milliner's dreams. Waiting in a crooked line for Jan and Ken to judge the best hats, Zoe broke ranks and ran to them.

The future shone bright. Children would don Easter bonnets and flock to Kenja. At Ken's next Thursday class, Zoe stood before us displaying her miraculously still intact hat. As she cuddled to our whirling, howling dancer, we clapped her like no one had ever clapped before.

We had hired a stretch limousine to take Jan and Ken home that night – our way of thanking them for the privilege of being a Kenjan. We tripped after them, anxious for a glimpse of our beloved leaders in a very large car, and waved them off as if they were newlyweds.

$$\infty$$

Kenja occupied some rooms in the George Street building. One was Brian's administrative office, In his previous life he was a librarian. His skin was papery, hair sandy and his hands pale; a yes man whom Ken called his lieutenant. Brian considered Japan to be an evolved society and ceremoniously declared that Ken would be a National Living Treasure there and should be here in Australia. In this life, Brian counted Kenja's money and ensured bills were paid on time so no one would notice us. In the natural progression that was life in Kenja, Brian had left his library job to be a carpet layer and expert floor cleaner before rising to become Kenja's general manager.

Kenjans joined the teams that voluntarily cleaned, organised, maintained, donated to and built Kenja Centres. Some teams were formed as punishment and those members had to undertake the previously valuable task of cleaning toilets. Each team had a name, like the Soaring Bandicoots and the Red-faced Runners. Brian taught his team members the art of cleaning floors but, as much as they tried, or didn't, no one matched Brian's gleam.

Brian was also the leader of the recruitment team, of which I was a member. Recruitment was called 'lines practice'. Spirits communicate by putting out lines of energy to another person in order to communicate, and cut those lines to end the communication. (When Ken had introduced this concept to us, I remembered Mum cutting sewing threads and believed I understood.) A determined but hopeless recruiter himself, Brian encouraged us to shoo hordes of new people to Kenja.

As recruiters formed a circle for our weekly pre-recruitment meeting, Brian rubbed his hands together. 'It's so good to see so many of you here. Today will be successful. I can feel it. As you talk to people, remember Ken's latest data; don't take the emotional baggage of the last person with you when you speak to the next – cut lines.'

Someone, who obviously didn't understand Kenja, had complained to the Sydney Council that we pestered people in the city's Pitt Street Mall; they had, in turn, complained to Kenja.

'We do not,' said a flabbergasted Brian, 'we merely use our spiritual abilities to communicate with light, bright energies.' (And regale people with the promise of ending up just like us).

'However,' he added, 'avoid the Mall.'

His hands reached one to the other, 'Now …'

Deana joined our circle. She was late. Lateness was totally unacceptable, and a minute was indisputably late. If one couldn't get one's body somewhere on time then how could one possibly rescue mankind? Deana apologised, and Brian indicated that tardiness is not a good example for children. All eyes turned to Zoe.

It wasn't as if Zoe was deliberately used for recruitment but, if parents wanted their child to be as happy, well balanced and plainly joyful as she, then they would be well advised to try Kenja.

With each word, Brian's paleness had turned pink and pinker with excitement, or dismay. He stared at my tracksuit. 'Annette, you can't wear that!'

My face dropped.

Brian compromised. 'Oh, let Nadine do the talking then.'

Nadine and I would bowl over as many people as possible in Sydney streets, invite them to Ken's lecture, and secure their phone number. Out of the Centre, Nadine abandoned me and commandeered one side of the road. I was stuck with the other. Strangers grew successively taller as I shrank. I barged up to them, said hello and fell in step with them. That was easy and they tolerated me, until it came to eliciting their phone number.

'Why do you want it?' they irritatingly asked.

'So you don't miss out on a seat!'

'I'll phone *you*.'

I lost the commanding position of a true Kenjan.

At our post-recruitment meeting, Brian hid his failure to collect phone numbers in his sympathy with my zero tally.

'Next time, Annette.'

Ken's weekly lectures were unique. Spirits created in the here and now, and each lecture was magically new. As Jan said, 'We don't need Hollywood. It's all here on a lecture night!' Each lecture was given a new name, and Kenjans would pack the room for this 'Be Kind to Your Human' lecture.

In the ladies' toilet, cracked walls impinged into the restricted space. It was meticulously clean. Extra toilet rolls were stacked in each cubicle. Pieces of soap were placed on the basins to be collected, along with the toilet paper, at the end of the night and stored for next week's lecture. Old mirrors had trapped images of women behind mottled silver; these silent faces watched with a hint of *deja vu*. Kenja's women outnumbered basins and vied for space, squeezing a glimpse of the mirror through arms held high, brushing, teasing and spraying hair. Despite being assured that Kenja women do not need perfume (we do not smell), most of us splashed on the best we could afford.

Nearly 30 new audience members were expected. To reach our 'Hollywood' space, visitors had to negotiate the cornered corridors in the George Street premises.

Expectancy lit up the downstairs entrance. Bathing in the flush of our floors, a Kenjan directed guests to the lift, where a momentary gloom settled; we couldn't do much with that. Brian beamed with pride at its saving grace: his floors.

Upstairs, devotees stationed outside the lift pounced as the doors opened. 'How pleased we are you could make it! Can I usher you down the corridor?' We did so anyway. Aiming to impress, some charged at full speed around corners to the puffing dismay of guests. Having negotiated the shine to our lecture space, guests were met with, 'Whom do you know here? How nice it is to see you tonight.'

We knew how to welcome people.

Inside the room Kenjans, bits of sparkle in a plain space, waited. Nadine hovered over the supper table, the bookings tables twinkled, the noticeboards beckoned, and the flower arrangements enticed. The name tags showing visitors where to sit – between Kenjans – were in place.

Professionals were vetting newcomers, ensuring there were no doctors or mental health professionals present; they should have been checked when they were invited. Each professional carried an appointment book. Fingers were crossed, metaphorically speaking, as each Kenjan hoped their own guests and those of their processees would have come; newcomers were potential processees.

I glanced around the room, heeded the anticipatory buzz, walked back out the door and continued walking to join the nervous, smoking women idling around the corner out of sight until the lecture began. We were the ones with no guests.

Brian pursed his lips, adjusted his tie, tried not to rub his hands together, mounted the dais and called for quiet. Us loafers rushed to sit as our fellow Kenjans shot to attention; we were everyone's example. Surely our guests would be impressed by our efforts; and the best, Ken, was yet to come.

Jan opened the night. She looked different: her long hair had been cut into a short bob, her skirt and jacket were mismatched, but her voice remained as lofty as ever.

'Ken's life has been devoted to this thing we call processing, a truly magnificent gift to mankind. One session literally changed my life. Ken is here tonight to talk about this science we call Kenja.'

Jan usually spoke about herself but this night she cut to the chase, and with outstretched hand, announced Ken's apocalyptic presence to the hysterical applause of Kenjans.

Ken hoofed it to the stage. We were enraptured. Wound up and eager. His eyes penetrated the invisible and the invincible.

His lectures always included a demonstration of the Tone-Scale levels, and from then on he seemed to skillfully wing it. For hours, he regaled and teased and challenged and empathised and strutted his stuff. Sometimes a listener disagreed with him. Ken listened, agreed with his listener, and then demonstrated that although they were right, Ken was in fact righter. If they insisted on interrupting with questions, they were asked to leave. If they objected – after all, they had paid to hear a public lecture – Ken claimed that they were in his private space and threatened to call the police. No one survived that threat and they were escorted out the building to Ken yelling, 'Give them their money back!'

I had heard it all before yet sat enraptured. I knew the real name of this lecture game; Ken called it 'Gotcha'.

He left the dais. People booked in for sessions.

Ken said that whatever we put our attention on grows. We grew Kenja with love and a touch of insouciance. It still had remnants of its alternative past, a trace of casualness and summer haze. It was but a few years old and although spirits operated way beyond hope, humans didn't. Our collective humans had expectation in abundance.

∽

When the money from the sale of my house came through, and my debts were paid, there was little left; enough for an oomph-less mustard yellow car. Yet I saw fortune and bought a flower run. I paid $100 for it and immediately feared I'd taken a fatal financial step.

My daytime flower run failed to live up to its financial promise – it might have been me. My night run, selling roses in restaurants, was in Kings Cross, Sydney's infamous suburb with its eclectic mix of day and night, its soiled streets and graceless trees. On Friday and Saturday nights I marched up one side of the road and back down the other, shunning eye contact with those dubious enough to have their feet on a Kings Cross street. They were full of prostitutes, trawling men, insolent teenagers, residents inured to the shenanigans of The Cross, and scurrying souls anxious to get the hell out of there. If I clapped eyes on any of them, they were certain to offload their putrid energies on me. I had enough trouble to deal with, without adding the cluttered of Kings Cross to my woes; the life of the streets wasn't processing session material for me, merely the vagaries of everyday life that I should deal with in my daily half-hour wall-walking.

One lucky night I sold all my roses to my first customer and went home early. One, unlucky, night a barrel-shaped man in a red cap bought a rose and asked me to deliver it. I tiptoed inside a rooming house used by prostitutes who could afford to offer their services out of the cold. The place stank, graffiti covered walls, my feet sank into carpet soggy with – I dreaded to think. I stood stock-still until another man who, judging by the looks of him never bought anyone anything, approached me, smirked, took the rose, and with a flourish sent me scampering outside. Dumping the remaining roses at the front door – you can have the bloody lot – I went home and wall-walked.

Gosford and the surrounding small towns, on the coast about an hour's drive north of Sydney, was a better flower run and cost $600. The parents of my ex-beatnik conspirator, Mary, had retired in Gosford. The odds were that I would never see them, and I didn't, yet the fear of walking into them dogged my time and I abandoned Gosford's shops. I blamed the ignominy of an ex-teacher flogging flowers.

In seaside towns I looked inside tourist resort cafes, wanting to stop and idle, sip coffee and chat to someone but, embedded in a fear of wasting time and indulging myself when I should be applying Ken's data and making money, I walked on.

Grabbing sunglasses, tramping from one business to another, I grew to like my long industrial run. Comfortable in my niche, men in overalls joked about buying flowers – nudge-nudge-wink-wink – and I veritably winked back.

I should have invited my customers to Ken's lecture but found excuses. The last time I had asked a teenage couple, the young girl took her boyfriend's arm, leant and whispered to him, looked back to me, said no and pitied me.

At night, crossing toes, feet and anything else I could reasonably cross, I counted my expected profit and donned my sole nice dress. The restaurant run was distant and dark and I trembled for my small car. Women often said no as the man reached for his wallet. Many smelt the roses and looked querulously at me – where's the perfume? Some asked about the significance of various coloured roses or did I sell black or dried ones and, as if this was a perfectly reasonable request, would I deliver one 20 kilometres away? Others ignored me. Once, I had sat at tables in restaurants with … my head clamped tight. I recalled Ken, and sold one.

Flower-selling grew to become a proper business, set up in a converted factory. Under the rusty tin roof, outside light glassy through cracks, Kenjans wrapped, stretching to hear reminders of Ken's data. This upgraded venture had been launched by Jan and Ken. With their benevolent smiles they had resembled royalty or, at the very least, the upper echelons of the Tone-Scale. A special guest, a rare outsider who supported us, shook hands with as many of us as possible. Jan and Ken made multiple rallying cries for our success – all against the backdrop of spectacular, abundant, floral arrangements.

Our financial future lay in this venture's success, although we were told to stop calling ourselves Kenja flower-sellers. What was this organisation that had people hawking flowers all over Sydney? Run-ins with local florists were laughed off. We didn't hawk; we delivered the flowers. Flower-selling became bigger and bigger, and sellers, happier and happier. Close to our goal of being the biggest purchaser of flowers from the Sydney Flower Market, our supplier had planted more roses to keep up with our demand.

This enterprise was at its peak when Stefan visited me in Sydney. I had been there for almost 18 months. He was nearly 17 years old. We sloshed round, tramping up and down the rows of benches. Stefan cast curious looks at the cracks in the walls and I, increasingly verbose, apologised for the state of the place. Next week we'll paint the walls; it's much nicer when there are lots of flower-sellers here; everyone in Sydney knows about Kenja flower-sellers; you should have seen how awful this place was before we fixed it up. I hoped the roses, my hype, something, any little thing would open his eyes to the glory that was before him, and hence Kenja.

The Sunday of the two-day seminar was then open to the public and Stefan attended. He thought Ken made sense. In public Ken usually did. Fearful he was rejecting his salvation, I insisted we have a session together. It was the last of the day. He sat opposite his bone-still mother, whose glazed eyes secreted the thousand-mile stare.

I never saw Stefan's look of despair as he left, and found solace in the kerfuffle of Kenja.

The most dedicated attended Ken's Wednesday night class – those omitted bolstering the importance of 'chosen' attendees.

In this class Ken deliberately paced onto the dais. Here you put up and shut up, no holds barred. Here was tough and thrilling; the really important things, our many stuff-ups, were handled in a manner exclusively and excitingly Ken. His Wednesday class motto was: 'If you can't stand the heat stay out of the fucking kitchen.' Unexpectedly, the Centre on an unwrapped ocean, Noosa, closed. During one Wednesday class, Ken informed his assembled that it was embroiled in the energy of the drugs that abounded there. Drugs, sex or rock 'n' roll – who knows? An error big enough to shut down a Kenja Centre was not vital information. Someone had slipped-up and everyone paid.

Several families had been involved in Noosa and some moved to Sydney, as did Marilyn, now an ex-director, who joined the rank and file sitting in front of Ken. During the day she sold flowers. At night she bore the covert derision of her peers.

For Mother's Day, a huge day for flower-sellers, Marilyn organised a truckload of mallee roots that were deposited on our commercial driveway amid a spinning of dust. Flower-sellers spent every spare minute, night and day, artistically sticking flowers in, on and even under these, creating gifts of floral genius. Some of Marilyn's efforts had collapsed before delivery but, on the strength of her personality, she sold the lot. One of her customers rang complaining about paying an outrageous price for one gerbera in a mallee root. But who cared?

Flowers-sellers had made our premises comfy and arranged a sitting room with a couch and cappuccino machine. Marilyn had regained her respect among her fellows; she was our most successful flower-seller. Having trouble fitting her Mother's Day preparation between Kenja commitments, Marilyn had slept overnight on the couch. Not long after Mother's Day, when flowers had withered and mothers had tossed them into bins across Sydney, Ken lashed out at her in a Wednesday class. By sleeping there, she had degraded the energies there. She knew that. She was *not* the boss. The rules apply to her, too. He had made his point – know your place – and for the first time, I saw Marilyn cry.

The following Wednesday, Ken called Marilyn to the front of the class to use her to demonstrate the latest session focus. He would process her in front of us. As chairs were scraped and swept out of the way, Ken led this slim, adoring and publicly dumped woman to the centre of the room and asked her to lie down on the floor. He lay next to her, leaning over her, eyeball to eyeball, in session. Transfixed, we watched her lie captive in her tears and Ken's silence. She was back.

We *were* a tad smug. Kenja was on the way to success – the closure of Noosa a hiccup. Flower-sellers began handing out business cards promoting weddings and corporate services.

On another Wednesday Ken strode onto the dais, his eyes as hard as flint. No one had booked in after his last lecture. 'I had the audience eating out of the palm of my hand and you fucked up. You are stuck in your pathetic identities. You can't have the game of Kenja. Don't piss on my game, sweethearts.'

Ken turned his attention to Rick.

I recall a photo of Rick with a laundry basket overflowing with flowers balanced on his shoulder, his face strained to one side. Ken encouraged him from the beginnings of flower-selling through to its success, and took full credit for this success. It was Rick's business but it was Ken's data. He was proof of the efficacy of Ken's 40-year quest; he rode Ken's wave.

Anyone present think Ken unfair? That things should have gone on as they were? Nice and cosy? No one could outshine Ken and get away with it: Marilyn had, and had been put back in her place. Flower-sellers ran to Rick, not Ken, for approval of their financial flush and frisky bunches. Usurpers unwelcome. Rick was deposed. His business closed down. He objected. I sneered; you want to be a Kenjan? I guessed the real reason and applauded Ken's lack of mercy.

Shortly after, in a Wednesday class, Ken had his admirers in stitches; apropos of nothing, he had removed his false teeth, dazzled us with a toothless, ear-to-ear grin then replaced them. Who needs good looks? Not Ken. Then he took the unusual step of inviting Jan to the dais. She had realised a dire glitch: flower-sellers entered restaurants, places that served alcohol – eek – damaging our sensitive energy fields. All that processing down the gurgler. Demeaning to Kenjans. Degrading to the Kenjan name. She put a stop to this right there and then.

Without night runs our finances took a nosedive. Panic. No money. No Kenja.

We had joined together and created something imposing. It was being wrenched away.

'For your benefit,' murmured Ken, 'to find out how resilient you are.'

In the absence of new flower runs, some men had set themselves up in business as handymen and painters. Their ranks expanded. Other Kenjans sold different items from their baskets. Some maintained their pre-Kenja employment, but flower-sellers retained a special place in the minds of Kenjans. And Ken had challenged them. Again his saying, 'If you can't stand the heat, stay out of the fucking kitchen,' came to mind. Following the demise of our venture, flower-sellers arrived at the market at the crack of dawn, purchased flowers individually and, using the boots of our cars as benches, wrapped them in the car park.

At that time of the morning, pre-lipstick, minus combed hair, I nurtured my flowers as if they were children, sprayed them and removed flawed petals. Shouting across open car boots I begged others to remind me of Ken's data, for which I was grateful – it never sat where it should in my mind.

At first I thought this a fall from grace, but I was a Kenjan and the glass was always half-full. Sitting in a market café, darkness rising to reveal the day, I looked to my friends and felt better. I no longer looked to Marilyn, she had stopped selling flowers to be a Sydney professional. She would establish the most successful Centre outside of Sydney, Canberra.

If one could stand the heat, the kitchen rewarded.

Dark stories had surfaced. Something terrible happened with a birth that Jan and Ken had attended. Ken let fly one night with a barrage of expletives aimed at the mother, otherwise this might have remained hidden. Their direct involvement in births soon stopped and trusted professionals attended instead. A little boy had died following an accident. Ken singled out a Kenjan man who had known the child with the words, 'I know you still blame yourself,' and watched him reel.

Some didn't make it. Their choice. One man died of cancer, despite Ken assuring us that cancer was an entity and could be processed away, and even despite his being processed by Ken. Weeks before his death, he came to class and stood in front of us with an arcane stillness so desired by Kenjans. When he died we observed a minute's silence for this spirit that had, by our definition, decided to flunk life and opt for death.

Another young man brought about his own death by avalanche in New Zealand's mountains because he dabbled in other belief systems as well as Kenja. I liked him and his devil-may-care attitude. Walking through a park amid tree-rippled light, almost holding hands, he told me of his intended ski trip. As he spoke, an image of his death, under tons of snow, came to my mind with the ferocity of a shotgun blast. That he was missing was quickly discovered but we waited to find out what happened. When Ken told us he was dead, killed by an avalanche, I scooped my heart up and hid it away.

As far as I knew, the failures of individuals were few and we were many.

We were parents with gap-toothed, grinning children. We were ballet dancers, pilots, secretaries, bankers and hairdressers. We were a woman in white whose intensity eclipsed Jan; a closet lesbian and a gay lawyer who would be normal; a member of Amnesty International who believed Kenja would beat it at its own game; a beautiful and newly sophisticated ex-bikie. We were the oboe-playing academic who left academia for Kenja, the university researcher into cancer who did likewise; another lawyer who now fixed locks; the geologist who sold scarves; the scientist who would be Kenja's most devoted mother; the rock star who became a businessman; former members of Australia's armed services who had run out of puff; a young Chinese woman who would renounce her ancient culture, change her name to Briony and process her way to feeling like an Australian; the artist whose work had hung on the walls of Victoria's National Gallery, before renouncing art for a shot at Ken's eternity. We were the runts of litters who would be Wonderwoman and Superman. We were the nobodies who would be somebodies.

Before this avalanche of wildly enthusiastic Kenjans, my Nina and Stefan slipped aside.

~

Kenja was in its Hundredth Monkey Phase. As told to us by Jan, all the monkeys on an island were, one by one, taught a skill. As this teaching reached the hundredth monkey it spread from monkey to monkey, and island to island, with no need for individual tuition. Kenja would grow like the Hundredth Monkey.

Jan was steering us from our hippy roots on her quest to create a new culture; difficult to achieve in Sydney at the best of times, and Canberra now provided a level playing field. The new Canberra Centre was Jan's baby and her success story.

By mid-1985, Canberra was established with Marilyn in charge. Before long, Natalie, director of the struggling Brisbane Centre before Nicholas took over, joined her. Tall and slim, Natalie stretched her long body and raised her head with the anticipation of a diva – she had, pre-Kenja, aspired to sing opera. Her long-term involvement meant that she had what it takes to weather storms and lead, without it going to her head. In Noosa, Marilyn had had an edge that matched Ken. She lost it that night of subjugation in the Wednesday class but sufficient edge remained to serve Kenja; she would not rival Ken again.

Marilyn and Natalie built a Centre that was vibrant and diverse. Both were warm and lovely and adoring of Ken. These chic women became the hallmark for Kenjans to aspire to. I watched as they arrived in Sydney for our newly named seminars with … well, let's just say my sympathetic persona was noticeably absent.

By then we were playing touch football and basketball and hockey and netball and tennis and athletics. We even lost with unparalleled zeal, delighting each other with how hard we had tried, the lessons we had learnt and how abundantly we paid tribute to our opponents.

Our days were long and hectic, we needed to ensure our bodies were up to the challenges that we believed lay ahead; physical activity would raise our fitness levels – it made our days even busier.

To be visibly tired was a demonstration that Ken's data did not work. When I failed to feel the required enthusiasm, I pretended; that way I remained, for all to see, high-tone. As Ken said, if one simulates a state of mind or emotion for long enough, then it becomes real.

The Canberra Challenge, instigated by Jan as an opportunity to showcase Kenja via our newfound athletic prowess, was billed as 'Four Days of Challenge in Sport, Culture and Communication'. The early Friday arrival in Canberra was followed by an all-day rehearsal of Jan's latest show – she wrote one every year – which we performed at 5.00 pm and 8.00 pm that night. Saturday, sports day, was followed by Ken's evening lecture. On the Sunday, Ken gave a one-day seminar followed that evening by Kenja's Choral Championships. Monday morning sporting activities were followed by a presentation ceremony.

'The Challenge is our Olympics!' said our Jan.

The logistics of organising and feeding the united Kenja in Canberra, by Canberra Kenjans, was carried out with an aplomb that only sometimes ended in tears. To fill the theatre three times (two shows and Ken's lecture) from the young to the old, they flogged tickets anywhere and everywhere. Flowers-sellers begged their customers to buy some. Kenjans leapt before strangers in the street, went down on bended knees to peers and colleagues, harangued neighbours and nagged families. They discussed the pros and cons of grabbing people outside churches – who probably needed us the most. They even boarded buses, sometimes in red noses, and draped themselves inside and outside of every public venue imaginable: movie stars have nothing on us and, forget doctors, process!

In the event, the theatre was packed each time. Packed! I stood with my peers at the back of the theatre, holding still the psychic picture that said how much they, the audience, will love us – and they did, and lined up to book into Ken's lecture.

On the brisk Saturday morning the four state Centres gathered, each team dressed in their state colours, in scattered sites around the Institute of Sport oval for the athletics Opening Ceremony. Sydney's blue swamped all others. Yellow Canberra looked acceptably impressive, Brisbane, less so. A vivid red Melbourne rivalled history itself in what not to do. Four blobs of colour, at 90-degree intervals, hugged the boundary and stared across the grass. On cue and resplendent, each Centre walked a lap of the oval, perking up as the seated groups rose from the ground and feverishly waved. Ken, goodwill incarnate, and Jan, hands joyously on her lips, rose as one from their sitting position. Each pulsating group stopped before a risen Jan and Ken and sang especially composed songs to the two who, by then, called themselves The Founders Of Kenja.

Sadly unequal individuals competed against each other in athletic events that ranged from hurdles to egg-and-spoon races. With elaborate gusto we held stopwatches and starter pistols. The few bystanders smiled and how could they not? Our joy was contagious but, in the end, unacceptably dotty and this audience didn't follow up and join up. It was all in the eyes of the beholder, and we were well and truly beholden.

I had resisted the Challenge as too expensive, over the top and tangential to the real Kenja, only to find myself ridiculously happy at its end, but poorer. I was not alone. Some complained about the cost. Ken said, 'What can you confront?'

Apart from our flawed selves, there was nothing *to* confront.

chapter 8

Slippery Slope

Only one new Kenjan would be at the next seminar. At our pre-seminar meeting the ever-present Kathryn, who had failed in Melbourne, hassled me for bringing my despondent energies along. How could we create a light, confident seminar that would produce upgraded Kenjans who would, in turn, attract new people when there I was, dragging the energies down? I sat churlish; she sat in anxious determination, stuck with the tissues in her hand. Our discordant relationship was strangely comforting: I was beginning to like Kathryn.

Nadine, Kathryn and I had become accustomed to each other. Glancing at Nadine, who had become a professional but quickly failed, I wondered why she had bothered – although I knew the answer; striving demonstrated commitment, and professionals were special. She had begun the business of proving that she had what it takes to soar to the top again. I had barely spoken to her for as long as she was officially above me. Contact wasn't banned; she was busy. Once again I could enjoy her big hugs and bigger fervor.

The individual photos that had, of late, been taken before and after seminars were on display prior to the start of this one. Nadine and Kathryn pored over the latest observing with shared smiles, what they saw as the differences in each of them since the last seminar. I watched, and noted the very obvious differences between the two women: Kathryn was tiny and Nadine was not, Kathryn tightened herself to distraught, Nadine's emotions ran overboard; one was teacher's pet and the other nobody's pet. Ken said we were like the phoenix that rises from the ashes, newly magnificent.

On tenterhooks, I sat among my peers waiting for Ken. I looked round, begrudging the financial success of some Kenjans. Ambition tinkled my lips. I sneered at those still stuck in calamitous Melbourne. Monthly, they proved their devotion by attending Sydney seminars. For 12 hours they sat squeezed in a rank, airless bus with toilets that stank, then fell into all-night cafes and crawled back to their seats, nursed their swollen feet and, feigning lightness, tried to recruit a fellow passenger – a nightmare to the person in the next seat.

Seminars no longer had the informality of the past when, at the end, we sometimes sat on the floor at Ken's feet. Now we were grown-up, and sat on chairs. By the time this seminar started I yearned for the first session, and waited impatiently for the formalities to end: more special songs for Jan and Ken, endless introductions and welcomes.

Ken walked quickly to the dais. I rose into oneness, applauding him until he stood still. His eyes encompassed all. Although they were light, I perceived them as black and all-pervading. Kenjan eyes sought his; I slipped into the momentary silence. When Ken spoke I put fearfulness and self-pity behind the swelling radiance in my eyes and was swept along. Sometimes I wondered, was I really in love with Ken?

The more scathing and direct Ken got, the more I liked it. One Wednesday class he had boasted of his sexual prowess; he had one relationship with a woman he called a knife-wielding nymphomaniac; once upon a time, he had a different woman for every day of the week – the easiest thing in the world was to get a woman in bed, especially nice ones.

Jan, he told us, was fabulous in bed, until he cleared her tragic sexual past and her sexiness disappeared along with her sexual hang-ups. He seemed to have some reservations on the value of this.

'Who sucks their husband's dick?' he demanded in another Wednesday class. We answered by raising our hands. 'How many men have you fucked?' One woman came up with over a hundred. Confused, I invented a number to impress Ken. Thinking about the men in my life, my memory was as gooey as their semen.

Pleased with our enthusiastic response, Ken continued. 'Do you have orgasms in your head?' On an orgasmic eruption scale of one to ten, when one is the feet and ten is the head, at that point, I knew mine to be puny.

When we dealt with sex – eliminated the significance of nasty and disappointing couplings of the past – we could have miraculous orgasms and fantastic relationships but, in the meantime, there was work to do and flowers to sell, and sex to abstain from.

For this seminar, Ken had researched electronics. Our bodies consist of electronic circuits that sometimes run wild, creating havoc within us. He had the solution. These sessions would be aggressive, our bodies would clang and jump and session partners must tie their chairs together.

Electronics were associated with sexual energies. And if there was any area in which we were radically screwed up it was sex. We had tried so hard, without success, to clear it.

Prostitutes were overwhelmed by the sexual energies of electronics. Unaware spirits have, for centuries, commandeered the bodies of hookers in order to experience sex, through them, with as many men as possible. Not for money, as the women naively believed, but to find the perfect penis. Once, in some lifetime or other, these lost spirits had experienced the ultimate one. Craving to re-experience this perfection, they have adhered to generation after generation of prostitutes, hoping, with each one, to find that primal penis. Believe it or not.

In these two days, sexual rage thundered through ruptured souls. Chairs rattled and shook with the contorting of our bodies as we sat in the processing rows, experiencing rip-roaring, electro-magnetic shocks of heartache, frenzy and grief and (sorry Brian) chairs gouged scratches in our floor. The room reverberated but we were as quiet as could be. We had been taught the art of silently screaming, letting emotion out without the noise.

As this seminar finished, our bodies stank and eyes glowed. We gave Ken a standing ovation. He held his flowers, acknowledged us and bowed his head. As he left the room his black, black eyes saw everything.

It seemed Ken was right when he said that I had much to clear. At the end of Melbourne's 12-month course I had said to him, 'Processing is so good I'll run out of things to deal with in session.'

'Not with Uncle Kenny!' said my Uncle Kenny.

I was a remarkable processor and processee, so still my breathing almost disappeared. When Ken said, 'Go into the eye of the pain in session,' I found an endless well of guilt, blame and regrets.

When I was ten, the mother of the young girl I sat next to in Sunday School died. No one told us children, but rumour was rife. The daughter returned to Sunday School and I couldn't look at her. In church, I concentrated on the wrought thrashing of the lead soprano of the Heidelberg Presbyterian Church choir. I never forgot the intensity of the adults who cloistered the child's pain – nor her.

Two years later, my young, tangle-haired piano teacher who sat patiently as I tried beating the metronome, disappeared out of my life. I thought she didn't want to teach me anymore. She, too, had died. Death was generally hidden from children: the world should not upset us; our worried adulthood would arrive soon enough.

At 14, I had a crush on a black-haired, impudent boy. As he entered our shop I raced to the pianola, shoved a roll in, furiously pedalled and hoped he thought it was me. He stopped coming to our shop and I pined for him. No one told me he was dead. I overheard it a few years later. He had been adopted and was unhappy, and I wondered: had he committed suicide? I never found out. Years later, I wished I had divulged my crush on him, and given him something to smile about. In session, I grieved for him.

In my late teens a friend, Ruth, invited some friends to her place. She lived in a bungalow at the back of an old house, never defined, by me, by daylight; my rare visits had been in the dark. I didn't go that night. Nor did anyone else. Perhaps we made the same excuse – I hadn't promised ... Ruth died that night, accidentally burnt to death; she had gone to bed leaving clothes drying too close to the heater. She had died alone in a room that was, due to her careless friends, bereft of a night's chatter. I blamed myself for her death.

I had another friend, also called Ruth, who lived in the middle of an apple orchard. She was gracious, kind and ugly. I had rejected her and spent many sessions assuaging guilt.

My abortion and miscarriage found their place in my regret; emotionally interred options on the prowl and up for grabs.

Ken said our painful spiritual past held us back. When he instructed us to find another lifetime, or two, in session, I did. In one lifetime I had limped along, an unloved old woman with bound feet. In another, I was a snake-handler killed by his snake. I had been lynched; I had lynched. I had been dictator and serf, soldier and nurse, concubine and master. Each time I experienced the pain of these lifetimes I was overwhelmed by the tears I shed, but also uneasy; these images seemed hollow, but still, they existed in session, and I cried over them.

Mostly, I concentrated on this lifetime: my terminal failure as a mother, my awful ex-wife and ex-teacher status, with lack of love and money good standbys. I wallowed in pain and put labels on it – Mum, Dad, Nina, Stefan, money, love, *ad infinitum* ('to infinity'). In session, like molten lava, anger and tears flowed from my body, my eyes danced till no music could be found in them. Then I sat in emptiness, and my rage built up.

As time passed I could have run out of things to deal with, but ... not with Uncle Kenny. While I had my roundabout of problems so did others, like Nadine's unending religious family woes and Kathryn's inexhaustible mother. Alex had arrived in Sydney, worked as a professional and failed, giving him plenty to deal with. Even Nicholas, who Ken once called 'clear', was in trouble a lot.

❧

The more you give the more you get, said our Ken, and I still gave for the disbanded knot of me and Nina and Stefan.

During a Christmas lunch, my mother, children and I sat earnestly together. Mum hid her pain in a rush of kitchen preparation. My children sat opposite my elusive Kenjan eyes. Conversation consisted of pass the potatoes, or the mint sauce, or the gravy. No one noticed the old lace tablecloth, or Mum's annual mumbling bemoaning the breakage of the dinner set that matched the best crystal and cutlery. I failed to notice my children's attempts to bond with the mother they no longer recognised.

Returning to Sydney, I buried myself in the hustle and bustle of Kenja.

On her way home one night, a stranger materialised from the shadows and dragged Nina towards the dark. She yelled, struggled, and he fled. She rang me for help. I asked Nina to come to Sydney and when Jan offered to process her, I was thankful

Jan said it was a magnificent session. Nina had handled her destructive entities, the ones that wanted to experience violence. Nina, on the other hand, said she had wasted her time as nothing had happened.

I didn't ask Nina if it was cold that night, or late, or had she heard footsteps, did she see her attacker, was anyone there when she got home, and who had cradled her? A distant mess of 'Clarence' the clown, and the heart of a mother, heard Nina and rushed to help. Yet unable to retrieve for her the mother she had cried out to, I glided back to the safety of my still burning hope.

Nina returned to Melbourne as she had travelled to Sydney: alone. She would not become involved in Kenja now. The only chance she had to rid herself of those entities was for me to process on her behalf. As I had been taught, the same group of entities attached to family members but only one person in the family needed to 'clear'.

If I worked harder, liked Jan more, sold more flowers, had more sessions, pleased Ken, then I wouldn't keep sliding back down the energy scale to apathy. The top of the scale, unbounded enthusiasm, seemed light years away. Now my clearing was fundamental to Nina's future happiness. I couldn't waste a minute.

☙

My children were a trace, a flake of shed skin. But still, my need to communicate outdid my capacity to impart. I sent them some cards, which Nina kept. Each consists of a few stilted words scribbled in dank arcades that no self-respecting Kenjan would be caught dead in. At first I signed off with Mum, then Annette. My Polish surname held me to a past of war, slavery and indescribable destitution and so I had abandoned it and reverted to my maiden name, Stephens. Perhaps without that complex Polish name ... something was holding me back from clearing quickly.

In Melbourne, my children had given me Christmas presents. Stefan gave me a Picasso print depicting a pair of hands holding a bunch of flowers. He was nervous, hoping I'd like it; he knew I liked flowers. Nina gave me a vase for my flowers. Despair leaked from my recumbent heart. They had unknowingly found in my love of flowers an entry point back to me, too small yet to define.

ↄ⌢

The larger presence of children in Sydney resulted from the exodus of several Kenjan families from Noosa after that Centre closed.

They were divided into age groups: under-fives, under-fourteens and teenagers. Children had regular sessions with a child professional of a similar age; the under-fourteens processed the under-fives. Teenagers processed together. Payment was not compulsory but many, in lieu of money, gave presents and treats. Under-fives and under-fourteens attended clowning, including seminar clowning. Many under-fourteens attended Ken's Thursday class, and were nurtured towards seminar attendance; some attended the Sunday of the two-day seminars. Privileged teenagers could attend both days.

Kenjans held these children in high regard; they were closer to their spiritual abilities than adults. Kids were eligible for two-week school-holiday seminars, consisting of activities and some processing. At least one two-week seminar was devoted to training children as junior professionals. General rules applied to children, including cold showers. The ultimate justification for the demanding life of children was the acceptance that everyone, child and adult, was in Kenja by spiritual choice, conscious or not – and could not only stand the heat but welcomed it.

Jan believed that everything for the children was of the highest order; that the emotional and physical health of Kenja's children was paramount. She mourned not having children of her own. Ken told her that she was lucky and didn't need any; she had the children of Kenja. They would be perfect, in recognition of her and Ken, and stay above the common fray. No bad drink, bad drugs, bad boys or girls for them.

Kids would remind us of how we once were – with the clarity and light of a clear spirit. Unborn babies, through their mother's sessions, would heal in the womb and newborns would sit on laps while mothers had their sessions.

Parents who had spent years making decisions regarding their children's welfare had to re-evaluate their priorities. Children's ties with the parents had to be, not broken, but realigned – via Jan and Ken. To achieve this, Ken was smilingly ruthless. Jan sincerely busted her guts to get parents over the line.

Then Ken suggested that children cleared easily, but their parents held them back. Free of these stumbling blocks, kids would clear quickly and psychically flow the benefits of their rapid change back to their parents. When many children were separated from their parents, parents were ostensibly given a choice: those who didn't follow Ken's wishes would lag behind and we would scorn them, while those that did would thrive and glow. These children were gathered together with Kenjan adults, some of whom were parents. The living arrangements of the majority of Kenjans who did not have children remained the same.

Maybe it was that great hidden decider – public perception – that changed these arrangements. Teachers at the public school attended by Kenjan children had apparently raised concerns. After a short time children returned to live with their parents.

A Kenja school was discussed but would not eventuate. Not that we needed one; we believed that all schools in New South Wales were already incorporating Kenja into their curriculums via a manual of creative movement. One young woman had been awarded a two-year grant by the Commonwealth Schools Commission to write the handbook. With generous dedications to Jan and Ken, it combined Ken's teachings with Jan's clowning.

If love is to sacrifice something for another, then Kenja parents loved and gave abundantly. Many had given up their livelihoods and homes to follow their dream. Our scientist created science lessons and others devised art lessons. The children's social activities were squashed in between their educational commitments; building blocks tumbled, science fizzed and banged, and barbecued sausages burnt.

In clowning, red noses huge on small faces, Kenja children stood before us, transcending the shabby, sometimes smelly, clowning clothes; the hems trailed, trousers were rolled up past knees and slowly slid back down – until someone suggested we provide kid-sized and clean clothes.

Young children loved Kenja but sometimes they wanted to be as they were, before their parents became Kenjans. School-age children were led away from their old lives. As they adapted to their new Kenjan lives, they were like a row of Humpty Dumpties, afraid of falling – perhaps no one would put them together again, at least as they were.

Teenagers navigated puberty isolated from their non-Kenjan peers with their skin eruptions, learner permits, fake IDs, rituals, discovery, angst and the biggest bogey of all: drugs and sex. Kenja teenagers would be different and recognise and reject abusive or demeaning behaviour. They would be the fore-runners of a brave new world; potential friendships with schoolmates withered through neglect. But still, they *were* teenagers. Kenja could quell nature but not kill it and undercurrents of teenage rebellion were dealt with. Parents couldn't understand the child's reluctance, even outright resistance. After all, Kenja provided them with everything. Ongoing defiance would see the children as being un-Kenjan and their doting parents in trouble, so they were stuck with their resentments. Mutiny died in its tracks. Teenagers bowed to their Jan-and-Ken-cloned minds.

Jan, stuck with her orphaned nurturing, was soon in charge of the communication with parents and children. Ken stood, absolved of the liabilities of mothers, fathers and their offspring.

∽

One family who had come to Sydney from Noosa quickly became Ken's focus and he showered them with praise – the usual burning bridges and promise of redemption. Soon they were in the hot seat, the centre of a remarkable degree of attention.

This father, said Ken, mourned a life lived in an alcoholic haze and 'blanketed' people. Blanketing was a definition of suppression whereby energy was used to create a fog that sat on people. Jake was a master of this talent, which he stubbornly refused to give up – regardless of how much Ken yelled at him.

Ken accused the equally problematic mother of being a witch. Marnie had always loved clothes and had once envisaged a different life for herself, intending to dress the denizens of Noosa and beyond in her brand of chic. She was given her chance to design clothes for Kenja workshops and, for a time, found her niche, until it was decreed that we could no longer wear her clothes because they made us look as if we were in uniform. She found a new way to devote her talents to Kenja and became the Kenja seamstress, in charge of sewing show costumes.

I saw a witch with a heart who set her life aside with a determined love. Ken paid some attention to her son, but reserved the bulk of his attention for his younger, ten-year-old sister, Vanessa. Marnie would not hinder the light shining on Vanessa. She loved this light: its source, Ken, and its focus, her daughter.

But Ken said that the continued interaction between the train-wrecks that were her parents would inevitably harm Vanessa. Most of the destruction of this marriage occurred in the privacy of Jan and Ken's office and private processing rooms. However, enough was aired by Ken, in the hot house that was our Wednesday night class, for us to know exactly what was happening.

One night our walls streaked with sweat and the ceiling dripped. Drenched, we struggled to ignore it. Ken stood next to a slight, shy and trusting Vanessa. He paced, watching her and us. Vanessa was, he said, the embodiment of love, a child who knew all about love with a future too great for us to envisage. She stood on the dais in front of us, a brown-haired 'Alice in Wonderland'. Toes turned in, she looked to the floor then glanced at Ken. This shy, beautiful and reserved ten year old was the chosen one, the child guide whose innocence would nourish and give life to us. Ken said that everything in front of her was hers to own, and her luminous eyes gazed to us. As the class session concluded, Ken finished talking then moved from centre stage. Vanessa returned to the dais and stood before our watchful adult eyes. We knew to clap; some held back. Ken moved forward, applauding her. We did the same.

Before long, Vanessa had more and more sessions with Ken at the Centre, on weekends at his house and, soon enough, she sometimes spent entire weekends there.

The unspoken words 'Vanessa's in session with Ken' coasted through our ranks. Here at the Centre? At his house? She seems to have no life. What does Jan think? How many wanted to raise doubts? How many decimated these doubts with the swiftness of a falling axe? I never raised the issue with another Kenjan, nor they with me. Talking about another person was gossip and gossip was covert character assassination.

Ken spent hours in a locked room with a ten year old. Sometimes I looked daggers at both. Sometimes I admired her. Ken lauded Vanessa. I watched. He showered accolades on her. I dutifully clapped. My resistance was my fault and I tried to shrug off concern with the words, 'Stop being so unkind, Annette.' My thoughts were whisked away before they had formed, and I succumbed to the most powerful persuader of all: the mass of Kenjans standing at the end of class, eyes wide with wonder at how far our beloved Ken would go for us.

He paved the way for the acceptance of the leadership of a child by directing attention to his humility in accepting Vanessa's equality. By virtue of her youth and trust, she helped us accept her pre-eminence. Looking at Vanessa, doubt about the desirability of heaping so much on such young shoulders dissipated. Ken would look after her. Children sitting in the ranks soon flowed their innocent smiles to Vanessa; adults unleashed their childish ones.

We were the elite; conceit blended with awe and replaced doubt. Ken flashed his wonderful smile, and we drowned the question of her age, and adored Ken. If we must idolise her, then we would.

On Thursdays after Vanessa finished school, I often saw her sitting with Ken, eyes linked to his, in a coffee lounge near the Centre. Once, while recruiting, he called me in as I traipsed past and, with reddening face, I sat with them. She may have been at the forefront of a brand new world, but this slight child with the expressive eyes ordered soft drink, played with the straw, and slurped the last drops.

Vanessa attended a local school along with some other Kenjan children. She once noted that answering questions from her classmates, about why kids were coming from Noosa and attending school with her, was easy. But when asked why the children in Kenja lived together, she found it hard to answer. Asked if they were all one family, Vanessa said yes.

We were a mysterious, spiritual and untouchable family, where children would never be without parents because there were many. And we had mummy Jan and daddy Ken.

When children returned to live with their parents, Vanessa and Marnie moved into a house with another Kenja mother and her daughters. They painted the rooms a beautiful dreamy yellow. Each day the lemon-house girls went to school together then came into the Centre. But only Vanessa processed weekly, or more, for very long sessions and at Ken's house on some weekends. For our futures, said Ken.

Then, one night, Ken declared that Vanessa was his research assistant. Jan's equal.

Our silently-breathing room gulped and held its breath. Some looked to Jan for guidance. Jan sat in her seat, in the ranks alongside us, challenged and defiant. She straightened her tiny body, drew in breath, held her head high. In clowning she stared us down and said we were privileged. Our beloved leader was taking us in a new and daring direction.

How many of us ignored the risky question: was Vanessa naked in sessions with Ken? Ken often said that nudity has no significance other than what you give it. For a Kenjan to interpret the nakedness of a child or adult in session with Ken as being in any way inappropriate was a reflection of that person's opinion, and incorrect.

I don't know when I sensed Ken was in love with Vanessa. At first I thought that he was behaving just like a man in love and left that destructive thought hanging mid-air. Each Thursday night the captive, fluid and darkening eyes of a beautiful child stood alone on stage, looking at the space she thought she owned, while Ken owned her.

Vanessa knows everything, Ken said to us. Everything.

The perfect backup team, her mother and her father, smiled.

chapter 9

Home Sweet Home

In October 1985, Nina and Stefan's father died. Nina was 19 and Stefan was 17 years old. For the year and a half I had been in Sydney, Nina and Stefan lived at the back of my mind; sleekly censored emotion, slick words too small to find.

Mum had told me Josef was ill, but that information never seeped into my remote self. He had cancer. When captured as a teenager and taken to Norway, he had worked in contact with 'heavy water'. I never knew what that meant. Heavy water was produced as a by-product of fertiliser production and was needed for the German nuclear energy project.

I visited him before he died. He looked like the damned. His pain was there in his eyes, seething through the barriers of morphine and a lifetime's repression. It was all there, too late and terrifying. He died, sooner than expected, with only his children present. Nina and Stefan went home alone, they cried alone. Mum notified me; I returned to Melbourne and organised the funeral.

He was cremated, and wanted no memorial. With my head ringing with Ken's data, I stood before Josef's mourners and delivered his eulogy. I believed he had chosen this spiritual path and wished him well on his journey. If those present were hostile to me they didn't show it.

Josef's funeral exists in my memory as a fragment of his eulogy. We hope to live on in memory and no amount of present understandings alleviates the affront, to him, of my failure to recall, in death and in life, much of the life of the father of my children. I cannot access the details.

I returned to Sydney, loaded my few possessions into the boot of the sluggish yellow car and drove back to Melbourne. I would look after Nina and Stefan and be the mother who would comfort them.

The flat in Elwood, where Josef had continued to live, had begun to disintegrate; the external walls were falling to heaps of dust on concrete. The herb garden had long since died and the Hills hoist wobbled. The new owner replaced the carpet in our flat but darkness still won its small battle with light in the lounge room.

My neighbours had moved. I remembered the old ones and wished they still lived there. The elderly Mrs Gruenberg had lived upstairs; she and her husband owned a house down the street but didn't live there. One day, Mrs Gruenberg stepped in front of a tram and her elderly life changed.

A widow, Mrs Braun, and her son had also lived upstairs. She and her husband had moved in when tenants still had to pay key money and renters intended life-long tenancy. Her lounge had Russian knick-knacks all in a row. 'I'll teach you how to cook *pierogi* ("Polish dumplings"),' she would say. But that's Polish, I would think.

My Hungarian neighbour was beautiful, poised, manicured and worked like a Trojan. Worn wooden steps concertinaed from her upstairs flat to the backyard and on both sides of each she placed a pot of geraniums, all the same size, the flowers all pink, and she repainted the pots uniform pot-red. Mr and Mrs Jackson poked their heads out their back door and nodded at the flowering staircase. His advice to me, when three-year-old Nina had a convulsion, was to put her in a mustard bath. Yikes! A bath half-full of hot water with loads of mustard added to it, a veritable sauna for sweating things out. The Jacksons financially struggled, until one day Mr Jackson got a job and they moved.

Only two former neighbours remained; one was the keeper of the pots.

Determined to rid the flat of the finality of Josef's death, aware of the dangers of wall-walking amongst perilous memories, I scrubbed walls clean and stood, eyes blank, staring at them, hoping to unleash the years of pain embedded there. Out went the heavy antiques and effects collected by Josef, his bits and pieces of life. Cups, glasses and old clocks don't eradicate pain, they absorb and reflect it, and secrete misery into the air. Convinced a thought and memory-free space would benefit my children, I processed everything, but mortality still lingered in corners and drawers.

⌒の

If Ken was a living national treasure, Kenja Melbourne was a living national flop. To count the number of core members you needed only two hands; on a good night, all ten toes (well, maybe three hands). Relocated to the heart of the city, Melbourne welcomed me back because I could be counted on to have a regular weekly session and maintain their mediocre finances. Looking around, I saw little to sustain a spirit and even less to nourish a human.

In Sydney, unlike Canberra where Marilyn and Natalie seemed permanent, directors were dismissed from their post on a regular basis, until eventually this was nominated as a rotating position. Melbourne was a revolving door. Each new director arrived in Melbourne with high hopes. There were different faces but each had the same degree of desperation. Then Nadine arrived from Sydney as a newly appointed Melbourne director; her tightly enclosing hugs still full of love and compassion and hope. This was her Centre too.

Hours were spent opposite Nadine in session, face to face and knees to knees, trying to process myself through Josef's death. I blamed myself, cried, railed at him for having died and, in doing so, left so much unsaid. I didn't understand I was grieving. Nadine had no idea either. She interpreted my crying according to Ken's data: more depressing entities.

Sullen, indignant at the failure that I considered the Melbourne Centre to be, I remained passionate about the aims of Kenja. But I was regressing, not clearing, my energies heavier than ever. Even Nadine struggled to maintain an interest in my repetitious troubles. She performed the ritual of disparaging my flunked recruitment, to no avail. Why, I asked myself, could I not communicate effectively about Kenja?

Melbourne's flower-selling runs were cheerless, and unprofitable. I entered supa-dupa blocks of glass, rode up and down elevators, smiled thinly at neatly coiffed receptionists then tramped, dispiritedly, to the next office block.

Back in the Centre, I focused on the floral arrangements and the noticeboards. The latter advertised Kenja's social functions and the teamwork of its members. I had found a task to devote myself to, and hide my general deficiencies behind and spent hours poring over coloured cardboard, cutting, slicing and placing – Melbourne's artist in residence and doyen of endless flowers. Sometimes I thought the only thing I really enjoyed was my noticeboard with its numerous dancing scraps.

The love of Melbourne Kenjans for each other was snowed under by its cares, although our social nights were sweet. One was a Barn Dance in Eltham, where my photographer friend Sue and I had once debated the state of the world in mud brick houses, discovered the local artist's colony and teamed up with urgent men. The hired hall was decorated with hay, strategically scattered. Women wore gathered skirts; men wore jeans and cowboy boots scrounged from second-hand shops. In this slowly impacting and noisy room, we kicked up our heels and ricocheted the night away. Our efforts would be picked up and reverberate throughout the psychic universe. Five people could creatively change the world, Ken had said – once.

Each month I went to the Sydney seminar. Wedged in the seat in that lousy bus, my feet got hot, smelly, swollen and achy. I stood in a crooked, heaving line with other interstate attendees as we were welcomed, buoyed by applause.

Back in Melbourne, nothing changed. I missed the excitement and vitality of Ken and counted the days until the next Melbourne seminar and then, weren't we adorable? Once, we lined up at our small entrance in Melbourne's busy Bourke Street making two lovable lines, our hands outstretched forming a tunnel so Jan and Ken could sashay their way inside, while we sang the welcome we had only minutes before finished sweating over. Jan laughed with the joy of our efforts while Ken just laughed and passers-by stared.

Ken still reminded me that I was degraded and hung on to my miserable entities because I wanted to and my children were doomed to the same fate as me. I wanted to help them and no longer knew how.

The reality of my living with Nina and Stefan hadn't dawned on Nadine; my children took medication and had a drink. Drug-taking was an inviolable offence. Families were a pitiful anathema to healing and a major cause of our aberration; we couldn't live with them. Well, we could if family members didn't drink alcohol or take medication, stopped dumping miserable energies on us, cleaned up their own act (virtually impossible without processing) and praised Kenja. Otherwise we simply would not change and would be wasting our money in Kenja. Sooner or later my living arrangements would be queried.

My finances inevitably deteriorated. I had never missed a session, or class, or seminar. My failure was Nadine's responsibility. She should guide me with a liberal dose of tough love, but her human cared for me and hugged me.

Veering between fear for herself and me, she berated me. 'Get a job, Annette. Are you really trying to prove Kenja doesn't work? You know everything is put in our way to make us fail. Are you going to let those rank old energies of yours win? Get a job!'

Invigorated, I pored over the Situations Vacant in *The Age*. An Italian restaurant needed a dishwasher on weekends. Dressed in my best clothes, my lecture outfit, I arrived to the quizzical look of the owner, who suggested I looked inappropriate for the task, and did I have any relevant experience? Spurred on by Nadine, I said I didn't usually dress like this and I'm really good at washing dishes. I started that night.

As I sweated over the dishwashing machine, the cook gave me coffee and, despite the hard work, I was content. Heat, sweat and the interminably full dishwasher created a cocoon in that frenetic kitchen. Only once did it expand. I glimpsed a man and woman seated at a table in the restaurant, inclined to each other, glasses raised. I smelled her scent, his arousal. As the candle flickered the image licked itself into my mind.

Nadine knew the restaurant I worked in was licensed but tacit agreement saw us ignore this. But then my friend fell short of being a brilliant example and crashed as director of Melbourne; her failure to drag me to better things had contributed to her downfall. Nadine returned to Sydney to a polite, smiling ostracism.

Ken said that both processor and processee could clear in session. The good processors remained detached from their own problems. I did. No one was nicer than Nadine, but she usually went into session *with* me; by the time sessions finished she was red-eyed and tear-streaked. My next professional might be a better processor. Nothing personal – a spirit is a spirit, and unsentimental.

∾

In 1986, Kenja Sydney was reorganised and divided in two. Jan was no longer the official director. The professional section was newly named the Personal Evolvement Centre. Professionals became accountable for that and a Sydney professional was appointed as a director. The classes, lecture, seminars and social activities were co-ordinated by the Kenja Personal Abilities Centre. The KPAC committee was an alternative ladder to climb for those who eschewed professionalism, and a means of demonstrating readiness for it. Jan and Ken became consultants to Kenja, attending on the 'kind invitation' of Kenjans.

It was all couched in rosy terms – now that we were high achievers, we could take responsibility. Nothing was in Ken's name. I privately suspected that the money trail had been merely redirected, that everything else was waffle, nothing significant had changed and we all knew the real deal. There was never any doubt about who was the boss.

As we sang our lovely songs to Jan and Ken and learnt our oft-peculiar lines from Jan's musicals, others had begun to notice our blooming, goggle-eyed demeanour. A woman Ken called a black witch had attacked Kenja. She represented a church group. Ken said that she was as black as the ace of spades or, worse, the devil.

In November 1986, in the *Concerned Christians Growth Ministries Newsletter*, Reverend Adrian Van Leen hauled Kenja out of the dark. Ken had addressed the Professors World Peace Academy of Australia and had proudly printed his speech in a Kenja publication. Inaugurated in 1983, the academy was a front organisation for the Unification Church, the 'Moonies'. Van Leen pointed this, and his serious concerns about Kenja, out. He noted that one Canberra Uniting Church had already issued a statement about Kenja and that Mandate Ministries in Sydney published an article querying Kenja and that Brian, on behalf of Kenja, responded to the latter with a letter in Kenja-speak and threatened legal action.

Then, on 12 May 1987, the blazing headline, 'Mother's Plea to Cult Leaders, Give Me Back My Daughter,' led the Sydney *Sun's* Section Two. This mother had flown from London to find her daughter, who had come to Australia on holiday and subsequently rejected her family for Kenja. The journalists had sought out Kenja. Ken bragged to us that, by the time they left, he had them in the palm of his hand.

Ken said, 'They can't touch me!'

So far, nobody had.

⌒୨

A lady named Marcia was originally a Melbourne Kenjan. Some of her friends had also joined up. They formed a subset of women and children still in touch with Melbourne style. Her children burst with energy. Ken revered them as role models for us musty older members. Despite their attempts to disregard teenage style and appear smartly dressed, but not smart enough to stand out in a crowd, they managed to turn up their collars and mess their hair. However, at social functions their youthful ebullience was forced into modest clothes.

In the world's greatest game, what kids missed out on the swings they made up for on the merry-go-round. Insulated by Melbourne's seriously childlike elders, why wouldn't they feel anything but privileged?

The Centre also had, as a part-time participant, Jan's gentle mother who took us for choir and who, one day, expressed doubt about Ken. Shocked, I put it down to her age; older people were past *real* understanding of Ken. She was not fully involved and retained a strong sense of who she was. I saw her as our surrogate grandmother and perhaps Kenja kids were her substitute grandchildren.

Marcia undertook professional training, impressed Ken and, six months before *The Sun's* blazing headline, was installed as one of two Melbourne directors. Dark-haired and tall, with her breezy self-confidence and sophisticated clothes, Marcia looked more the part than her predecessors. To augment my flower-selling income, I became her cleaning lady. I had stopped dishwashing as it was low-tone and very un-Kenjan. The extra money helped pay for my weekly session with her. Everyone benefited. My session helped Marcia to maintain the crucial number of sessions she ran in any given week. Ken congratulated Marcia for, if not increasing her session numbers, then at least maintaining the status quo, and Jan cooed because the Melbourne Centre had not slid backwards.

I particularly warmed to Marcia on a day of mutual exertion. In hockey training, muscles aching, breath gasping and bums surging, we swung our hockey sticks and if the stick tapped the ball, it trickled. My sense of fellow feeling increased with the playing of netball. I hoped she might deem it undignified for us older females to play but no, she was a director and under her guidance we would move forward.

Once she declared that, despite our broken lifts and accident-prone seminar preparation, Melbourne's transport strikes, Victoria's bushfires and more, Ken's latest data on 'primitive energy' saw the last Melbourne seminar go off like a rocket, and prayed that Melbourne would also explode with new recruits.

There *was* something about Melbourne, an unseen hindrance. I knew what it was – my hex. When I finally cleared I would regain my rightful place at its head and then, free as a breeze and light as a feather, Melbourne would shine.

Who, in their right mind, would want to sit through Melbourne lectures anyway? Marcia paced a desultory room. Air prickled, resentment hid behind light facades. Time slowed. Someone arrived. A discreet 'phew' was followed by panic – this might be the *only* new person! Time slipstitched, another two members of the public arrived. Chairs were removed, the three guests seated between enthusiastic Kenjans. An unconscionable 30 minutes late, the lecture began.

Sitting in our limited semi-circle I did my best to encourage Marcia. I laughed, I applauded, I approved. Marcia could've been speaking to a 100 people; we never let standards slip. When the talk finished we should say two words, 'Book in!' That was an order from Jan.

Clasping a cuppa, I couldn't shut up. 'Oh, wasn't that just fantastic ... my life has changed ... now I run my own business ... oh, yes, well, umm, I'm a flower-seller ... you won't believe how good a session can be ... isn't Marcia fantastic? Oh, please book in for just one session ... I promise you it will change your life ... ask anyone here tonight and they will tell you exactly the same as me ... perhaps your friends would love to come to next week's lecture?'

I gulped down a mouthful of tea, then re-launched. 'Oh, let me grab Marcia for you ... is there anything you didn't understand or want to ask me about? I can tell you as much as she can ... more, in fact!'

They left, without booking in.

Ah, but when you play a creative game, the universe, as Ken said, provided; there was plenty of leftover food to gobble up when the lecture audience had gone.

By then Jan was responsible for the numbers game. Ken *was* smart.

Regardless of her dedication, fortitude on the hockey field and despite pulling Melbourne up, Marcia moved to Sydney, taking her children with her. I understood that Sydney was where it all happened but was uneasy about their departure. Some parents who had taken their children to Sydney from Noosa had even left. I wondered why. I had no answer. Returning to Sydney wasn't an option for me. I loved the city of Melbourne. I was born there. My children were there.

My latest professional, determined to succeed where all others had failed, took over from Marcia and determined to get me on track. I knew what that meant; questions about me, my life, where I lived. I still lived with my 'medicated' and 'alcoholic' children, and had done so for almost two years. For a time I hesitated. Determination, anger, a resistance I barely remembered fell back into me. I couldn't leave my children again and wanted a normal life with them.

After six years I still believed in processing, but I had begun to notice things. Kenja had lost its hippy, happy past and the carefree hope that accompanied that. It teetered between prim and proper and slapstick. I mourned its changing. As much as I loved Ken, misgiving had inched up. People had left. It was far too expensive being a Kenjan and we spent too much time in pointless endeavor.

Jan was far from infallible. I recalled the Kenjan man who had left and threatened to start up his own Kenja, complete with the Kenja name. It wasn't legally protected. Not only that, the Melbourne Centre was still in my name – what an oversight. Jan collected anything that displayed our logo, including Kenja badges and newsletter. 'These are our history! Why don't we value them?' she cried. Ken prepared us for the impossible: the loss of our beloved name, Kenja. By the time he had finished talking we couldn't care less – it's just a name, it's not who we are. Kenja's legal right to its name was upheld and all was well.

I had barely changed in the years I had been in Kenja; there was a time when I believed I had; slowly and with difficulty, but surely. The hardest thing to mould to thought was the feeling that the greatest game on Earth was going nowhere. What we put our attention on grows in our minds, said Ken, and negativity was growing in mine.

I couldn't keep my love for my children suppressed any longer. It had begun to hurt, to shake at unseen boundaries, to look to the other side of veiled drawbridges.

And so ... I decided to leave. It should have been the most difficult decision of my life, facing the certain failure and insanity that snared all who had given up and left, but it wasn't.

Christmas was approaching. Christmas is family. I had no idea that I was ready for the truth about Kenja.

$$\mathcal{C}\!\!-\!\!\mathcal{O}$$

I briefly wondered if I should refer to myself as a Kenjan since I had left. I still accepted the belief system and aims of Kenja. I vowed to use Ken's data in order to maintain my Kenjan self. I would still detach from my body and maintain this for every minute of every waking day. I wouldn't think of the past or future, in fact I wouldn't think at all. I believed that a Kenjan has no need of thought; a spirit can simply look and know. I would be conscious of every minute as it happened in the here and now and never sit in shame, blame, regret or failure. I would forget love and understand friendship. And I would maintain the challenge and question what I could confront and confront it. I would create the identity I needed to survive and it would be successful, vibrant and desirable. And of course I would wall-walk. For this, I needed neither Ken nor Kenja. I was a spirit, capable of knowing that which I needed to know. I would psychically, miraculously, absorb Ken's latest data and allow my belief system to sustain me.

And I would be a mother again. A Kenjan one, but a mother all the same.

At the bottom of the heap in Kenja, in the world outside, I believed I was the tall poppy; a dumping ground for the perverted and envious. People, unconsciously, understood I could clear myself of energies and so they challenged me to clear theirs too. The world outside constantly tested Kenja; only when they discovered that we would not be stopped would they give up and accept us.

The masks of others suffocated me, creating heaviness and headaches. At home, I waited for Nina and Stefan to go out, then I wall-walked. The energies I collected on my body seemed more grotesque than ever. The pain of expelling them made my bones stretch and body lurch. Resolutely I continued, extending sessions to an hour but, despite my intentions, sad memories of my life in Elwood with Josef, Nina and Stefan were always present.

I still sold flowers. It was a Kenja flower run. My bedraggled flower runs would barely pay for any Kenjan classes and sessions, but still, guilt stained my thinking. Ken wouldn't like that, so I stopped and my earnings dried up.

The Education Department, to my surprise, informed me I was still a registered teacher. Early one chilly morning the phone rang and I returned to the classroom as an emergency teacher. All my teaching had been in inner-city schools with their multicultural and working-class mix. This was a nice middle-class school with children who sat perfectly still. Twenty-five pairs of calm eyes looked expectantly to me. Anxiety rose and I feared failure. Somehow they would see through me. I sat, then stood, then paced, then sat, then stood then paced again. It was a Year six class, 11-year-olds, and the day began with Maths. I remembered zilch about fractions and the class deteriorated into Old McDonald's hee-hawing farm.

Winter finished. Few teachers were ailing with coughs and colds. The phone stopped ringing.

For my next job, after a short training period, I was dispatched to appointments in the suburbs to flog the product: vacuum cleaners. I tried to implement the sales techniques and scare the prospective buyer silly, frighten them with the bugs in their beds, shame them by demonstrating their home had always been, in fact, filthy. One prospect, a nice lady, vacuumed a section of carpet with her inadequate, tired machine and, seeing our monster at work, apologised for dirt embedded in her unhygienic carpet. I should have politely recoiled at that point – something to do with added impact.

My ineptitude was noted and the number-one salesman, a genial fellow in the staff room, accompanied me to my next appointment. Standing outside a modest house, I doubted the occupants either wanted or could afford the machine. He did his job well and the elderly couple signed on the dotted line.

'Annette, all you need is a little more time,' they said.

I couldn't sell. Look at Kenja recruitment. I left.

Selling display houses looked more promising; I loved houses and still dreamed of owning my own. The appropriate identity of a crash-hot saleswoman just might be found in my old shopping haunts. Revisiting that seaside suburb, Brighton, caught me by surprise and plunged me back to the time when I was a teenager in an old mansion. The swiftness of the experience unsettled my Kenjan mindset; it instinctively fought back. I had no understanding of this behind-the-scenes battle; my fortified cult mind was far stronger than the remnants of the old Annette. It was durable because I spent my days strengthening it.

But, unbeknown to me, doubts created by this chink – and, who knows, perhaps there were more – could, under the right circumstances, be activated.

Rummaging through discount racks in Brighton's expensive shops I hoped for a cheap makeover. Something had got lost though; when I tried the clothes on at home, lacklustre beat style.

I had worked for the developers for several months when the possibility of building my own house was mooted. Finance was not a problem, they assured me. I could live near Werribee, across the Westgate Bridge – it was miles from Elwood where Nina, Stefan and I had lived our lives. But my Kenjan deep meaning of frequent bridge crossings niggled. Several workers had tragically died during the construction of the bridge and I feared that, deep down, I still identified with death and disaster. That didn't augur well for me and my house.

Sitting at a large antique table, in meetings dedicated to encouraging sales consultants to sell well, I liked the brothers running the business. They treated me with courtesy. Like Kenja recruitment, my sales figures added up to zero but they maintained their faith in me. I seemed to be doing everything right, but postponed the house.

◡◡

Strangely shocked, I watched Nina and her boyfriend on the couch smooching in a world as small as their touching bodies. I tried to explain to Nina and Stefan how we needed to lighten our energies. That there is only one place that understands this, that understands our humans need to play sometimes. They responded neither positively nor joyously. In fact they barely responded to anything I said about Kenja.

Mum's phone calls disappeared from mind the minute I hung up. She was a determined ringer of people. 'I ring them every week,' she'd mutter. 'They never ring me,' and I was not an exception.

My family understood that I had dramatically changed, but believed I had made a choice. That something sinister might have happened to me was inconceivable, and I had a reputation along the lines of: she's always been a worry to her poor mother. My joining Kenja had hurt them. We never got beyond that, and I was still, mentally, a Kenjan.

I did visit a cousin. After two hours of stiff enthusiasm and polite enquiries as to the health of increasingly far-removed family and friends, the visit ended and was not repeated.

My two long-term neighbours visited and struggled to recognise this new Annette. I was fearful of ending up a little old lady on the pension, no longer able to afford this rambling, altering dwelling. However, a new neighbour seemed friendly. I couldn't connect but was grateful for the attention. She had misplaced her purpose in life, left it in New Zealand and wanted to return. My opaque self had nowhere to go.

At Melbourne's National Gallery I stood with my hands in the water that runs down its glass walls. In my late teens I had discovered the original gallery in a columned building on the city fringe and often stood before one painting, transfixed by its gentle indistinctness. My painting, David Davies, 1894, 'Moonrise', was not on display in the new building and I was strangely disappointed; it encapsulates my dreaminess.

Nearly three years had passed since I left Sydney. What had I achieved? While I was at the gallery, my thoughts tottered, veering inexorably back to my old life and my visits with old friends.

While I was in Kenja Sydney I had visited my school friend, Laura. (To this day, I cannot recall how we met up again while I was Kenjan.) She had a new kitchen in her beautiful house, with a pool, and two luxury cars in the driveway. I couldn't relate. I tried to connect, dredge up our mislaid past but something was wrong. Without commitment to a purpose like mine, what value could a life have? Laura had refused my pleas to attend a lecture. I didn't push it; better she didn't ask questions about Kenja or, worse, my feebly touted success.

In Melbourne, I met up with my other school friend, Lynne. Ashamed of my old car parked outside, sitting on her white couch in a fine old Edwardian house in a beautiful treed street in Hawthorn, I stared at everything I had wished, and had sessions, for. I tried to look bright and my head clamped tight. With her open smile, ease of movement, Lynne had none of the manic enthusiasm I was accustomed to. She spoke of growing her hair again, and in this entirely normal conversation I was lost. Lynne showed me Mirka Mora's astonishing angels. Mirka gave angel workshops at a gallery where I could make my own; I would love Mirka's workshops. My dormant love of beautiful things flashed to life. I looked at Lynne, and fought myself.

The pain I experienced standing in that gallery bled through skin in search of … what? A deluge of thought and pictures argued: images of my children, my life and dust. There was always dust. Dust rising, the smell of dust … it was everywhere, always had been. I looked at the floor and my mind congealed. My slow bleeding was loss and loneliness, yearning and shame. I did not belong. I never returned. I never saw Lynne again.

In the May 1988 edition of the *Women's Weekly*, I read an article entitled 'Combatting the Cults that Prey on Our Children' in which Kenja is listed as a Personal Development cult. I could privately doubt Ken, but public criticism was different. This criticism wasn't a quibble, it went to the heart of the reality of Kenja. I had long mastered the knack of 'thought-stopping', the instinctive purging of thoughts and ideas that threatened my Kenjan mindset. I threw the magazine away. This was the tall poppy syndrome Australians are famous for, cutting others down to size. I knew Ken as the most creative man in the world. Misrepresentation was the price Ken was prepared to pay for us.

I tried desperately to put my consciousness out to absorb Ken's latest data and keep up with him and Kenja. But Ken's latest words never jumped magically to mind. There was only a distant, imploring voice in my head saying 'reach and withdraw'. Where I needed to reach, I could not. Ken was the only person who understood the real me; his was the most unconditional love in the world, the ideal love. No one else had the courage to love like that, wanting nothing in return. I missed him, mourned him like a death, quiet, brimming, aching.

While I was in Kenja my ambitions had spread far and wide. Now my life consisted of Nina, Stefan and I as well as wall-walking in an Elwood flat.

Nina was busy with her boyfriend, dressing up each weekend and going out. Stefan spent his time with friends; he enrolled in university but couldn't continue. Too hard ... the last few years ... father dead, mother back. For all they had gone through, their affection for me remained. What could I confront? Not that. Their anger, bitterness, tears and recrimination, yes ... not that burnt-at-the-edges love.

Nina sometimes smiled. Stefan was a good boy.

More days. More nights. More wall-walking.

One clear day I glimpsed the tall ships re-enacting the First Fleet, their sails catching the breeze. They appeared silent and still but were on an epic journey – just like me.

Beyond recognition of my precarious state, beyond past, present and future, I existed almost beyond thinking and almost knew that that was a godsend.

Shrink-wrapped in shame, I hid from friends, from neighbours, from family. At night I stood naked before my mirror, coldly eyeing the creeping of time. Isolation oozed to bone and dried my mouth. I recalled that quote from *The Family of Man*, 'I am alone with the beating of my heart.'

Paranoia returned. I focused on small things, the cleanness of my kitchen sink, dust in hidden places, the flowers and leaves I picked from the garden and placed on our table, finding pride wherever it desperately lay.

Details swamped, encompassed me, my mind scrambled through them. The question of why life away from Kenja was unbearable, was unasked and unanswered. I slipped into the space between mind-worlds. It is a perilous place in which to drift: one is meant to make the crossing. Without information and understanding I was stuck in the middle. Nothing supported the creation of a new mindset and my Kenja one was under pressure in a world it could not understand, rammed up a silent, shuddering scream.

I slid to a smudge on my new carpet.

chapter 10

The Way Up

Hearing the voice, my human ran the gamut of fear, apprehension and joy. I knew the voice belonged to a Kenjan. It was late 1988 and I was 46 years old.

I had not heard from Kenja since I had left, one year earlier. When a Kenjan left, some were inundated with phone calls from their professional and friends in the hope they would return. But once accepted as an ex-Kenjan, they were shunned. If Ken put someone out, they were immediately ignored. There were exceptions and I believe that permission was sought, from Jan and Ken, to approach me; it was the Melbourne Centre's first Eisteddfod and the Caulfield Town Hall auditorium had to be nothing less than chock-a-block full.

All the states had their 'thing'. Canberra had its gala event, the Canberra Challenge. Sydney was Kenja's inspiration; that was more than enough. Melbourne now had its own four-day event, based on the Challenge. Instead of daytime sporting events, Melbourne had cultural activities. The timetable followed that of Canberra's Challenge with two performances of Jan's current show, Ken's evening lecture and his Sunday seminar. I would be just another bum on a seat at the evening performance of *People*.

Advertised as being direct from interstate triumph (namely the performances of this play at the previous Canberra Challenge) my ticket cost $15. Straining forward in my seat, I couldn't understand a word the performers said. Jan had taught us the art of projecting our voices; however, the skill was not evident in this presentation. Clapping anxiously, I told myself, with a small degree of stealth, that 'this is fantastic' and swiped away my thought that it was not.

Melbourne hadn't changed. It didn't take much to work that out despite the full house at the show. Kathryn greeted me cordially and

Nadine easily. Others were polite; I was an unknown quantity until Jan and Ken gave their nod of approval.

At the end of the night, Nadine hugged me. The enduringly prominent Kathryn asked the magic question: would I like to book in for a session? I knew they'd ask.

Back in the Melbourne Centre for my session, I didn't tell anyone about the disastrous acoustics of the show. I lied and said that it had inspired me. I just wanted to process again. Taking a nerve-wracking chance, I asked if I could please return to Sydney and be a professional again.

If the truth be known, I have always needed someone behind me – even in the best of times. I could hold down a job, work like a beaver, do all the practical things like wash and sew and cook and tell stories to my children. But I hid behind those I considered strong, and if they were men, then I was a Very – Good – Little Girl. And Ken most certainly was a very strong man.

I had doubts about returning to Kenja, but I would have processing, and Ken. And Nina and Stefan were adults: 22 and 20 years of age. Both worked so they could maintain the flat in Elwood – and they had their nana.

Within days I received my answer. The spiritual universe had rewarded my tenacity. I had never given up. I had never stopped being a Kenjan.

ↄ⌀

Professionalism was a rite of passage to entrenched commitment. Sam, Evan and I were the current crop of new professionals. Professionals were, by then, called Meditation Consultants and processing, Energy Conversion.

An elite athlete, a marksman, Sam was as quick and straight as the shots he fired. He had always been a wonderfully enthusiastic Kenjan. With his lean head high, he and his Kenjan girlfriend, Lillian, hurried to class with the undue haste of lovers, steeped in their private life of new saucepans and matching towels.

Sam was reaching for the top of the ladder. Lillian sold flowers. He was a professional and she was rank and file, a drone. She spent a seminar processing to eliminate her attachment to Sam, vomiting, screaming and bristling at Ken. So what if she looked like shit? She did as expected and left Sam to rise to his new heights. Lillian became the Kenjan chef, and whatever was left after Ken had zapped her could be found in her cooking.

Evan was a recent Kenjan. An accountant and brilliant pianist, with his puppy-dog eyes and flat brown hair, he was the eternally hurt little boy who had recorded every single episode of his favourite television series, *Get Smart*. The cows would come home many times before Evan mastered the art of recruitment but, on the other hand, he inherited a lot of money from the early death of his parents.

The three of us weren't thrown to the wolves, as I had been when I became Melbourne's first professional. Professional training was given by Jan and Ken contributed with his data. The length of this 'course' had condensed and we were trained in two weeks.

'The most important weeks of your life,' said Jan.

Professional sessions were conducted Monday to Friday from 7.00 am until Kenja's evening classes began at 6.30 pm and all non-seminar weekends. While professionals ran their daily sessions the three of us were with Jan, who ran us through the formalities of professional processing. The professional section held a book sacred, our 'bible'; it contained the written rules of processing including the contentious locking of doors, a complete list of the processing commands regularly devised by Ken, and instructions for the ethical conduct required of professionals. We should guard it well, never remove it from the Centre and ensure it was returned to the guardianship of Brian's office. The thumbing of its secret pages initiated us into the elite realms of responsibility. We attended all of the professional's meetings, dedicated to recruitment and general business, and attended Ken's weekly Thursday afternoon professional class. Brian explained the required paperwork and, in our spare time, we recruited. We had sessions with Jan and Ken.

In my first session with Jan she said to me, 'Annette, now you are the head of your household ... well, your mother is still alive but obviously old. Your children are adults and their trip is their trip. Annette, if you were to walk past them in the street you wouldn't take any notice of them.'

My spine stretched up. Yes I would! I sensed her manipulation. It hurt but was suppressed.

We had been in training for less than a week when Ken looked contemptuously at me. 'After all this time, you still have no idea of this game. Look at those clothes, and you want to be a respected representative of Kenja!' I dumped my wanting Melbourne attire and bought a nice white shirt and fawn pleated skirt, but kept my hot-pink evening skirt. I would not do as Jan suggested and buy second-hand clothes, even though my fellow professionals advised that there were some really nice second-hand shops.

During the second week, I had the session with Ken. Since that session long ago, I never recoiled in confusion at the end of a session at a semi-naked Ken. In the few subsequent sessions that I had with him when I was a Melbourne professional, he was fully clothed when each concluded.

Ken was an extraordinary processor; the minute I sat in session with him, the air I breathed seemed to undergo an instant cosmic shift. It was as if an invisible conduit sucked me in. As the session continued the conduit filled with the energy that flowed from my body. I clung to his eyes, entombed, until time itself disappeared, my breathing disappeared, my life disappeared; there was only the sense of lead-like energy compacting in a finite space, and the knowledge that tears were wetting my face. Ken and I were locked in the deepest stillness. I believed that Ken respected my capacity to enter this state, readily and deeply. I failed every other test: making money, recruiting, looking happy when I wasn't. However, I was fabulous in session. As it ended, I looked at Ken and said, 'That was the best session of my life. Thank you, Ken.'

We three new stars were also welcomed to our elevated ranks, by Brian, in his capacity as Kenja's manager. As the training finished so did our closeness. Our attention was back where it should be – on processing and Jan and Ken.

Our professional careers were kick-started by receiving 12 clients that we called our processees. Ken took these from the existing professionals who stood, poker-faced, while being shorn of their clientele.

For Sam, the honeymoon did not last long; he left suddenly. Jan said, portentously, that he had taken something with him. I feared it was our bible.

At our next professional meeting Ken, uncharacteristically, grilled us. Normally the fact of professionals leaving was dealt with privately; regardless of the hype blaming the failed professional, this might be seen as Kenja's failure, and was therefore buried.

Ken stood in front of a seated me and leaned forward.

'What do you know about Sam leaving?'

'Nothing, Ken.'

My head tilted back.

'Why did Sam leave?'

'I don't know.'

Ken mellowed. 'Did you help him?'

'No, Ken.'

Head to one side and quizzical, he asked, 'Can I still trust you?'

'Yes, yes, Ken.'

His voice was soft and teasing.

'Don't fuck with me, Annette.'

I shivered, as if I just might.

Sam returned for a session with Ken. A respectful hush fell upon the Centre as they sat in session. We hoped for the best; Sam was one of us. As Sam walked away we sighed with relief, but never saw him again. Sam had been given his chance. We cut emotional ties with him.

But Sam left a legacy. He had been involved in a company that manufactured the most gorgeous teddy bears with silk ribbons tied round their necks. Practically every female bought one and the fact that we still had, through these cuddly toys, psychic ties to Sam went unnoticed.

Brian still ran the office, handled the money and made sure we were conversant with Kenjan methods. Professionals kept two sets of appointment books, one for personal use and the other for the Taxation Department. Both were in pencil until some bright spark decided that biro might look more convincing for the Taxman. Brian shredded anything financially sensitive. The total number of sessions in any given week was recorded and displayed in Brian's office in code; 11 sessions was recorded as one, 12 as two and so on.

All bookings, for sessions with professionals and for Jan and Ken's seminars and classes, were recorded in pencil in loose-leaf folders and later shredded. No receipts were given. If a receipt was requested, that person was declared a security risk and closely monitored. No money was taken in advance except for seminar deposits. If someone requested the deposit be returned, it was. When it came to Jan and Ken, professionals had higher interests than the what, how and why of Kenja's cash flow. Ken now had a personal assistant and Jan, an assistant. These positions, plus that of receptionist in Kenja's front office, were valued and sometimes given as rewards to selected Kenjans, and were a stepping stone to professionalism. Personnel changed, either as praise or punishment.

⌒♁

When the Sydney Centre moved, some were sceptical. The new Centre was opposite a hotel. Even though the smell of beer might infiltrate our entrance and condense on our stairs, Ken assured us we were so far ahead in the game of life that those doubtful energies would not hurt us.

Jan had long envisaged that we would be recognised as a professional training organisation; Ken's data would be the feather in every CEO's cap. We had tried, but our old building laughed at our pretensions. Now there would be no more apologetic glances while ushering guests along Brian's playful lino.

We renovated, top to toe, under the inspiring name of Operation Michelangelo. Brian contributed money, to verbose praise from Jan and Ken; after all, if not for them ... and anyway, with a new and bigger Centre, he'd earn it back. Devotees lent money as they had for Canberra,

Melbourne and a convention and training Centre in Canberra based on Kenja ideals and established by two then-staunch members. Each time, members were promptly repaid.

To outsiders who sneered that Commonwealth Street, Surry Hills, was hardly the grandeur of the Italian Renaissance and our Centre not exactly majestic, we flaunted our inscrutable 'just you wait and see – this is a Renaissance' looks.

Brian, Jan and Ken had an office each, and Jan and Ken had commodious private processing rooms. We boasted also a large sitting room, a hall-sized multi-purpose lecture/class/social events space, a shared office for the professionals and a new processing suite consisting of a large room locked from the outside and lined with rows of individual cubicles, as usual, secured internally. Everything was freshly painted, the kitchen new, the bathrooms renovated. The finishing touches, including the Kenja logo, were upgraded from Kenja's colours, nondescript pink and blue, to brilliant aqua and hot pink.

New premises. New functions. New teams. The new Security team paid homage to our new grandeur by protecting women from shonky strangers in the questionable streets surrounding our Centre. No one could leave the building without the protection of this group of men, and a new facet of self-discovery, whereby men could be men, began. Security escorted us to cars and cabs with a degree of control *sometimes* appropriate – well, if you want to call a spade a spade, they came across as animated control freaks captivated by their walkie-talkies.

This rigmarole ensured that Jan's New Women (us) were safe on the streets after midnight. With the Security team, gallantry became part of Kenja's bag and most women loved this; 'bag' being the latest expression in Jan's journey to immortality. Nadine and Kathryn loved the escort. I hoped for a bit more style, but kept my eye on the main game; I was back.

∽

Ken and Jan rented out their apartment in a hilly, leafy street in Double Bay to the female professionals. One tenant was Kathryn and another was on her way out of professional processing as her client numbers were woefully low. Helena was a recent professional and I was the fourth occupant. We paid our rent to Brian.

Despite the balmy late nights, Kathryn huddled right next to her heater while we bickered about the disarray in the household – don't look at me, I'm never there! A combined household purchase, a fruit-juicer, was our Achilles heel. We nit-picked about who had the right to use it, who washed it last, why isn't it in its proper place and if you don't pay up then don't use it.

One day, Jan unexpectedly inspected our flat and found no food in the fridge. 'Buy some,' she said. We did but it rotted. How could Jan be unaware of the fact that we never ate at home? During the week we left home at 6.00 am and ate breakfast at the Centre. Lunch was usually eaten on the run. By then, Lillian prepared meals in Kenja's kitchen that were for sale before the evening classes. Kenja activities also kept us away from home for most of our weekends.

When Jan and Ken hosted a barbecue at their new *million dollar* (Ken's italics) waterfront home, I peeked inside Jan's sadly stocked fridge. Their house magnificently topped a cliff and had a path that leads to water. Ken gave us a guided tour. In class he had informed us that Jan was lucky because she had the whole bathroom to herself while he made do with the en suite. His room was enormous. Jan's room was small; a child's room with a single bed, neatly made, and above the bed was a picture of a warrior on horseback.

The poignancy I had sensed while standing at Jan's bedroom door was pushed aside in our expectant, busy days and nights.

Each morning my flat-mates rose easily and charged down the hill to catch a cab to the Centre for 6.00 am.

'Hurry up, Annette,' said Helena.

'I'm coming!'

'*I'm* going to go for a jog before *my* first session.'

'I know!'

I sat clammily next to Helena in the cab, half envious of her early morning wakefulness, half scornful. She was a current golden girl and on the rise in Kenja; she veered between suspicion of and pity for me.

Inside the Centre, my human emerged hoping my processee arrived with a mouthwatering breakfast.

I was responsible for my processee's mental health, just like a psychologist really, counselling them on life. I was lucky that one of my processees was Deana. She had taken me under her wing when I first sold flowers. She and Rick had not survived Ken's ruthless closure of the flower-selling venture. Rick had left Kenja; however, Deana and her daughter remained ardent devotees.

She arrived quarter of an hour early for her weekly session to prepare our snack: two large juicy mangoes cut and decorated with parsley to be followed by chocolate biscuits and a cup of tea. She was still lovely, soft and practical, and walked after me carrying our breakfast on a tray. I stifled yawns. Inside our cubicle she pressed $100 into my hand, of which I kept $56; the balance went to Brian.

'Oh, yummy, thank you,' I said in real appreciation of our breakfast.

We ate and talked and smelt of mango. Deana and I didn't have to pretend with each other, as I did with some newer recruits; we understood the old ways, when Ken was a whirling, howling dancer. Then to my surprise, Deana and Zoe left Kenja. I was disappointed as I really liked them both. Perhaps I had failed with them?

Reports were written straight after each session. These recorded the processee's conversation in the half-hour chat immediately before the session. Important were the names of Kenjans who successfully recruited so Ken could praise or promote them. Those who failed to noticeably change, thereby invalidating Ken's data, were singled out. Criticisms of Ken and Kenja, and anything that might represent a threat to Kenjan security were duly noted. Nothing was sacred; parents reported on their children in order to help them. Information from reports soon formed the basis of records kept on Kenjans – just in case – and included our glowing testimonials that could be cited if we left and said something nasty about Kenja.

After one processing session with a young mother named Shelley, I rushed to the shop around the corner, grabbed a cappuccino, a pack of cigarettes and furtively lit up. This 'smoking around corners' was new. Things had been better when Ken smoked. He stopped and told us to do likewise. The cigarette was weak and I dragged hard. I missed the old cigarette-smoking, swearing Ken. He had undergone a metamorphosis, thanks to Jan, and wore business suits and ties. I grimaced, stubbed my cigarette and, determined to recruit, approached a woman.

I had dashed out without writing my report on Shelley. By the time I did I had forgotten what she said. She had talked about her daughter and said something about the child's behaviour. Something about it being out of character. Unsure of what Shelley said, I ad-libbed. I certainly didn't mention anything about a child. Parents were in enough trouble as it was, forever in Jan's office, bowed over her desk, tense as athletes on starter lines.

That was time I saw Shelley. Ken gave her to another professional. I had failed with her.

Soon enough, the wind was blowing down Kenja's corridors. Something was radically wrong. Parents were in deep trouble. Jan held long meetings with them behind closed doors. Everyone, Jan included, emerged white and crumpled.

In addition to this, Ken could be heard in his office verbally whipping Shelley, of all people. Shelley and her husband and daughter left suddenly. I had thought they were a Kenja success story. Both had visibly grown in strength. Ken's jet-black eyes fired up as he berated them for leaving. Their leaving threatened us. Even I thought Ken was a little melodramatic.

Canberra, Jan's baby, grew, but from as early as 1986 numbers in Sydney had remained fairly static. Perhaps something changed while I was in Melbourne. (The possibility that people failed to respond to our drawcards, Jan and Ken, was never entertained.)

Jan was building the new public face of Kenja. Ken gave her a playing field and, being a good little girl, she lost herself in it. Kenja would be more Australian than Vegemite. Not the wide, sunburnt country of folklore, but a slice of urban community where opportunity abounded; Australia as it was – in the 1950s. Kenja's professed values of honesty, awareness, striving, friendship, moderate frocks for girls and short back and sides for boys were, to some, quaintly appealing. Sadly, the rest of the world rushed to the future. Kenjans noisily promoted, and practised these standards; ignorant that our ideals were commandeered to ensure obedience.

Jan hailed Ken as the Michael Jackson of the psychic world, while at the same time leading us to an increasingly conservative image. She led us in the direction of an exclusive private school when once we were, almost, rabble-rousers. Jan's forte, aspiring and flying in the face of reality – Kenja's cultural transformation – was not Ken's. He couldn't care less about melodious new cultures and soirees and elocution and 1950 frocks. Possibly what's under the frocks? You can guess where I shoved that thought.

I wondered why Ken, who rarely attended our social nights, had agreed to them? These were Jan's idea of a proper formal evening. Mr Goody meets Miss Gumdrops. These nights appeared moronic to outsiders, who either patronised us or thought us really cute – until they became Kenjans.

'We don't need Hollywood. It's all here on a Saturday night,' said Jan.

As well as professional processing, professionals contributed to the Kenja workload. In this capacity, they called themselves the Time Bandits. They organised the weekly public dinner dance because we profited by gaining more processees. One particular event was called 'Our Extravaganza'.

Envious of those still locked eyeball to eyeball in session, the only valid excuse for shirking any task, I rushed from my sole afternoon session to hurl tablecloths on trestle tables, scrounge fresh flowers, shuffle mismatched cutlery and shove candles in little glass holders bought from Two Dollar shops.

Slipping on my hot-pink satin skirt and pearl-crusted evening jumper, I snipped off loose threads. I was 47, and comforted by the absence of wrinkles and my still slim body.

All our hard work in the previous week recruiting – dangling social nights as electrifying opportunities to advance one's life – had resulted in a paltry handful of new people. Before the guests arrived, professionals gathered together to reinforce our goal: to book them in for sessions.

Nicholas, currently in Sydney – he had at one stage been a director of the Brisbane and Melbourne Centres – wore a new tie and had polished his shoes. Nadine and Kathryn wore strapless, crackling satin dresses. Brian, in a shiny suit, donned his usual hand-rubbing identity and insisted on insisting. 'Isn't it great to invite a new friend to a really fantastic social night. Have a fantastic night everyone. I *know* we will. Just remember to hold our psychic picture still and people will come tonight out of nowhere. You'll be surprised. You really will!'

Suddenly the flowers *were* vivid, the serviettes chatty – success was, after all, a core promise. Ken's words came to mind, 'Everyone agrees with us, they just don't know it yet.'

Nadine and Kathryn were seated at a table collecting money. As I paid my entrance fee a pearl fell from my jumper. I wondered if I saw mascara and eyeliner on their pale faces? I looked again. I was mistaken. A hint of desperation, not there in our early days, had imbued the flowers with wilt and snuffed out candles.

As the night progressed, Nadine and I stood together. She snapped her fingers, frowned and fixed her gaze. The hastily organised program of events was running late.

'Begin the Beguine', circa 1940s, burst melodiously into action then stuttered and stopped. Sitting at our wishfully elegant tables, under unforgiving fluorescent lights, paper serviettes on laps, Brian, Nadine, Kathryn and I sat together. Safely chatting.

'I just love lemon and pear fruit juice. You should try it, you'll love it too,' said Brian.

'I must,' said I.

Nadine jiggled in her seat; her skirt crackled. 'There's nothing like our social nights anywhere else in Sydney.'

Kathryn half opened her eyes, 'I know.'

Brian, in a flashback to his days as a lover of the written word, enthused, 'I really think we should all read the daily paper. You know, as Kenjans, in fact especially as Kenjans, we need to know what goes on in the world outside.'

Brian! It was imperative that, as good little Kenjans, we knew as little as possible about what goes on outside.

He rushed to talk to the new people and looked disgracefully eager chatting to one of the female guests.

Kathryn, horror-struck, responded as a responsible Kenjan should. 'Where's the food!'

On cue, Alex flourished a tea towel and deposited food in front of us, taking our attention off our niggling thoughts. Brian eventually returned to our table and Kathryn, dramatically, sighed.

Conversation stopped as we ate. Lunch was a bigger luxury than an excess of four hours sleep. Many ran out of time and some, like me, ran out of money. Not Nicholas though, our perennial maître d, he circulated non-stop and ate on the run. I looked at him; he was the only professional to have never been told to stop conducting professional processing sessions. He was still lovely Nicholas, no longer applauded as the first to clear, but still devoted to Ken.

The tape recorder spurted into action and dancing partners swanned to the floor for the formal waltz. Gowns moved in a multi-coloured twirl; bodies moved like androids. Nadine bustled as she danced. Kathryn moved with exaggerated flair. With the line from her shoulders to her fingertips a perfect arc, her head to one stiff side, she led her partner instead of the other way round.

Gretel, whom I really liked, stood next to me, counting down the minutes till she mounted the podium with her violin. Pre-Kenja, Gretel was an architect and talented amateur musician. In her late twenties, she was beautiful, gracious, ethereal and committed. Her eyes were gentle, her talent prodigious, both were given to Kenja. Gretel was now a professional.

Looking at newly formed relationships, wondering which of them will be the first to hit professional heights as a couple, Gretel said, 'I know it's okay to have a relationship now as a professional, but I don't like it.' She had given up a relationship to be a professional. I recalled Gretel and her boyfriend coming to one class. She wore a flowing Indian dress. They sat down, their shoulders touching. Ken began before he reached the dais. They could not sit together. They must have his data for themselves before they could share it. They moved apart, and stayed apart.

Playing the violin, she rose above the silliness of the night. She wore a gypsy scarf tied around her waist. I was uneasy at this non-Kenja touch. As the notes faded, the violin dropped from her shoulder; she hugged it to her strangely unsure body. We gave Gretel a standing ovation, momentarily banishing her uncertainty, but as she moved from the limelight our eyes met; she indicated disappointment with her performance.

The evening tapered to a close and our guests left. Nadine and Kathryn's dresses ceased their crackling, the Time Bandits packed everything away, and time, suspended for these hours, resumed its tempo. It was business as usual and we formed a circle for our post-event meeting.

With Brian conducting our meeting in hushed anticipation, it was revealed that no one had responded to the evening's magnificence by booking in for a session.

⌒◯

Ken was late for class. Gretel looked at her watch. I looked at mine. We looked at each other.

Jan said that Ken was still in his processing room processing Vanessa; researching his latest data for the seminar that weekend.

'She gives everything,' Ken had said.

Oh, does she? I had thought.

Sitting next to Gretel, who held her professional appointment book on her lap, I recognised that her energies were better than mine, but when it came to recruitment ... Jan was still on the dais, prattling, filling in time.

Where are you, Ken? I silently, and impatiently, demanded

He finally bounced into the room and settled into his chair. A girl sprang to remove the plastic wrap covering his nibbles. The cling wrap clung; the girl fumbled. Ken raised his eyebrows.

He then began with a rambling repeat of his rapid promotion in business; it was because he took responsibility. When something went wrong he yelled out, 'I did it, I'll fix it,' and soon people looked to him for guidance, as he seemed to be responsible for everything. He informed us that he would introduce a new subject, something he had never talked about before. 'Tonight I'm going to talk about death.'

We had all heard it before but no one said so. Have a death a day, experience the pain of it now. Why wait till the bitter hour? Play psychic target games with death. Experience every death you've ever had, now, in the past and in the future. Become a master of death. Wink at death, taunt it, piss on it, ask death if it can confront *you*? Rarely did I take my eyes off Ken, except for a glance as my peers got slaughtered. This night I did.

Those who were currently in Jan or Ken's favour sat with casual collectedness, a draped arm and fierce eyes, apart from Kathryn who remained terminally tranced. Most slumped to limpness; all-knowing minutes before, they had slipped into smog. No one crossed their arms or legs. This was forbidden by Ken as it demonstrated an unwillingness to listen.

Riveted to Ken, Jan had her feet up on the seat of her straight-backed chair, knees pulled under her chin. Ken screamed bloody murder at one of her current favourites. Jan ignored it; nothing would divert her attention from Ken.

Ken called Vanessa to the dais. Now a slim, dark-haired, silent-eyed teenager she stood on stage, magnanimous and benevolent. In a swollen room before shrunken people she acknowledged our applause. She was used to this.

After class, as Gretel and I left the Centre, she said, 'You know, I always put my hand up, even when I don't agree with Ken.'

'Yes,' I replied with a small buzz, recalling Ken's comments on death, 'I do too.'

Is that what Gretel meant? Something was out in the open.

～

Once more the rustling began, but it was nothing substantial. We never gossiped. This time it related to Vanessa. Demoted, put out of professional processing, she remained Ken's research assistant. The words swam to corners and idly circled. Shhh. She had been up and down the teenage professional ladder. One month she was superior to her peers and the next she was reduced to ordinary teenager, promoted and dismissed with the same efficiency that Ken applied to adults. Her schedule was inhuman, but as Ken said, 'Those who lead us in Kenja pay the highest price.'

Despite apparent amity, some of Vanessa's peers secretly disparaged her. Regardless of the prize of being in Ken's good books, no one wanted to be in Vanessa's shoes, with little time to herself and seemingly forever with Ken. Perhaps she was scuttling their chances of reaching the top? None were immune from Ken's dividing and conquering.

Passing Vanessa in the corridor, I couldn't help but see the black circles under her eyes, but when she stood in front of us her shining outdid fatigue. For years she had stood in front of her audience as our example, a challenge to us: what *can* you confront? With a blatant, sometimes self-satisfied grace she was Ken's chosen one and initiated into secrets.

Ken had taken to denigrating his two sons. Matt had long been gone from our ranks and his other son, Ben, was an off-and-on participant. Ken claimed they only hung around to collect his money when he died. One day he informed us he was leaving Vanessa $80,000 in his will.

'She deserves a reward, doesn't she?'

'Yes, Ken.'

For some time we had been encouraged to put a little something in a plate in gratitude for Vanessa's hard work. She had begun to irritate me. Could we *please* have a class or seminar or something without Vanessa in our faces? She seemed to be more like Ken's girlfriend. He took her out on dates, like daddy's little princess.

'I offered Vanessa a glass of wine in a restaurant the other day,' he laughed in one class.

A bombshell had been dropped.

Ken looked at us; his eyes stopped time.

Kenjan jaws gnashed; Kenjan bodies stiffened; Kenjan hearts jumped to Kenjan mouths.

'I want to clear her on the energy of alcohol. After all, I can have a drink because I'm clear on that.'

I'd heard from a Kenjan service-provider that Ken quite enjoyed a drink and I had listened derisively.

Ken casually, contemptuously almost, scanned our response.

We sat still and quiet. We were as one.

This pleased him.

He smiled.

That satisfied us.

All was still well in our Kenja world.

Ken was, in the end, KEN.

'Isn't that what we all want, isn't this why we process, so we have the choice to say yes or no to everything? When she's older and she meets a young buck,' he laughed again, 'and goes out to restaurants, Vanessa will not succumb to the demands of alcohol abuse like others her age. Isn't that true?' he said turning to Vanessa.

Her uncertainty touched all.

In another class, Ken said.

'I'm clearing Vanessa on sex.'

You could have heard a pin drop.

'No man will ever take advantage of her; she will be smart and aware of the nature of sexual games and not face the usual normal sexual degradation on offer in the big wide world. Isn't that what every woman wants?'

'Yes, Ken.'

'Have I ever touched one of you women? I treat you all with total respect. Isn't that right!'

A collective accord rolled through our ranks.

Ken turned to other teenage girls.

I glanced at Jan; enigmatically, she watched Ken.

'How many of you girls am I helping to clear on sex?'

There was another collective confirmation as girls raised their hands in agreement with Ken.

'Yes,' continued Ken, 'when they have relationships, these girls will have the very best life can offer, having already experienced all possible traps. I will have cleared them completely in this area. Isn't that right, Jan?'

'Isn't that right, Vanessa?'

Bewilderment hurled itself into my mind as I recalled a semi-naked Ken at the end of that long ago session.

The words that Jan had once said to us in a professional class, 'You have no idea what hell my life is,' came to mind.

So did Ken's words, 'Those at the top pay the highest price.'

I battled with my confusion, and won.

༄

Whatever Vanessa had to clear, she was not clearing it. Ken had failed to. Jan had processed her, to no avail. Whatever it was, Ken was making a massive hullabaloo about it.

Surprisingly, Ken asked me to process her. I sat opposite Vanessa in session and saw a desolate, young woman, and felt edgy. At its end she thanked me; her feedback was guarded. It stayed put, the hidden question with no answer – the uneasy trio, Jan, Ken and Vanessa. Doubt sidelined by my privileged status; I gave our 'goddess' sessions.

Then … Vanessa turned blushing cheeks towards a young man whose testosterone had kicked in regardless, apparently, of sessions. With his heart hunched in his agile and polite body, Sean should have been wearing jeans and t-shirt, instead of ironed shirt and short-assed pants. Their attraction was obvious – that first, awkward, deliriously divine, tongue-tied love. To Ken, Vanessa gave a beatific smile. With her young man she gazed and giggled. A shred of Vanessa's desire for a young man was intolerable, for her sake, of course. There would be no rush of teenage hormones for her. How in God's name could she be our example if distracted by this blundering, excited young man?

With his black eyes bruising her heart, Ken plugged Vanessa's affection for Sean, resulting in two very desolate teenagers. For weeks the smitten youngsters mourned at their own funeral and we, their pallbearers, hummed a sad, sad song.

Sean became Ken's gardener and weeded his plants and trimmed his branches and listened to Ken's words until he agreed that, indeed, young love might interfere with rescuing the world and was therefore unacceptable. Soon Sean was like a parcel that had arrived at the wrong address and now sat in the lost box. Vanessa raked the ground with downcast eyes. The teenagers cast decreasing peeks towards each other. Then stopped. Our Ken could be a real bastard.

Shortly after, Vanessa pushed past me, clothes crushed, body hard, resentment in her wake.

I grabbed her. 'Vanessa, how dare you, the number one representative of Kenja, show up to class like that.'

She looked coldly at me and edged away.

I pitched forward. 'Of all people, we expect so much more from you. Don't piss on this game!'

Brutal resentment smouldered in her cheeks, but she ironed her dress and later thanked me.

Despite her demotion, Vanessa was still praised for her contribution to Ken's data and our clearing, and frequently stood before us for her acclaim. She stood with her shoulders back, head lowered. Over the next few weeks, Kenjans watched her change to immutable. She was concupiscent, in complete ownership of the space that, one day, she may wish had never been hers. Ken left the dais and sat in the ranks. Vanessa stood alone.

It was Ken's unassailable moment too.

～

Jan's sister, Claudia, learnt the hard way about the road to spiritual freedom. They had lived comparable lives. Jan's career had changed from 'physicist' to actress. Claudia was a scientist who turned to classical music. Claudia became Kenja's composer and wrote the music for Jan's musicals; some of Claudia's compositions were hauntingly beautiful. Both women were slight and brown-haired. Claudia's features were more severe than Jan's. The biggest difference between them was that Claudia was one of us, and was not in imminent danger of losing her clown's humanity. In clowning, her clown cried with and before us. Jan had long ceased to refer to her ill-starred clown, Gladys. The sisters were close but Jan was Claudia's Kenjan superior.

At first, I had thought Claudia second rate but had warmed to her. We went back a long time, to Melbourne's very first seminar. Her talent saved her but her recruitment was regrettable. She was also hopeless at flogging flowers and sometimes couldn't afford to attend classes.

When she allegedly stole money from Kenja, Jan demonstrated her words, 'I have to be particularly ruthless with my sister. It hurts but I must.' Claudia was disgraced. She admitted to being the lowest of the low, a mockery of the Kenja game, and was threatened with temporary expulsion.

The opportunity was taken up by Jan and Ken and this became another great Kenjan cleansing. A spade is a spade. Theft is theft. Alex, thrust from his cushy gardening job by Sean, owned up to taking home a plate of food and forgetting to return the plate. Nicholas, proudly honest, confessed to having once stolen a Kenja badge. When it came to pencils and rulers, I ran out of counting. Our ambushed criminals returned their booty. A pile of trivia. No one, me included, ventured that we had all paid for it in the first place.

Ken's wrath melted to largesse – aren't Kenjans all basically decent human beings? Claudia paid back the money, proved herself worthy of being Jan's sister, and a Kenjan, and was appointed our receptionist. She was also a young woman who met her match in my fellow professional, Evan.

Evan was, by then, Kenja's resident impresario. He was a terrific, if at times distracted, teacher prescribing his students a daily dose of Hanon's *The Virtuoso Pianist* and scales and more scales. Our pride reached its zenith as we sat, dressed in our very best, entranced during Evan's Kenja piano recitals.

As the musical activities of Kenja expanded, Claudia and Evan became its musical co-directors. Claudia was chief conductor of the Kenja Simplistic Symphony Orchestra. Its name was appropriate, some had barely fingered a musical instrument five minutes before curtain time. Through the orchestra, Kenjans experienced the thrill and pride of playing together unimpeded by expertise or the tittering of strangers. Claudia stood in front of her serious, joyful and inept players wearing Jan's trademark expression of ecstatic compassion, and making difficult decisions such as how to cover the total absence of wind instruments as Evan's piano was already filling in for the second violins.

There was little call for another pianist, so I played tambourine in Claudia's classical choices. Frustration won out as the conductor, baton tapped and arms aloft, took us meticulously into obscure pieces. I silently gnashed because I wanted to throb with passion for familiar classics. But the choir! Bellowing Beethoven, tunefully or not, with one's fellow choristers is one of life's great joys. When I auditioned for it, Claudia cleverly pounced on the one out of ten notes I got right and drowned my voice by placing tuneful singers on either side.

Kenjans raced to take up musical instruments. Nadine and Kathryn took up the violin; at 31 years of age, swaggered Nadine. Kathryn lamented that she may have to cut the nails on her left hand forever. Alex took up piano and he and I battled it out for practice times on Kenja's sole piano. Dear Nicholas took naturally to the pose of a virtuoso pianist, level one – it was all in the mock-up (we knew that). Music lit us up. If we weren't growing in numbers we were booming laterally.

Claudia and Evan misjudged the resilience of the moment. The buoyancy of Kenjans was not shared by Jan and Ken who considered that some of us were becoming smug, complacent and losing track of the real game of Kenja.

Jan and Ken had a flat in the city and sometimes stayed there after class. Claudia and Evan used it. Other relationships were allowed to develop at this time but this one came to an abrupt end. It had dirtied, illicitly, Jan and Ken's sheets! Perhaps they had been unlucky and were caught out the first time? 'Apoplectic' describes Ken's response; Jan's oozed betrayal. The lovers did their penance. It was tough and cruel and heartbreaking to watch. It seemed senseless, vindictive even.

In time we were relieved to see their hearts no longer entangled with the musical notes. I wondered why this was not seen as a good match? Both were intelligent, accomplished, had a shared passion for music and were totally committed to Kenja. It couldn't possibly be that Claudia knew too much about our leaders to risk her closeness with another?

A year had gone by since the last four-day Eisteddfod, and all states were busy preparing for the next.

Jan's life before Kenja may have been a lead-up to the main event but watching her now, it was clear she had missed her calling. During rehearsals for the musical, she slipped through our ranks like a leopard. I admired Jan's dedication. Perhaps it was partly to herself but, without us, there would be no demonstration of her ability; and although she was changing – more ambitious, more demanding of herself and others – she still recognised us, her Kenjans. Before the Eisteddfod, Jan challenged us to fit everything in. We did the lot. Painted backdrops, made costumes and props, organised lighting, rehearsed lines and songs for the musical, music for the Simplistic Symphony Orchestra, our solo instrumental recitals and choir, plus our poetry and Shakespearean recitatives. All without missing out on classes and seminars and sessions and sporting activities and everything else. And the host city, dear Melbourne, had, once again, to fill the Caulfield Town Hall auditorium three times and, to my admiration, rose to the challenge. It was panicky and exciting. We were truly exceptional.

At the Melbourne Eisteddfod, we performed with bravado; it *was* all in one's mock-up and we could create whatever one we wished – that we all created identities of dedicated pleasing was irrelevant.

Bone fide judges assessed our performances and Ken awarded an energy score. Playing something lovely by Schubert while casting helpless shrugs at Evan, I expected the 'average' score the judges gave me, but Ken gave me a ridiculously high-energy score. I didn't deserve it but I dared to hope.

At the conclusion of our four hectic days we gave Claudia and Evan a special acknowledgement. To us, their friends, they bowed and blushed. To each other they gave a polite and distant nod.

chapter 11

The Way Down

I had guessed right. My high score did mean that I was designated. I was a chosen one. Back in Sydney, Ken dramatically increased my number of processees. My peers struggled to regain the expected composure, but they understood that the game of Kenja was more important than the individual. Soon I had 23 clients. I spent an average of 30 hours a week in session, still as steel; the more one processed, the faster one would change.

Cashed up, I bought a new suit. As one seminar finished, Nicholas and I rushed straight into a five-star hotel in the heart of Sydney, where we lazed and drank coffee. Coffee breaks in hotels had long been an illicit pleasure. I wanted to dally in those comfortable chairs, under soft lighting. Perhaps I left my mind in that hassle-free room because in the rush to find a cab, I lost my jacket. I stood, dazed by rain-blurred lights, in pelting rain, sodden and mesmerised by loss. Nicholas gently led me to the cab.

In December 1989, one year after I returned to Sydney, my elevation to the post of director of the Sydney Centre was announced. And my ascendancy was quickly terminated in March 1990.

Some anticipated my downfall; others were astonished. How had I, of all people, managed to get to the top? No one publicly denounced my appointment. Ken always knew best. Perhaps somewhere in my urgently shining self I knew it couldn't last. Numbness became humility, then, all too briefly, arrogance. I was part of the elite, among the chosen and I, the eternal being, hoped it would last forever.

At class, the director was acknowledged by name and applauded individually. Often, during sessions, I walked the aisles separating the rows of processing pairs in my stockinged feet, breathing as lightly as possible so as not to disrupt the sacred mission of spirits unfolding before my eyes. I held the balance of human frailty in my hands.

Ken had taken a fancy to requesting lists that detailed our fears and hates. One set specified, in gruesome detail, the murderous punishment we would mete out to our worst enemies; hanging someone from the rafters seemed tame compared to graphic descriptions of skinning enemies alive, or a vindictive mix of tenderness and torture. In the wrong hands these could be misconstrued, let alone the subject of legal proceedings.

Another set of lists highlighted everything we disliked about Ken. He was smart and brought opposition to him out in the open. In several Wednesday classes, he asked us what we disliked about him and, for our class session, instructed us to focus on, and hence clear, our reservations – and, lo and behold, we realised we had been mistaken.

It was my job, as director, to shred these lists and some of the written reports on individuals that were regularly given to Ken. Like my predecessors, I should have also had a private weekly meeting with Ken to discuss the important ins and outs of Kenja; he must have overlooked them.

Ken had stopped giving Kenja's weekly public lecture. Jan chose the substitute speakers and according to their place on the energy scale the lowest-level speakers spoke first. This, in theory, would result in a progressively lighter and higher-tone cascade of communication. Up to a dozen of us, mostly professionals and team leaders, rushed to the stage, hot on the heels of the previous speaker. I, despite being the lowest-toned of the lot, was the director and therefore spoke last and urged people to book in.

At my first lecture in my executive position, I went completely blank after a sentence or two. I had no idea what I'd said or what to say next. I stood before my peers in mute apprehension. I fudged, and got lucky. The following week, it happened again. After two intact sentences, my collapse of mind occurred and, coming to my senses, I said in a panic, 'Book in for a session. Suck it and see!'

Brian, in his endearing haste, said, 'Annette, that was just brilliant.'

'Ha!' I retorted.

One day the world briefly opened and Ken allocated a new person to me. I had never given a formal 'first session' before. Who was she? Not whom she thought she was. Her name was Carla; soon she would know herself as a spirit.

Carla knew nothing of what a session entailed. She knew it was called an Energy Conversion session and that this first session lasted two hours, cost $100, and I was the professional Meditation Consultant conducting the session.

I should have known the end results because I stuffed up the beginning. She should have made the coffee, an unconscious gift to me but she was nice and I, so eager, made it – and carried it. Liquid slopped in saucers as, entering the professional processing suite, I fumbled with the lock then, inside the room, double-checked that I had the right cubicle. Carla entered first and sat down.

'Do you mind sitting on the other chair?'

'Sure, now will you tell me about a session?'

I ignored her question; she folded her arms.

Picking up a blank questionnaire I assured Carla this was part of the procedure, and that it was brief. She answered these initial questions promptly. I learnt that she was 53, divorced, had no children and was a lapsed Catholic. Her career was successful and her family and friends supportive, but something was missing. Looking directly at me she said, 'I suppose that's why I'm here.'

'Next question, Carla, is about your alcohol and drug history, including medication but not antibiotics. You haven't taken anything like that in the last 48 hours, have you?'

'No, you asked me this morning.'

'Fine.'

'Why?'

'It affects the sensitivity of our energy fields. Carla, what drugs did you take before the age of five?'

'I can't remember.'

'I know, it's difficult ... '

'I suppose the usual childhood illnesses ... I had a few chest infections ... and had medication for that.'

'How often?'

'I probably had three or four a week.'

'Three or four what?'

'Asprin, I suppose.'

'For the full five years?'

'Of course not. I can't remember. This is ridiculous!'

'I understand Carla. It's just that we need to know the energies we'll deal with in session.'

These questions were repeated, 'Aged 5 to 10 Carla? 10 to 15 Carla? Through 45 to 50? And this week Carla? Now, let's start with your alcohol history.' The five-year segments of her life were repeated until we reached the present and, once again, Carla answered.

There is a fine line between a person becoming irritable enough to need the session and too irritable to be bothered at all. As Carla snapped her answers, I knew she almost couldn't be bothered and I trod carefully. She was confused, relieved, angry with me for asking, and subdued by her niceness; the closest she came to telling me to get lost was to ask why the door was locked.

'Oh, Carla, we're not trying to lock you in, these sessions are very sensitive. Someone walked in on one once so we decided it was best to lock the door. As you're aware, a lot of people come and go ...' as I spoke, Carla gave me the benefit of the doubt, and all that mattered to me was her.

'Three more questions, Carla, are you seeing a psychologist or psychiatrist?'

'What difference does that make?'

'We don't interfere. One does either one thing or another. Have you ever been involved in satanic practices, black magic and the like?'

'Oh for God's sake, Annette, do I look the type? No, I haven't.'

'Do you have a criminal history?'

'No!'

'They do seem strange questions. We need to know what we're dealing with ... did I show you our ethics? Quite simply, Carla, we don't deal in areas we do not feel we are able to handle.'

She looked at me. I smiled. Carla was already dear to me, a spirit about to take the first steps to clarity.

'Before we start the session, what area of your life would you like to look at?'

'After my husband left me I was, well, hurt, even though he was a real bastard – my brother uses women, too. My sister lives with me and that's really difficult. I can't bring anyone home to my place; everyone I do bring home gets the cold shoulder from her. I need something for myself ... I don't have enough time ... I have to work long hours ... I can't not do that as I need the money ... it's ... well lately nothing seems to be going right ...' Her expression pleaded with me for understanding and I was compassion personified.

'Would you mind taking your shoes off?'

She popped them neatly under her chair.

My explanation of a session was the standard one; it is the natural action of two spirits and the transfer of energies. That we are spiritual in nature had been touched on in the lecture she had attended. Sometimes, people get over-loaded with energy. Here we don't put a value judgment on that; we allow that energy to flow out.

She listened quietly. I explained that for an hour we did not speak or move. If she needed to speak, or needed the toilet she was to ask me to stop the session and if she insisted, I would accompany her. She must look into my eyes. The eyes are important because the spirit communicates through them. I explained to Carla that she might recall events, see mental image pictures, feel light or experience a release of energy or emotion and, if so, she should just let herself run with it. My training in Kenja, I continued, enabled me to be motionless, mind and body.

As a spirit I would detach from my body and observe us both. My stillness would make it safe for her to let go, although I didn't tell her that.

We looked to each other. My empty cup sat on the small bench, Carla's half-full, tepid coffee next to it.

Carla appeared uneasy; she was ready to start.

'Is it okay that we do the session?'

'Yes.'

'Is it okay I process you?' She nodded and I asked for a verbal response.

I might touch her heart or head if I felt she was experiencing an energy block. I asked her, 'Is it okay if I touch you to clear energy if necessary?'

'Yes.'

I pulled my chair closer to her and caught her eyes in mine.

I would not give the formal command; she had outlined the issues she wanted to deal with.

'Okay, start.' I commanded.

Ten minutes into the session Carla interrupted, 'Annette, I feel strange ...'

'That's okay.'

Carla relaxed. I observed. I waited and watched. Her face wrinkled, her tears dropped. I offered tissues. As I reached over and touched her heart, her filled eyes sought mine; a negligible smile crossed her face and the hour ticked on.

'Thank you, that's it on that part of the session.'

'Now we have the concluding processes. I say hello, you say fine, I say thank you, like a tennis game – hello, fine, thank you, hello, fine, thank you. You've been through a lot and the concluding processes are designed to get you back in the present time, back in the here and now. If you've gone back into your past you could be anywhere.'

'The next part of the process is to be aware of the walls, floor and ceiling, feel their mass and density, and when you've done so, look at me.' Again I explained: this also located her firmly where she sat.

'Okay. Look at that wall,' I said, pointing to it. She did and looked at me.

'Thank you. Look at that floor ... Thank you. Look at that ceiling ... Thank you. That's great, Carla. Look at that wall ... Thank you.'

The repetition of the word, thank you, sounded polite, but wasn't. Each instruction was a command, not an invitation; each 'thank you' signified that this specific action had ended. Similarly, 'is it okay ...?' is not a question to the body sitting opposite the processor; it is the seeking of agreement from the spirit opposite and without this spiritual agreement the session will not be undertaken genuinely and wholeheartedly.

'The next part of the process is to look around the room, find something you can experience, duplicate it, own it, name it and give it to me. So, Carla, if you look, for example at the picture, you really feel it, look at the beautiful landscape and understand how the picture feels, then in your mind you give it to me.'

Carla relaxed, almost smiling with disbelief as she repeatedly complied. She didn't know its real meaning: Carla, the spirit, was psychically giving me presents.

During feedback, processors are silent, hence non-judgmental.

'It was amazing, Annette,' said a slightly bubbly Carla. 'At first I thought nothing was happening, then everything went a bit funny. You know ... when I was young my sister and I were always fighting and Mum always took her side. I grew up being ferociously jealous, I suppose ... I don't know ... somehow I just kept on seeing my sister and couldn't stop crying ...' She looked to me. I said nothing.

Time ambled.

'I thought this would be about my husband – does that make sense?'
Silence.

'Is this what other people experience?'

Carla wanted a response, my validation. I was tempted to break a processing rule but ... no ... not that.

'Annette, I feel great ... amazing ...'

'Is that it Carla?'

'Yes.'

'Would you like a flug?'

'A what?'

'It's a Kenja word for 'flowing hug'.'

Smiling broadly, she stood up and hugged me, and as we held each other tightly Carla agreed to another session the following week.

I forgot the cups, left them sitting on the floor at the main door. An annoyed Brian noted that someone had let the team down and degraded the processing suite. I shut up.

Carla didn't show up for her next session. I rang her. Having done a session, she was eligible to attend Ken's Thursday class. She said she would try to make it.

'Carla, I know you'll get so much out of it,' I tried not to plead.

'Annette, the session was great, maybe in another couple of weeks I'll be able to make it to a class.'

That will be too late, I thought, my face showed the strain I felt – for both of us. She had taken a step and no one should slide back after that. By coming to Kenja one gave allegiance to Kenja and, once given, should never, never be withdrawn or … I rang her every day but to no avail. 'Of course, we can change the session time, Carla.'

Carla, please come back! Her next session was booked for three weeks later. She didn't show up.

'Hi Carla', said a not at all bright-eyed me, 'Missed you, how about this time tomorrow?'

Shortly afterwards, Jan told us to stop ringing people every day.

Oh, Carla, I thought. Oh, Carla.

☙

Ken began taking processees from me. He never looked at me, merely noted how little change he had observed in them, and gave them away to someone else. I wanted to cry out but sat silently, like a good little girl. Over the next two weeks my numbers were reduced to ten, and Ken stopped giving me sessions. The inevitable happened. I was sacked as director. Surprisingly, I remained a professional.

During my brief stint as director, Vanessa's mother, Marnie, had reflected on Vanessa's 16th birthday. The greatest danger in Vanessa's young life, she wrote, was alcohol and drugs, and Vanessa had avoided those. Perhaps Marnie's most touching sentiment was that Vanessa has achieved one of her mother's most coveted desires: she has 'been instilled with enough strength to say no'.

Nothing had changed. Vanessa still spent hours in session with Ken. Ken's processing room was more luxurious than Jan's, with large comfortable chairs and an overhead fan.

After my demotion, I joined Gretel in cleaning these rooms. Like Mrs Mops we displayed, to each other, our expertise with feather dusters and household spray, and the knack of lightening the energies in the room by breathing nice ones all over the place.

It was late one night. We had finished cleaning Jan's room. Ken was still in session with Vanessa. Gretel had a headache. I was sleepy.

Ken's processing room was locked. We knew not to knock. Gretel's head thumped; she seemed exhausted. A fellow female professional took her place.

Vanessa opened the door. She was naked. Ken called us in. He was lying on the floor wearing trousers and a shirt. Vanessa returned to his side.

She looked like a goddess. I saw the pubic hair and breasts of a young woman. She had no qualms and gracefully stepped over his body.

I gaped in shock but then … Ken obviously had nothing to hide or he would most certainly hide it … nakedness in session was not unheard of … I thought everyone was bare in session with Ken anyway … and with Ken the usual rules were different … had Vanessa always undressed for Ken?

'It has been a particularly heavy session,' Ken said. 'Look how well she clears the energies off me.'

I sensed his challenge and rescheduled my response to empathy.

Vanessa performed the task of psychically clearing the energies off Ken's body. Naked, she stepped over him, bent and touched him with grace and lightness and, like rain in drains trickling away, cleaned those energies up.

What were the covert realities of Vanessa's life? Had our initiation into these coincided with her achieving the legal 16 years of age? Oh, God, I was questioning Ken's behaviour, his decency, his morality; wondering if he had anything to hide?

I shot these thoughts dead.

This image would stick, though, like damp cloth to ice; if it threatened to rise to consciousness, a tweak of my body saw it safely back in its hiding place. Whenever it did come forth for a split second, I responded with coldness, a lickety-split of hate for Ken's contempt and for Vanessa, doe-eyed, dutiful – the prey, mingling and complicit.

Ken said to come back later. The fan whirred. We left the room and said not a word. Ken was right, made privy to his secrets, we kept them safe.

つ◌

Cluttered in Jan's office for Ken's professional meeting, windows closed, the air slowly changing from dense to foul, we resembled the Three Bears. Daddy Bear in his big chair, Mummy Bear in her medium-sized one, and lots of little bears on straight-backed chairs all facing Daddy Bear. The women present considered themselves the rightful Goldilocks, unmindful of the ending – Goldilocks fleeing the bear house.

Nicholas, Gretel and Kathryn and I sat with our peers, still breathless with anticipation after all these years. Mouths were slack, hair lank, our ever-present diaries at hand. Note pads in laps, Ken's high achievers were ready to record, word for word, his newest, crucial data.

Sometimes, if Kenjans dared to look, they might see Ken's penis moving in his suit pants. On this day, I peeked. I saw. Trousers rustling, Ken began.

'Ignore the press,' he said. 'Give reporters the information you want them to have and, if unsure, answer a question with a question. Never forget that when dealing with the press you validate and you acknowledge Kenja.'

I wondered why the press would be interested? But apparently they were – and Ken did not like it.

He turned to Jan. He mentioned her marriage, the one I had no idea existed until then.

'Jan was married to a bloody poofta, a bloody poofta,' he taunted.

'Please Ken, please, no! No, Ken, not that!'

To watch Jan beg in front of her charges was surprisingly moving. I wondered if Ken really cared about her any more. A mix of fear and curiosity uncoiled.

Nicholas, Gretel, Kathryn and I each wanted to be the focus of Ken's attention, to be the most important person in the room. In this room we were clearing spirits and put our humans away ... until Ken brought one trustingly out.

Kathryn struggled to stay awake. Ken stopped talking and focused silently, motionlessly on her. She knew what he was doing. There was no way the entity currently controlling her could withstand his merciless psychic pressure and it crumbled. When he finished, Kathryn's eyes opened wide as she said softly, 'Thank you, Ken.'

Ken leaned back in his chair, sipped his drink then sucked on an orange segment. He said, 'Create life, and do the unexpected!'

God in heaven, a glass was dropped and by Nicholas, of all people!

This was interpreted as a 'covert piss' on our game. Perhaps all was not well with Nicholas and he, unconsciously, responded by mocking Ken's comments?

Kathryn swept the mess in a corner.

We crouched in our seats.

Ken reached for his cup.

'When you clear your dark side, you are instinctively ethical; people trust you.' We bent forward to his long talk. '… surrender what you think is you individually and then recreate it in harmony with Kenja.'

Kathryn's eyes resumed their drooping.

Ken looked quietly at her.

She opened them and wriggled herself to single-minded attention.

Ken waited. With Kathryn he had all the patience in the world.

'I slept with you when you were 18, didn't I?'

My emotion briefly surged and thought momentarily raged. 'Ken?' 'He never touched anyone …' Had Ken and I …'

I looked at Kathryn.She winced, the tiniest of flinches.

He laughed, 'It was the only way I could get her away from her mother. I've never seen a woman so trapped with her mother. I cut the ties she had with her mother and attached Kathryn to me. It was the best solution I could come up with at the time. It worked!'

Ken settled back in his chair, surveyed his assembled acolytes and looked back to Kathryn.

'You've been in love with me for a long time, haven't you?'

Tears gathered. One rolled. 'Yes, Ken.' Kathryn dabbed her eyes.

Oh, but the betrayal of secrets is good for one, despite pain slashing human faces.

For years, Kathryn had given Ken all the love she had never given to a young man, to the children she might have nursed, to the children she might have given birth to.

I tried to calculate: when Kathryn was 18, was Ken with Jan? That didn't bear thinking about.

Ken continued, reintroducing an old process for this session. 'The purpose of the current process, the Human Process, is to clear the energies of the human. The intention is to clear the human on this lifetime and hold them in their human time track. The human is the key to our future and vice versa. We reached into this universe to learn from it. The command for this process is "I'll experience your human and you experience mine". You will never understand human love until you've cut lines with everyone you've ever loved. Love is the disadvantage and the strength; cut lines with love in the past or you won't have it now.'

By then we were primed and ready to go straight into our sessions, craving our silent release.

When the session ended, Ken said. 'Open up and be vulnerable and honest. People can relate to that. You are warriors, players in the game of life. A good warrior has no allies, they just play their game, stack the deck, choose their time and place and create the vacuum for an opponent to play their hand. A good warrior is foot soldier, general, medic, statesman, politician, diplomat, priest, profiteer and clown. A warrior is not locatable, is prepared to win or lose – you can lose a few points and win the battle, even give your opponents a few points so they're less vigilant. A warrior never loses affinity for his opponent; that way, they are always in charge. Be willing to lose everything, you will get it all back because you are playing the most creative game on this planet. Never forget that you are players in the game of life. Players in this game of Kenja! Destined for the highest echelons. Players first, second and third. Nothing less!'

Kathryn, the fired-up player in the game of life, tossed her tissue.

It was decreed that professionals and selected Kenjans would, for the duration of Ken's latest processing command, process naked in their professional and co-processing sessions; we needed to get the energy flowing through our genitals. After our early co-processing sessions in Melbourne when only one, the processee, had occasionally disrobed, nudity had taken a back seat. I was always naked in the sessions I had with Ken, but not in the sessions that I had with Jan. In these naked sessions with committed members, mine never ended in furtive sex, nor did the majority, but I can't speak for everyone locked in the hot house of cramped cubicles.

Mid-week seminars were initiated on an irregular basis, followed by the existing timetable at night. Forty or so Kenjans participated. These had the same daily format as weekend seminars. In some of these, everyone processed naked. Mattresses from our gymnasium classes were lugged to our space; no hard floorboards for us.

Nudity in seminars was limited to the sessions themselves. Listening to Ken and eating lunch, we were fully clothed. In naked sessions touching was forbidden. The after-session flug was given when dressed. We would keep our nakedness secret because, in the long term, exposing others meant divulging our own involvement. Short term: there was nothing wrong with what we did.

As our emotions hit new crescendos we were racing through levels, playing the game of warriors, inhibited by nothing – least of all each other. For me there was nothing sexual in writhing, crying bodies haunted by the mistakes of the past, trying to clear in a room imbued with the tang of genitalia and sweat.

Neighbours complained of the noise and we were reminded to scream silently. Had naked images reflected through the windows? We began covering them with paper.

Some, but not all, of these seminars focused on sex. In one that did, windows fogged up. Pores steamed. Tears sprang from deep places. I don't think there was anyone in that room who had not had an experience of sex as dutiful, or belittling, or less than consensual, or outright abusive, or confusing, or trapped and denied. In the privacy and hope of that seminar we gave our emotions free rein.

Then Ken stopped us mid-session. The eyes of men and women, ragged and ghostly, reeled towards the boss.

Ken had seen a man touching his male partner's genitals.

'The reason for sessions is to avoid the long and messy business of clearing by living the experience in the real world. A body is nothing, it has no significance other that what you give it. You have no need to grope and fuck. That is why we process!'

Distracted, tugged from their pain, partners struggled to regain momentum.

My partner, Paddy, a middle-aged man, wanted to receive a session instead of giving one. Contempt mounted as I faced this man as we lay on the floor in a caricature of misery and damp cardboard.

Ken said that spirits can simply look and know. I looked at Paddy and knew. Opposite me lay a man who had been a guru. People had listened to him, until he listened to Ken. How does a man retain his self-respect when he has none of the external trappings that demonstrate success? No reliable income, struggling to support himself, no normal family life. How does such a man accept being a follower, forever bowing to Ken's earth-shattering ideals, seeking security and hope in Ken's words and support from his stargazing evangelists? How many times had Paddy deferred his own hopes?

Ken also said, like attracts like. Life had come down to Paddy and me, with our faded souls and empty eyes and wearying trust.

I looked and knew, but the words did not form.

Sweat beaded Paddy's face.

Ken yelled at him. 'For God's sake, Annette's had more than enough from men in her life. Let her get rid of her anger.'

Who but Ken cared that much for me?

Paddy snapped out of his lethargy.

I cried and silently screamed for the loveless sex I had experienced in my life. In agony for the men I could not remember. Fighting back the fear that life was passing me by.

I plunged into the mosh-pit of intimate sessions.

Late at night I left the Centre and, entering that strange mix of neon and moonlight, my conservative manner and dress belied the warrior within.

A secret series of sessions, six professionals forming three processing pairs, were instigated. These were considered highly privileged by its naked professionals. Ken sat fully clothed at the head of the row, facing the standing row of processing pairs. He observed and timed the sessions, which lasted for about two hours. He also 'group processed' those present. In the same way one person processed their partner, Ken's superior ability saw him capable of processing everyone in the room at the same time.

In one, Jan and I stood opposite each other, thighs opposite thighs, pubic hair opposite pubic hair and was it, also, hope opposite hope? With our eyes locked together we saw beyond flesh. Ken seemed to have no pity for Jan of late. Tough game this is, Jan baby. That night I saw Jan as a nakedly hurt human being.

Whatever I had seen would not survive outside of those four personal walls. Back in the daytime real world, Jan professed her caring for her Kenjans, including me, but I didn't believe her.

What, I asked myself in another session, was one particular man doing with us? He was a long-term member but wasn't a professional. He and Jan stood opposite each other and I risked a glance. Briefly. Before Ken saw. I sensed why this man was processing with Jan. The words, 'they are lovers', remained unformed.

Many long-term Kenjans stuck to the old relationship rules; Ken had relaxed the rules but a relationship with one of us seemed almost incestuous. Younger women hoping for a mate had the bleakest options; there were few eligible Kenjan men. Beyond their desperate mission of saving the world, love and babies remained high on their agendas. Some, like Nadine and Kathryn, were Ken's white brides.

How many lied when Ken asked us if we masturbated? I did. How many nodded and said yes as he instructed us to never, ever, indulge ourselves? Holding copious amounts of stifled emotions within, which were struggling for release; my mind and body didn't discriminate. The sexual relief of tension was as good as other outlets for its release.

I had had no relationship with the opposite sex, let alone a sexual one since I had been a Kenjan. (Had I with Ken? Did it count?) I had long bypassed human comfort and yearned for it. No closeness, no touch, no other's breath on skin, only the quick passage of a forbidden masturbation and ritual hugs performed with a slight disdain, a haste – no lingering and its dangerous possibilities. Nor did I discuss this with my peers, including in professional sessions for Ken might parade this secret as pathetic examples of inadequacy. A Kenjan reduced to actions unfit for spirits. Most likely, masturbation might remind me of my emptiness, but I didn't know that. Ecstasy can become agony. In my private times, I silently screamed defiance. Jan and Ken could neither prevent nor corrupt the primal power of orgasm; I kept it to myself. It was mine.

In the last of these sessions I masturbated. Ken didn't stop me. It was swift, brutal and lonely. Held still by my partner's eyes, this young man's gaze never wandered from my eyes. Leaving that room, shame swamped, anger roared, then my Kenja training sliced in. Mask set, I joined my friends for an inconsequential chat.

～

Seventeen-year-old Michael attended a lecture with his father, whom we impressed with our clean environment. We insisted parents check us out; see Kenja's Ethics. In class, a real-human clown with dark, rampant hair perched happily on Michael's face. He sat before Ken and knew what he had been missing in life. A hero. One who could match it with footy players and doctors and soft-eyed 17-year-old bricklayer apprentices like Michael.

I have a photo of Michael taken at a social night as he performed in a sketch. He is on his hands and knees. His hands turn to each other, his eyes look to the floor. In the photo, Michael seems caught in a spell; if his breathing may break the enchantment he is charmed by, I fear that Michael would not breathe.

I barely noticed him until apprehension rose, incandescent, in our space. This tongue-tied, self-conscious teenager's sexual confusion had been flummoxed on finding himself in a session in an oppressive, locked cubicle, naked, opposite a clothed female teenage professional.

It wasn't long before Michael visited a prostitute. Following this, Ken summoned Michael to his office and Ken's screaming shredded the reception area. I stood hushed, trying not to listen, justifying Ken – he always had a reason. Michael was ordered by Jan to have an AIDS test, stay away for three months and if the result was positive, stay away for good. We should not give a passing thought to Michael, or the fact that this was not only cruel but irrational; AIDS is not catching, like the common cold.

How do you cope at 17 when you have found Ken and Kenja, the man and the organisation that you believe will enable you to realise your dreams when nothing in your teenage life so far has prepared you for the conflicting assault on your senses, your heart and mind that was, in fact, Kenneth Emannuel Dyers at his best in his steaming hot kitchen?

Michael survived the three months staying away and the result of his AIDS test came back negative. He thanked every God imaginable and came back to us.

Michael's brother, Max, became involved in order to check us out and sat, arms crossed, head shaking in disagreement; not a good omen for Michael. Ken raged at Max, standing in front of him, walking away then charging back. God knows what brought on this outburst but Ken's words whip-cracked to memory, I would never forget.

'Criminals! You mix with criminals! ... I would never go to jail. Never! ... I would commit suicide rather than end up there!'

I listened to Ken denigrating Michael in our professional class, 'He's not really part of this game ... and look at his family ... mixes with petty criminals. Kenja doesn't need people like Michael; he's just not where we are now. Is that okay with everyone here?'

Ken often asked if we agreed.

And that, I believed, would be the last I saw of Michael.

$$\sim$$

An angry, hating Annette with a look that could strip the glaze off Brian's lino was emerging. Since Michael had left, my list of misgivings about Kenja had grown.

When parents died, some Kenjans ignored their funerals; if there was an inheritance, I doubt they ignored that.

Brisbane and Noosa had closed. The Easter Parade only lasted a short time. And many years had passed since raffle prizes were things for us, for our humans; like gourmet dinners on the beach given by and for Kenjans.

One disciple had urged us to see ourselves as 'presents to the universe', when our adoration was silly but touching. Ken said that he was non-locatable. Was this a euphemism for saying one thing and doing another? He stopped talking once, mid lecture, shuffled vacantly around the dais for minutes, lurched to attention by the dazed stares of his Kenjans. Ken joked that he had Alzheimer's. I mused … feared … assumed ... denied.

Jan had melodramatically announced that now she really understood the economic recession was biting. Shops had closed down. Jan, where have you been? Another night she gave her considered opinion on the Three Tenors. Pavarotti had let the team down. And, oh dear, before Claudia composed our music, Jan had planned a performance incorporating Carl Orff's 'Camina Burana'. I knew this music. One song was a drinking song and I shut up. Imagine. Kenjans singing along to an ode to the demon drink. Someone else told her.

Ken's Wednesday evening class, which I loved, was about to be scrapped, substituted with team meetings and the Thursday class had degenerated to a short session following his, now short, talk.

Not that we went home earlier. Jan was clever at creating agendas and acting on suggestions: an IT specialist gave computer classes, the ballet dancer gave ballet lessons. Etc. Each required another meeting, each meeting led to yet another. It was considered un-Kenjan to refuse involvement in some extra classes.

We used to have a decent Christmas break but many failed to return. It was shortened. We didn't need real holidays; we could have psychic ones. Spirits could be on an island or in the desert soaking up the peace and quiet and then, after a few minutes, reappear refreshed.

Following our last Christmas performance, the annual Christmas pantomime devised by Jan and performed for Kenjans and their compliant families, Jan and Ken stood in front of us throwing handfuls of lollies. Jan laughed and Ken cared. Another conjoined Kenja moment. Hadn't they devoted their entire lives to us? Wasn't that enough?

Ken scoffed at one woman because she had fat legs. He jeered that the son of one Kenjan had the smallest penis he had ever seen and what will he do, ha ha, when he grows up?

Ken said that life is heaven and hell, sanity and insanity; it goes by in the wink of an eye and then what have you done? What have I done?

Another frantic Thursday, a crimson-faced Brian ran repeatedly from his office to the underground car park. A stranger had pinched Ken's parking space and had the temerity to dismiss Ken, who then attacked him, probably breaking something. He won't go to the police, he has no balls, said Ken, our man with the big ones. Ken was right.

Three months out of Kenja was a tough punishment. Those who returned came back to us, chastised, hungry for the embrace of Kenja.

All children completing seminars were now presented with a certificate stating that they had successfully completed their two-day training. Jan assured us that these would be much valued by an appreciative society, in the future ... Who was she kidding!

Ken changed some rules. He no longer routinely separated couples; instead he controlled relationships. He arranged one marriage. Some rules, such as no doctors or mental health specialists, had convenient exceptions. Some Kenjans, especially those with successful businesses, could disregard the full-on attendance that usually demonstrated dedication. I wondered about medication; once, anyone who took ongoing medication was rejected, but now I wondered ...

Were Kenja's raffles legal? I doubted our cockroach-infested kitchen had gone through the proper channels. What about fire safety? The Centre had two exits; the council instructed us to keep the back exit open. We kept it permanently locked.

Ken loathed homosexuality, he said once, 'let's face it, it's distasteful'. He disparaged those he called 'negroid' as being at the bottom of the food chain, basically primitive, yet when a group of Africans attended his class once, he stood as a crusader for equality. I doubted his authenticity then, but not Jan's.

We had processed on reactive, primitive, causal, electronic, spiritual and, God knows what, other energies. We had cleared bodies and subtle bodies and minds and group minds and reactive minds and somatic minds and the cells in our bodies and the cells in our brains and we had cleared universes. Since Nicholas, whose ascendency had long been annulled, not even Jan or Vanessa had been declared by Ken to be clear – pan-determined spirits; incorruptible and indestructible.

Once, we cared about each other.

And laughed together.

Hoped together.

Believed in Kenja's future, our futures.

The worst, though, was the shift in our belief system. It changed to the concept of spirits as having always been fully cleared; we only had to jettison entities. At night I worried about this basic change to my truth.

Sometimes the old Ken emerged and, enraged, verbally mauled someone. The new Ken was … what? There was an unnamed something about him … and, as for Jan, her mind was openly distorting, her caring convoluted, her eyes now clefts in a once pretty face.

After all this time, Nadine should be over her religious family, and Kathryn her, now late, mother. Alex was going nowhere. And what about Nicholas? Nicholas, whose knuckles had bled to please Ken, was in jeopardy of losing his professional status.

⁓

Holes invaded my senses, thoughts crept like thieves, but when I tried to focus on them Ken did something to allay my suspicions. Look how many people he put in the hot seat the previous class. That demonstrated his love.

Perhaps Ken was just disappointed? He has given everything for us.

I vowed to read L. Ron Hubbard's *Scientology 0-8*, purchased from Scientology by Brian. Half an hour's reading of this book was compulsory for professionals although I doubted anyone, other than Ken, could fathom it out. I couldn't understand the words; they moved on the page. Perhaps I was blinking them away? I squeezed my eyes shut in an attempt to bypass the vagueness I dwelt in and disperse the flickering air.

The pink and white wrapping paper concealing my Scientology book was torn off and replaced with silver paper. I re-covered my appointment diary with the same rustling paper. And my human prayed.

⌒⌒

My demotion meant that I could no longer live in Jan and Ken's Double Bay apartment; that was for Kenja's successful professionals. I now shared Kathryn's Double Bay flat with Gretel. Gretel and I shared a common futility – few processees – something we almost overtly recognised.

Late at night we talked about human things and planned our bright-eyed futures. In one late night dreaming, Gretel suggested I buy a scrapbook and cut out pictures from magazines to inspire my ideal future. It featured pictures of houses and comfortable furniture and secret gardens and a new kettle.

We would be normal people on a usual Sunday. Gretel and I would sip coffee in a human setting, in an unhurried place, with the smell of sea close. As we drove along a lusciously green road to Palm Beach, we hardly spoke, as if words would remind us of something forbidden – like an escape far away from poetry appreciation and hockey and tap dancing and sessions.

Nearing a smart café our shoulders imperceptibly sagged, our familiar eyes averted. This one was too good; we pronounced it too busy. We finally sat in a lesser cafe, stilted, under an umbrella. We were only having coffee! Our almost redundant animal instincts reared, we gulped our drinks and walked and smiled our faraway smiles as our feet felt the sand and our eyes looked in the windows of other people's houses.

Back in the straitjacket of professional failure, Gretel waited for the inevitable. After Ken demoted her, Gretel sold flowers. To my surprise, we still lived together; professionals didn't live with rank and file Kenjans. Arriving home, late at night, I spied her half-full basket of flowers. Gretel wasn't a flower-seller but a musician with a heart jingling with crotchets and quavers and mostly my sympathy was with her, except for the tiny bit of spiteful delighted at her fall. Despite liking Gretel, I remained a rung above her after all.

I arrived home one night and she had gone. There was nothing, not a note or an empty flower basket. I was terrified for her. Gretel will go insane, unable to cope in the world. We knew too much to survive outside.

Our humans liked each other, for Christ's sake.

Her parents' phone number was in Kenja's files; I assumed Gretel had returned to the family home. I rang her and pleaded for her to come back. 'Please Gretel, *please.*'

She cried, 'I can't, Annette, I can't.'

I felt a little softening in her. I wanted to grab it with both hands and hold and stroke it but she started crying again, said goodbye and hung up. I would never see or speak to her again.

Without Gretel, the flat felt hollow. Wordlessly I missed her. Without thought I missed her. Without feeling I missed her.

My energies were laden with dung, the rent was due and how was I going to pay it? The scrapbook sat in my room dreaming its own dreams.

∽

In my professional death throes I made a special effort. I suggested we involve the wider community in Kenja and take our message to clubs and volunteer at soup kitchens. Brian fluffed up and flushed at this wonderful idea. Ken did not.

When another Kenja Centre in Wollongong was mooted, I, who had not recruited a single person into Kenja, raised my hand. Evan's position as a professional, likewise, did not look good. He had proved kind and thoughtful and was a credit to Kenja but, well … so far … he was not our star recruiter. He, optimistically, and I, desperately, offered ourselves as the Wollongong pioneers. Ken thanked us for our offer, and rejected it. I was grateful; at least I had been seen to make the effort.

Perhaps Evan recognised the folly of us two flogging salvation from pink and aqua baskets? The proposed Centre never eventuated.

My remaining nine clients were the few women of my age and other long-term failures. Our despair stood out like blood on snow. Ken reminded us why we were there: to become the biggest and best, the power of one in our own small universes.

When it came, my dismissal was merciful.

During my last session with Ken, he distastefully, as if I smelt unpleasant, masturbated me. A going-away present? He was fully dressed, I wasn't. I faked an orgasm. Ken smiled. I tried to interpret this as denoting my specialness; as Ken insisted, he never, ever, touched any of us women. But nothing disguised the fact that the man I once believed had second sight, couldn't tell the difference between real and fake. I knew Ken had no interest in me. And I knew why. Stale. Old.

chapter 12

All Good Things …

Ken said that one of the worst things that can befall someone is to treat them as if they do not exist; we called it 'not-ising' a person. I wasn't blatantly ignored, but having failed and thus denigrated the Kenja game, I didn't warrant attention. And I especially didn't warrant attention because I had been given so much help from Jan and Ken.

I was initially allocated a professional, and then another, which was Nadine. She was still full of big hugs and good wishes. Surely the latest process will help. Working on Ken's basic psychic law – there is no need to experience that which has already been experienced – the spirit can, in session, experience loss and death and avoid this in the real world. Ken described this process as:

> … *by the discharge transfer of energies, mental image pictures and commands between two educators [Nadine and I, the spirits] using the student's [my] brain, mind, nervous system and in doing so clears reactive cellular commands which engender succumb.*

Ken called it cellular processing; Kenjan science at its peak, and my hope for the future. Out there in real life, anxiety surfed the waves nearest my poor psyche. I had to get flower runs, buy a new pair of shoes, move out of Kathryn's flat. Why didn't she move in again? Why did she always do what Ken said?

I moved into a flat with Lillian, who did nothing other than bitch about me drinking out of her precious cup. She eventually moved out and another woman, whose stint in the armed forces had terminally sapped her strength, moved in.

My small flower run allowed for classes and sessions but did not entirely cover the rent. I left home at 5.00 am to catch the train to the market. My heart felt like asphalt, my squeezed eyes watched nothing in particular. I hauled my basket, full of flowers that had not been wrapped with love, into the train ignoring the stares of commuters. Ashamed of my situation, at my age, I repeatedly sprayed the flowers, and this small task did its best to settle me. Soon I would be back at the Centre.

Once there, most ignored me. A few looked piteously in my direction.

On some weekends I couldn't face my peers so I walked through Sydney's Botanic Gardens. With one foot in front of the other in its own frequently distracted rhythm, my mind roamed from grass to sky, to echoing rooms with skylights, to the Brighton pier and Bach's measured, insistence that masters the tempest, and finds its way home.

My days slowly bled, one onto the other. Where were they and how had I filled them? My thoughts increasingly scattered. Dip here, dip there, lucky dip if something relevant emanated from my mind.

'You are smarter than you have ever been.' Ken told us. 'Processing has freed up your intelligence units.'

Trepidation had long been part of the dreamland I lived in outside of my body. It used to be peaceful there. Now it palpitated, too black to see, and the only lived emotions in the real world were fear and resentment.

My Kenjan routine offered little comfort. I could no longer afford Kenja seven days a week, but still prized Thursday class. Nearly two months after I had been sacked from professional processing, I 'floated' for the first time. It was a Thursday night. The session had ended. Ken had finished his words of wisdom and encouragement.

Skimming the surface like Casper the ghost on a mission, my feet only occasionally touched the floor. I had been gliding and winding between people for minutes before I realised that I was. Perhaps I had breezed along before? It was thrilling. I soared. I sashayed. I swung easily past my friends. Ken said, 'Life is an instructive gift from the Source.' At that moment, I knew this to be so. I smiled magnanimously, then anxiously. Then fear kicked in. My flying stopped.

No one mentioned my soaring to me, or begged for lessons.

Had I been involved with Transcendental Meditation I might have said I levitated. Outsiders may have linked my experience to processing. I knew only that I glided above the floor with the sureness of an eagle for an unidentified time and that, the next minute, the sounds of babbling Kenjans encircled me. My feet back on the floor, I stood in a muggy, agitated space, full of drowsy people waiting for their peers to form into teams and complete their chores.

Once I had watched Polish dancers glide across the stage …

The fear that I was going to be a little old lady in a rented room frequently impinged itself into my mind. I was nearly 50 and had nothing. What happened to you in Kenja when you got old? There was no Kenja home for the elderly. This grim future stopped my thought; my mind's existence had long been limited to a taut, arid space. I caught myself grumbling loudly in a supermarket aisle while shopping for one dollar's worth of lambs fry.

Oh, Annette.

Negativity was constantly on the tip of my tongue but then I had another session with Nadine and once more I hoped that success, for me too, was just around the corner. Once I had believed in Kenja. I tried to slam this thought shut. Once … My peers believed they were close to clearing. Most were successful, sold everything in their baskets. Kenja was in the midst of a growth spurt. (At its peak, Kenja had upwards of 200 members.) The newest Kenjans were smart, savvy and successful even before they joined us. The press had stopped bothering us. There was renewed talk of another Kenja Centre … Kenjans kept leaving, but most of those were kicked out. Ken said that they just could not have the game.

I stopped confiding in Nadine, her words of wisdom had proven completely inadequate. She never knew how often I walked the streets droning out loud to myself, unaware of my voice. Each time, the shock of realising that I had been resentfully ranting and raving stopped me in my tracks. I never considered that I had, apparently, achieved the state of detachment so desired by Kenjans, that of being separate from mind and body. I had seen people do this in my life before Kenja and considered them mad.

Then I had three sessions with Nadine that were unlike any I had experienced. I wasn't healing. I watched a story vividly unfold in my head over three strange, serialised episodes.

Aliens loomed large and almost transparent, they were gentle and soft with big expressive eyes and not at all frightening. In the second session, their environment collapsed around them in slow motion, unsettling the soft colours of their planet. The land turned to powder; time had no meaning. Defenceless against their fate, they waited, observing their strange and bereaved land. In the third session, there were only two big-eyed aliens left, then one alone against a pale sunset. Its tears dropped onto the ground. Two glistening eyes stared through me. I stared back, helpless.

I interpreted these sessions to mean we must hurry and clear, or face extinction.

Financial despair encroached. Full involvement, by then, cost about $300 a week. A session cost $100. The nightly classes, lecture and attendant costs added up to about $50, monthly seminars $200, the increasingly frequent mid-week seminars cost $500. Then there was the expense of the Canberra Challenge and Melbourne's Eisteddfod and Sydney now had an event to rival these, the Sydney Spectacular.

I had fought to maintain a full-time commitment, eaten the smallest serve of fast-food chips for dinner, struggled to maintain my self-respect in front of my peers, wanting to make it. I had left once and that had been a terrible year.

Things must have been bubbling up inside me because one day I'd had enough. Sitting opposite Nadine in the matchbox cubicle, I notified her of my intention to stop attending everything but professional sessions.

She was not the least bit happy.

'I know you can do it without backing off, Annette,' she grimly attempted to convince me.

'I can't. I've tried and tried.'

Our moods changed. Nadine got stroppy and I, angry and bitter.

'I am sick of the whole deal with money, I want to earn good money. I want a clean Kenja, I want to stop cheating the Taxation Department and that's what I am going to do.'

Not even Nadine could ignore the warning bells. Ken ordered me to a meeting.

Sitting behind his desk, Ken pushed his copy of the Tone-Scale under his blotter. I smirked. Oh, Ken. You need to look that up, after assessing us according to its ranking for how many years.

Assorted professionals stood in a semi-circle behind him. I was offered a chair opposite. Ken looked slightly amused. My compatriots looked like they'd swallowed nails.

Ken leaned back, swivelled his chair and began quite gently, 'What's this about us not paying tax?'

'We don't.' I said.

The assembled clucked.

I knew we cheated the Taxation Department. This wasn't about opinions, or Ken's data, that I *could* be confused about. Facts are facts. We systematically cheated.

'We'll you might cheat, but we most certainly don't.'

'Yes we do. I was professional and I cheated then, as does everyone. It's part of the deal.'

His words clipped air and his eyes flashed.

'Do you realise, Annette, you are accusing us of being dishonest?'

'We are.'

Blink by blink, I matched Ken, to a crescendo of contempt from his pompous warriors.

Fists clenched, he sent me out of the room. I felt potent. I had felt this once before, a long time ago as a teenage student; I had challenged a teacher's choice of songs for singing lessons – hymns. I refused to back down and she left the classroom in tears.

I left Ken's office feeling strong until fear catapulted ahead of each step. I had gone too far. They'll kick me out. Oh shit. It's true, though, we cheat.

Dependent on my flatmate for transport, going home was impossible. Failing to join my team members in their tasks would see me in more trouble, so I swept floors, put chairs away, assured members of the women's hockey team that, next match, I would cheer them on, and could not avoid the circus that was the kitchen. Washing up stacks of plates, pots and cutlery, scrubbing stoves and greasy tiles meant that the kitchen team was the least popular, and chronically understaffed. As people finished their allotted duties they were co-opted into the kitchen; everyone ended up as kitchen hands after all.

At home, it was I with my growing panic and blinkered pain, with my sleepy flatmate, in a small and loveless flat.

That night I destroyed every piece of writing I had that might incriminate Ken and Kenja, even including the heavily censored Kenja newsletter, and my remaining two sets of professional appointment diaries. My personal diary, recorded 23 sessions in one week; the other, for taxation purposes, documented only nine for the same week.

Sitting on the floor, fear vibrating through my eyes, I pulled everything out of the bottom of my wardrobe, threw it into a plastic bag, wishing I had a shredder, silently begging the council to empty the rubbish bins soon.

The next day, Nadine suggested we have another session.

Eyes locked onto hers, I silently explained to myself how, all my life, someone had looked after me: my parents, my late husband Josef, and now Ken.

Nadine pleaded for me not to back off and only just have a weekly session. It was nearly ten years since we became involved in Kenja together. Poor Nadine would be torn and in trouble, but I couldn't help that.

Leaving the cubicle I stood to attention, like a child when the teacher says, 'Freeze!' I didn't want to be a little old lady … my heart and mind congealed with the thought: I am so far up my arse and I can't get out. It's not a nice place to be.

೮

Sometimes the grass *is* greener on the other side.

In one of Mum's phone calls, I had cried that if I owned a car I just might succeed and another Kenjan had a cheap car for sale. God bless her, she sent me the money for it, and in doing so put herself more visibly in my mind.

Chocolate-sellers did well. A Kenjan woman made the chocolates; others sold them. I planned to do both. Convinced that the woman in charge of chocolate-selling would refuse to hand over her recipes, I feigned a casual interest. I tried to feel superior because, in better times, I was her professional and that should count for something.

Surrounded by the paraphernalia of chocolate-making, I experimented, hesitant and determined, until finally the smell of chocolate overpowered my kitchen and I cooked and wrapped and cooked and wrapped.

I chose Newcastle, a one-and-half-hour drive north of Sydney. Making and selling chocolates meant that I would be busy. With the three hours of driving per selling day, full-on attendance at Kenja would be impossible. I was making an effort to change; therefore, limited involvement would be acceptable, provided I had a weekly session with Nadine.

Stiffly entering buildings, I expected the frequently dismissive greeting but instead was met with surprise. 'What's in the basket? Chocolates! I love chocolates. Do you have ginger? Could you make me some? When are you back?'

Hair turning to salt and pepper, wearing my worn floral dress or my brown one, I ran around panting, ignoring the hellish weight of chocolate, smiling my vacant smile at the smartly dressed men and women who were my customers.

Stopping for lunch, nibbling sandwiches, miles away in the clouds, I found a measure of contentment, daydreaming about my own little house in a nice leafy street in Newcastle.

As my chocolate-runs settled down, I opted for another day of selling and chose an equally distant town, Goulburn, where I dreamt of another small house away from the highway, with a birdbath.

My Goulburn customers complained about the noise of trucks resounding through its main street. In Newcastle they wanted to know why I drove all the way up there, and did I really and truly like the place, as they would rather live anywhere on the planet except there, and how did I make chocolate and did I have a family?

My family was a photograph with its face on the floor. I answered a question with a question and mastered the art of saying 'Ohaherrrr … Mmm' with sincere obliqueness, and daydreamed the questioners into friends.

My flatmate, sinking in status with my unpopular presence, suggested I leave. I moved to a beautiful place, a flat overlooking the water in Lane Cove. My children would love its huge trees that stretched to and canopied over our balcony. Gaudy, happy birds flew across the water to sit on our rails and gobbled every crumb my friendly female flatmate and I left out. She had been involved in Kenja forever, always on the fringes.

I concentrated on selling chocolates and, for the first time in a very long time, lavished my attention on me. My clothes looked as if they had sprung from our clowning box, my hair straggled and the ends were split. New clothes were impossible. However, I could do something with my hair. So in a trendy salon in Newcastle, eyes agog and dress hanging, I asked for Jan's hairstyle, a short bob.

Buoyed by my new smartness, I went to Ken's class for the first time in ages, swishing my hair, on tenterhooks. Ken looked at me, looked away and said dismissively, 'New hairstyle.' I hugged myself, and loathed Ken.

That weekend I didn't go to the poetry group or social night or Paddy's silly restaurant with mundane food that we pretended was great because he was a long-term member and we should support each other.

Resentment was eating me up, gobbling up my generous thoughts, but I still floated, better than ever, feet rarely alighting, skimming past others. What did I do yesterday? Nadine had asked me in one of our sessions and I didn't have a clue. Annette sat on a dusty stool staring past horizons while her mind rampaged somewhere off the Brighton pier … but where was I?

Where should I be?

Sydney streets defied my limited logic. Not like home – another prod to a milky past – you can always find your way round Melbourne. Lost on my way home from the Centre one night, I stopped the car, looked at the street directory and couldn't read it. An optometrist confided that eyesight weakens as one ages. I looked in my mirror. Not old yet.

There was, however, something wrong with my health; I was hot one minute, normal the next, my heart palpitated and muscles twitched. Nadine thought I wasn't trying hard enough to change. A doctor found nothing wrong and asked about my lifestyle, so I left. I forgot to tell her about feeling hot. Had I asked she would have explained menopause. At my next session, Nadine earnestly defined this as yet another thorny entity.

My progress (I earned more money) gratified her so I attended another Thursday class. Some new team leader urged us to have another lamington drive. Spare me. Didn't they have enough money? I tried to figure out how much money Ken had taken from Kenja. From one unpaid flat to two houses and apartments ... and his share portfolio ... and boat, all in a few short years.

Nadine pressed me to do another seminar. I had missed a session; her processee numbers were low. I agreed.

We had the usual hooha. Someone had drawn indescribably dopey drawings all over the paper covering the windows, and called it art. I was twitchy from the start. Before Kenja, I had been plagued with migraines and sinusitis. I had suffered neither since becoming involved. By the time Jan's clowning class began that Saturday night I had a migraine. Nadine, with Jan's permission, took me aside to a processing room where she ran the 'headache process'. In theory, by locating and moving the pain, the sufferer realised that they can control the headache themselves. There was no need to lock the cubicle doors or run through agreements; this wasn't a formal processing session.

Like a wounded animal, I stared blindly at Nadine.

She began. 'What colour is the headache?'

'Black.'

'What shape is it?'

'I don't know. It's everywhere.'

'What size is it?'

I grasped my head with one hand. 'Vomiting always helped my migraines.'

'Stick to the process, Annette. What size is it?'

How would I know, I thought.

I said, 'It's as big as my head.'

'Move it somewhere else.'

'There's nowhere in my head for it to go.' I was crying.

'Annette, I can only help you if you help yourself. You know the rules. Stick to the process.'

'What colour is it?'

Sitting in a miniature room under harsh lights with the only person I could still call a friend, I invented my answers.

'It's brown … it's the size of a pineapple … it's red … the size of my heart. I pointed to behind my ear, to the back of my head.

Jan sent another professional to check on us. As she stuck her head around the door, Nadine whispered gloomily, 'It persists.'

Eventually, my migraine eased. I returned to clowning; the class had almost finished.

Jan congratulated me on not succumbing to that vicious entity. She had noticed me. I wept in gratitude.

I looked around. Nicholas and Alex had left, and Michael and Gretel and Marcia. Their leaving left me barren. Michael had no choice, nor did Marcia or Nicholas. They had been asked to leave. But Gretel and Alex had just given up. Insanity, as predicted by Ken, surely idled in the tampered depths of these five minds.

Brian, Nadine and Kathryn would never leave. Brian looked pale. Nadine and Kathryn stared past me, intent on Jan, bodies erect, faces white and eyes dark, in limbo in a room offset by dazzling pink and aqua.

I just wanted to go home.

&

Nina and the young man she seemed to be in a perpetual clinch with were getting married.

I would be there, at my daughter's wedding, without thought, cleaved and quartered, but I would be there, struggling against treacherous feelings, a rekindling of emotion too dangerous to recognise. I would be there because that's what mothers do; they tend and fuss and cross their fingers.

Tramping Sydney streets, I sought out a present for Nina. You can't go to a wedding without a present. Walking past shops I caught myself talking aloud. A nervous shuffle, a few seconds trying to recall Ken's invaluable data saw me back in the here and now, aware only of the present moment. Perhaps it was my human who cried when I decided that my wedding present would be the wedding flowers filled abundantly with love?

Stepping out of my car in Mum's drive, her neighbours peeked out windows and over her fence. The curtain rustlers thought me mad, and seeing is believing. I was introduced to a friend of one; the man and his profile, a car and an attitude impinged on the remnant cells of my brain and I would remember him.

Nina and her bridesmaids dressed on the other side of Melbourne in a flurry of loose hair and lipstick. I wanted to be there with her but ... when I arrived with the flowers my lips stuck to my teeth.

Before the ceremony, I hung around Mum, then around Stefan and his girlfriend, Jacqui. I drifted out of range behind other guests until my dearest Mum sought me out and stood with me.

Stefan stood next to Nina and gave her away. A slip of a girl in billowing tulle and a nervous young man in black stood in a rotunda, circled by flowers, in a verdant and quivering park.

At the reception I sat at a round table covered by a stiff white tablecloth with starched serviettes extravagantly folded, next to Mum. People I used to know long ago sat with us. Yet now we were strangers.

I didn't touch a drop of alcohol but I was tipsy. After ten years, no medication or alcohol, I had little resistance and was groggy on its smell. Hoping with all my heart that my words weren't slurred, I gave a speech.

Standing in old-lady clothes, a blue and beaded dress, my hair a tight French roll, overcome and struggling for coherence, I covered my blank patches by gazing into the middle distance. My love for my children was where? I felt it but couldn't call upon it. It was hiding in a new secret place.

Nina left the wedding reception wearing a white suit. Passing through a trail of people she stopped and kissed an odd, blue woman who, with mechanical mirth, tailed her to a bedecked and festooned car.

Oh dear God.

Panic followed. I had classes to attend and sessions to have when I returned to Sydney. I needed some money.

Psyche sagging, I drove from Mornington to Melbourne to purchase flowers, then back again. Sadly wrapped bunches sat in the back seat as, tranced out, I drove to an outer suburb on the other side of Melbourne. Slumped in the car, my glazed eyes surveyed the shopping strip and found it wanting. Without opening the door I returned to my mother's house to say goodbye. I had driven for five hours.

At five the next morning, half-an-hour out of Sydney, having driven all night, I went to sleep at the wheel and veered towards oncoming traffic. Wrenching myself awake, my car ricocheting, I sat terrified and kept going.

Back in Sydney, I attended Ken's class and had sessions, but had to stop again; not all of my customers purchased chocolates each week, and money only goes so far.

It was a very dark place for an impending little old lady in a rented room to find her way out of. Any further in and I might be jammed, stuck irretrievably up a fetid place.

༄

I drove to Melbourne for another Eisteddfod. In the dark of night my journey froze. In pouring rain on the side of the freeway I sat, dispossessed, in a faded green car. Lights rushed past. My engine responded to frantic ignition twitching. My overnight trip continued. Cars swished and trucks rumbled through the storm. Drivers flashed their lights. I flicked mine on. My windows fogged up; I opened them. Wind tore at my hair and slapped my face.

My children and their partners would be at the show. I told everyone, 'My daughter is pregnant. Nina is having a baby. I am going to become a grandmother. Do not, I repeat, do not try to book my family in for anything. Nothing.'

Jan had not selected me for a role in the show. Instead, I should be a high-tone black-clad stagehand and I did my invisible best. Sustained solely by each performer's enthusiasm, the show was jumbled and inane.

My children and their partners sat and watched the performance and arranged their faces into a semblance of approval – their eyes they could do nothing about. Four people together, one infused with the growing of hope, in a large and noisy room.

Nina and Stefan politely said that it was fine. I didn't believe them. They said it *was* fine and as they called me 'Mum', something indescribable surfaced in me. The endearment fought for air.

Mum! I am the mother of Nina and Stefan. Soon I will be a grandmother.

Nina's stomach was swelling with child and I was afraid to touch it. My rights to intimacy had been forfeited. My Kenjan floating eyes just stood there until Kathryn nudged me.

Trudging after her, my body struggled to move, my blinking was so bad that I was incoherent. Finishing my tasks, I found someone trying to book them in for the following day's seminar. 'How dare you!' I snarled. 'How dare you!'

'It's alright, Mum.'

Conversation faltered; stopped.

I watched my children walk down the steps as they left, then I silently screamed.

Back in Sydney the most terrifying image haunted me. It slipped to mind. My son would die in a car accident. He would if I couldn't stop this image. Stefan sat in a red sports car facing infinity, no screech of brakes or impending knell. Neither sessions nor wall-walking demolished it and my breath gave it life.

What we put our attention on, Ken said, grows like weeds, and my son's death grew in my mind.

Once I had made, by hand, beautiful patchwork quilts.

∽

I wanted to change Kenja; I wanted it to be more like it used to be, more like it was meant to be. It was meant to be wonderful, change the world, help mankind.

The unessential nonsense we spent our time on was Jan's fault. Ken still ignored me – after ten years of trying so hard.

At night I stared past televised images, disorientated. What do normal people do? They read magazines. I flicked through one, whose name I do not remember, blindly flitting across words. My eyes uncoupled as I read that whenever you are turned inwards to the extent of excluding the outside world you are, to a degree, in a trance. Sitting in session we looked inwards. Understanding cartwheeled to consciousness. Trance equals hypnosis. I realised that processing sessions are, in fact, hypnosis.

The following morning in a bookshop, searching for something on hypnosis, I scoured shelves for anything I thought could be relevant. As I was about to leave I saw it. It was larger than other books on the rack, and called *Combatting Cult Mind Control* by Steven Hassan. I wasn't paying $17 for a book. However, I paced the shop, went outside and paced the street, crossed the road for a cup of coffee and, trying to hide myself from other Kenjans who might transgress and lurk in bookshops, went back in and bought it.

These pages would hit home, their definitions both familiar and sinister. I read it secretly in my bedroom with a newspaper and magazine in front of it. And I closed my bedroom door as I was scared of being caught.

I rang Nadine, cancelled my session and booked in for the following week. I knew there would be no more, and hurt for my slowly aging friend with her unusually darkening eyes.

Hassan writes about the real person, the one before the cult that may be locked away but still there, extant, the point of entry possible, through their childhood. I tried to find the real woman who was my flatmate. Late at night I asked her about her childhood.

We sat opposite each other. She tucked her feet under her body. I sat on the edge of my seat. As she spoke a different person emerged, a nicer, lighter, dreamy woman, until suddenly she snapped back to her cult mindset and changed the subject. I wanted to tell her what I knew but was afraid she'd tell Ken.

I knew what to do, and began stuffing boxes with clothes, chocolate moulds and the saucepans that I had, in my gourmet efforts, burnt black.

I knew where to go.

'Mum, it's a cult, Kenja is a cult and I'm coming home'.

On the morning of my leaving, I ran up and down the stairs leading to my flat, lugging my large timber trunk down, scraping it, vowing to repair it – that's what I do best, fix and clean. Two more loads ... as I carried my slippery, plastic chocolate moulds they dropped from the box. They hovered, then tumbled and bounced off the concrete steps and, like yonnies on water, skittered across the path. My face tight, body hostile to itself, I scrambled to pick everything up.

Before leaving I rang Nadine. 'I can't do my session, Kenja is a cult, please don't contact me ... Nadine, no. I can't ...'

Home, and Mum, lay ahead, a 12-hour drive away. Locked in my car, one thought darted through my head. I left a saucepan behind, the smallest one I used to melt chocolate in. I loved that saucepan; my flatmate had better send it to me. Stuffed tight with this picture of a small, scratched, bent saucepan, my mind was safe.

In this trip that remains erased from memory, my mind sheathed in a comprehensible fear, I leaned forward and closed in on home.

chapter 13

Love and Mum

Mum opened her front door to see her daughter huddled and mumbling, 'I left a saucepan behind.' She ran to her next-door neighbour for help; how could she cope with the wreck stuck, immobile, on her porch? Returning home, Mum remembered the day when I was born and declared a miracle.

Her well-kept house hinted at pensioner in residence. A Petaluma hydrangea, once Mum's pride and joy, barely survived in a corner and snaking upwards a wisteria tugged at the front porch, a neatly wound hose sat next to the tap, and trees, too close to the windows, protected her privacy.

Inside sat the piano and crystal cabinet. Mum's pride in these, and the muddle of crystal and porcelain that spoke of her dreams, had wearied with time. In my room a single bed hugged the middle of one wall and opposite sat my childhood dressing table. Mum had kept it all those years, through Heidelberg and those multiple moves. I stared into it; a ghost stared back.

Adrift with unknown spawn, Mum did a perfect nothing. Instead of expert consultations in hushed tones she gave me time, love, three meals a day and, in her rough touch, more love.

For weeks I sat incoherently muttering to myself. I had tumbled into an abyss. I was crossing mindworlds, with Mum keeping a worried, respectful distance between us.

At times I experienced myself as being in two places at once. My body was on one side of the room and part of me, like pieces of clear plastic, zoomed and slashed through the air on the other side of the room. Ironically Ken helped. He said the most terrifying feeling he ever experienced was he, the spirit, separating from his body and being unable to get back but his interpretation was askew. It is a psychological condition, not a spiritual one. I remembered Ken's words and knew he had survived.

Mostly I hung on with a slim thought, my saucepan, its charred black handle and its rightful ownership.

c—o

An incomprehensible world slithered to sensibility as I sat in my room reading Steven Hassan's *Combatting Cult Mind Control.*

It is a complex and comprehensive book. I refer only to his ideas that were most influential in the months after my leaving. I thumbed these pages so often they fell out.

Hassan defines the difference between brainwashing and mind control. The term 'brainwashing' was first used by a journalist, Edward Hunter, in 1951 to describe how American servicemen, captured in the Korean War, rejected their values and denounced their government. The technique is usually coercive and, once away from the particular condition, is generally undone. In mind control 'hypnotic processes are combined with group dynamics to create a potent indoctrination effect'. With mind control a person believes they have made a proper choice.

Hypnosis, he writes, is complex and involves looking inwards (as in Kenja's processing and Ken's long talks) not out through the five senses.

Hassan defines four components of mind control: behaviour control, thought control, emotional control and information control.

Behaviour control in Kenja involved the regulation of clothing, sleep, rituals and rules, including the compulsion to recruit new members, cold showers, constant early mornings and late nights, and the punishments meted out for lack of vigilance. Processing, with its strict rules, was a Kenjan ritual as were the classes that glorified Jan and Ken and were hand-in-hand with the belief system.

In Kenja, thought control involved the use of words and phrases that made no sense to others (with the exception of Scientologists). Kenjan's beliefs became internalised, if not totally then to a large, practical, degree. Thought-stopping was taught via the belief system, namely, the required detachment of spirits. Kenjans were taught to train their own minds and be passionate Kenjans, living for Kenja, ever ready to defend it, immune from criticism of it.

Emotional control manipulates and limits feelings. Cult member's feelings are 'redefined'. Kenjans suffered for the benefit of mankind. Abuse, disconnected from other viewpoints, was seen as tough love. Both guilt and fear were used to manipulate. With fear, an enemy outside of the group was created; during my time in Kenja that was the hostile outside world and parents. Loyalty to Kenja came first. Kenjans were afraid of retribution if seen to fail at living up to Ken's expectations. Phobia indoctrination results in a panic reaction to the thought of leaving the group. In Kenja, the most common overt threat was that of insanity; the most insidious one was of complete non-survival in the outside world and it was left to individuals to fill in the blanks with their own worst fears.

With information control, says Hassan, one common tactic used by cult leaders is the 'need to know' principle. If members don't have a good reason to be in receipt of information pertaining to the group, then they are not privy to it. 'Levels of truth' refers to the discrepancy between information given to those outside the group and to members. When aware of the existence of the outside version, Kenjans were adept at assigning plausible reasons for it; these were not lies but a different 'level of truth'.

Hassan refers to mind control as a:

… system of influences that disrupt an individual's identity (beliefs, behavior, thinking, and emotions) and replaces it with a new identity. In most cases, that new identity is one that the original identity would strongly object to if it knew in advance what was in store.

I cannot claim unfamiliarity with the cult 'Annette'. My resentful and complaining self was brought out to form part of my Kenjan mindset alongside aspects of me that I liked, such as my love of the intimate connection of processing, my embracing of my clown and my respect for me as the mother who misguidedly suffered for her children.

Hassan points out that members cannot feel secure outside of their cult. However, it is unusual for a member who has left to return.

Memory loss is common among ex-cult members. It is usually short term and memory of the cult experience usually returns in time. Mine was pre-existent. In writing about Kenja, I write what I do remember. Dissociation is also common among ex-cult members. Unbeknown to me, I had long experienced this; it had intensified during my involvement with Kenja.

Believing I could tell him something new, I wrote to Steven saying that, although he had never heard of Kenja, he could have been writing specifically about it. I waited anxiously for a reply and when it came, Mum looked on, aghast, as her flibbertigibbet daughter jumped up and down.

His handwritten letter is dated 8.7.92:

Dear Annette Stephens

Thank you for your kind letter. I'm glad my book was helpful.

I hope to come to Australia sometime. I've been hoping someone will hire me to come there to do some workshops, media or do a counseling intervention.

I will keep your letter and address on file and let you know if anything comes up. Please keep me apprised of your activities. Of course, letting people know about my book is helpful.

Sincerely, Steve Hassan

Steve Hassan would come to Australia in 1993, where he was guest speaker at the Cult Awareness Conference in Queensland. I gave a short talk on Kenja. His visit to Australia had absolutely nothing to do with me.

ᕲᐢ

My recovery was painful, erratic and slow. You really don't want to know the whole traumatic experience; each paragraph would start and end with a reference to tears and some passages would consist entirely of them. I diagnosed myself as dissociated after reading Hassan, without delving into it. Something explained my state; that was enough. In time, I would even forget the word.

Taking Hassan's advice, I began replacing my Kenja vocabulary but for some time nothing rolled off the tongue as easily as Kenjanese.

For Kenja's 'second dynamics are aberrated' I settled on 'relationships are dysfunctional'.

'Use your knowingness to create the action' translated to 'spirits know everything so use this ability to develop Kenja into a vibrant concern.' That this could prove useful in the real world was highly unlikely.

'Havingness' related to the capacity to enjoy the good things of life, in particular those that can be bought. 'High havingness' meant that one had lots of it. Kenjans of 'low havingness' had precious little. After Kenja, my 'havingness' had nowhere to go but up.

Instead of 'create the game', I decided that, somehow, I would do the opposite and expose it.

Miles away from Kenja in a quiet house in Mornington, I braved the wrath of Ken and wore a black t-shirt and tracksuit worn in my earlier life as a stagehand assistant, the exception to the 'no black' rule. It felt shabby and coarse. Fearful that Ken, with his embered eyes and black intentions, watched, I discarded it.

Flashbacks were rampant. Most featured Ken, how I had looked at him and how I had trusted him. My nightmares were black. In one, a group of hunched figures with sneering, cindered eyes watched me, legs wide open, as my life force was bled dry. In my nightmares I tried to enlighten my black-lidded friends and woke up wondering if I was born in a sac of black amniotic fluid.

One day, when Mum's neighbour said, in frustration, 'Come on, darling, one drink won't hurt you,' I took the plunge. My tentative sip became several and that was all it took for me to become tipsy. Uncle Kenny drinks – naughty boy. The room was spinning.

If I caught sight of my reflection in a mirror my spirits sank; I dressed like my 80-year-old mother. In Mornington's cheapest store, I roamed clothing racks in snaking loops, grabbed a pair of trousers and fingered many shirts before making a decision; then, in a rare decisive moment, I swapped the trousers. Standing in the checkout queue realisation glided, like a snail from its shell, that *now* the shirt won't match. (I continued to dress like Mum.)

Unfortunately, I was a liability on the roads; quietly careering off course while driving my car had become a habit. Providentially, I had always toddled along nature strips and the wrong side of double lines trouble free. When I drove genteelly into the back of a parked car I sat stupefied. I decided to own up – Ken would approve of my honesty.

Each morning I scrambled to read my astrological forecasts and found truth in every (positive) word. I saw a clairvoyant. She told me the weirdest thing: I have a partial memory of a 'previous life' that had come to a terrible end. I dwelt on these words, related them to the time I had experienced, in a solo wall-walking session, Uncle Dan walk towards a very small me brandishing an axe. Some claim that seeking out clairvoyants, or religion, is merely replacing one thing with another. I was. I needed someone, other than Mum, to tell me life would get better.

By stealth, my world grew from the inside of my head to a recognition of something outside of it. Curious as to how Kenja hid its professionals from the taxation department, I obtained copies of my tax returns. As a Kenjan, I wrote my name at the top of the form and my signature at the bottom, but not the details. I discovered that I was officially employed by Kenja's professional section as a clerk. A clerk! But I was *the director*, and doesn't this mean something to someone – somewhere!

Then one day I decided to head into Melbourne to confront Kenja. Was the Melbourne Centre still there? It was. I rushed past it, fearful of turning my head towards its entrance and bumped into another ex-member. I gravely exhorted him to please, please never return. He said that if he did, it would only be to satisfy his curiosity; he could protect himself by making himself invisible just like he had learnt to do in Kenja.

His faith in the absurd goaded me on. Despite the holes in my mind, I oddly trusted my memory and recalled Ken's bragging of placating journalists. In Melbourne's public library I scoured Sydney papers and found the article in *The Sun* describing a mother's fears for her daughter who had travelled to Australia for a holiday where she had become a Kenjan. I looked at the photo of Ken with his smiling supporters and thought, Ken, you *are* deceitful.

I missed my Kenjan friends, especially the seemingly mascara-caked Nadine and Kathryn, and wanted to rescue them. I hoped to save Jan who would, in turn, liberate them. Despite the odds, Jan would in an earth-cracking flash of cognition realise the truth of my words and, on stage in a timber-splintered hall, together we would enlighten Kenjans who would then leave, en masse. Cult experts would wait in the sidelines ready to support my shattered friends. In a warm, rambling house, crammed floor to ceiling with books, with a garden exactly like Melbourne's Botanic Gardens, we'd all walk to the lake, feed the swans and take personal issue with our ex-guru.

It was imperative that I remember every one of them. I compiled lists, so their names would not be defied by memory. My first, *The Book of Lists*, named the members of Kenja. Manically I wrote their names and the occupation they had before their involvement, highlighting flower-sellers and handymen. *The Dumpee's Book of Lists* recorded those who had been professional, and frequent professionals, like Nadine and Kathryn. Then became *The Black Books of Lists* of those I believed would never know the truth. I drew beautiful coloured lines down the sides of my pages, wrote some names and savagely cried over others.

These flowered into the desire to write a book called *The Book of Revenge*. Two pages long, it began inauspiciously:

These people are experts. I went for two days and stayed ten years. That's what I was told. That's what I believed. That's why I went. That's why I stayed. I went for two days and stayed ten years.

My writing style (the above excepted) imitated Jan in full, heroic, saving-the-world mode; I would save the world from Kenja. I copied that part of Jan I had been most influenced by, her sense of drama and passionate rhetoric. I had to be someone. Pre-Kenja Annette was not, in Ken's words, an 'operational memory'. The cult Annette was, as he also said, a 'service identity'. The post-Kenja Annette was in search of variation number three – one that would knock the socks off the previous ones.

My vivid recall of some of Ken's data surprised me. I found myself, like Lady Macbeth, begging these words to leave me alone. I slipped backwards and forwards between the ease of my Kenja beliefs and the unkempt unknown.

I reached for my pen the minute I woke to record nightmares before they disappeared, the same with flashbacks. Sitting at my typewriter, the word 'hate' was repeated until, in anger, I punched no key in particular. When vitriol and pain soared, I named Ken 'my craven image'; when afraid of Ken's reach, I wrote 'slumbum'. These *bon mots* ('witty remarks') mixed with offbeat epiphanies. One equated Ken's 40 years of research to Moses in the wilderness, which is why (light bulbs flashing) Jewish people apparently considered him a rabbi.

My acute sense of betrayal was written and cried over. I obsessively listed Kenjan examples that slotted into cult definitions. I wrote of resolutions, then forgot them. Of anger and self-righteousness; of feeling trapped in a man's scorn and a woman's rank hand. I recalled Jan, her innocence lost, and one particular night in clowning when she had donned a pair of pink rubber gloves and, as she opened and shut her hand, her face contorted, her eyes twisted, her laugh distorted to a dry cough, her pink-gloved hand degenerated into a parody of evil intent.

On condemning Jan, guilt crowded my emotions, and my strangely belated sense of fellow feeling for her muffled adverse thoughts. I had seen her tears and felt her pain. I swung between hating Jan and Ken and making excuses for them.

Jan had little hope since meeting Ken, I decided, and maybe it's not his fault either. Perhaps he had been controlled as ruthlessly as he had managed Kenjans. If Ken had no conscience, it must be because the concept had previously been removed from his mind.

I mourned my inability to let go of Ken. I missed his certainty and the comfort of having the answers to the problems of humanity. The words were at hand. Kenja is a cult. Kenja had become entwined with so much of me that, until I could separate one from the other, I would grieve for the loss of the whole writhing lot.

Ken said Kenja is wheels within wheels. I was stuck in their ruts.

Ken said resist nothing. Why couldn't I resist *him*?

I tried to disengage from Ken's belief in the aberration of time because at my age (49) I might run out of it.

Months after leaving, some part of me hovered and was still separate from my body. My head constantly ached, thought skittered, speech slurred, eye contact slipped aside. My memory was difficult and I was unable to make simple decisions, such as did I want tea or coffee. Sometimes my eyes blinked rhythmically. Questions disappeared; I blinked intently at people and, trying to find the answer, forgot the question. I alternated between relentless dreaminess and raging resentment. Mum looked in horror as I rambled out loud while I remained blissfully ignorant of my voice.

I had hoped for so much from Kenja. After ten years I was no inspiration whatsoever but a brilliant example of malfunction. I returned to Melbourne with ten dollars to my name, no future, a fragile relationship with my family, pain and dubious sanity. But one day, unbeknown to me, healing entered.

On that day I sat in my room, inspected the walls then mentally renovated them as I had done in my life before Kenja. Mum's walls gleamed and sheer curtains blew and the beautiful but poisonous flowering angel's trumpet was replaced with bougainvillea that would bloom brilliantly along the entire length of Mum's fence.

⌒⌒

Mum aired her bedroom daily but behind her bed hid a year's layer of dust. Finding solace in that old standby, housework, I dipped the cloth into brown water, gibbering to myself how slack my mother was and she muttered back, 'Trust you to notice.' I disapprovingly dusted anything that moved and scowled at the mess in the crystal cabinet. Mum said, 'Oh, you won't want those when I go.'

Nina's marriage broke up and she and her daughter came to Mornington. We were four generations living together. Stefan lived with his girlfriend, Jacqui.

Mum, Nina, Stefan and I peeked at a patched-up start. Nina and Stefan were glad I was back but Nina and I were awkward with each other. Our link was through her daughter. Mostly I looked, too frightened to offer an opinion. What right had the worst mother imaginable to offer advice?

With Mum things were easier. Our conversations were like fallen twigs that landed, stranded. Mum proudly informed me, for the umpteenth time, of her driving to Sydney through the dangerous curves of the Razorback. Of the frequent visitors she once had long ago in Heidelberg. She still puzzled over one man (with parched eyes) who had stopped coming to our milk bar. 'Just like that! No explanation at all.'

'Did you ever visit the grave of my barely born brother?'

'Oh, I wouldn't know where to find it now, but I'll never forget that little white coffin.'

'I often thought of finding it. Whenever I was troubled I talked to him … do you remember the little girl who was murdered not far from us in Heidelberg?'

'No, but there was something about a woman …'

'Are you sure you understand about Kenja?'

'I'm just glad I kept ringing you up and leaving messages on your answering phone and got you away from bloody Kenja.'

'Do you understand about Nana?'

Mum never said the words that could scuttle me backwards; a combination of not wanting to err and a canniness I had not recognised. She never said how could you do that to me, to us?

We settled to our routine.

I ate. Mum watched.

I cried. Mum flinched.

I daydreamed and Mum knitted.

I tried to interpret her many sighs; they were of incredulity and despair and, sometimes, of delight.

Wagging her finger at curious neighbours, she whispered, 'Don't you dare upset Annette.'

Nina, Stefan and I discussed her approaching 81st birthday in hushed tones and decided on a surprise party. A gaudy sign waited, as did streamers with sticky-tape on their ends, the food, drink and riotous cake were hidden but Mum was still there. She was going to have her drink at five o'clock. Her routine would not be changed; we had pinned our hopes on that fact. Stefan in desperation growled at the old stick-in-the-mud she had become, so off she went with him to the pizza shop.

Approaching her front door cognition dawned. With suspended smiles and frozen surprises we stood paralysed as Mum clutched her chest. No dying on your birthday, Gladys, we uniformly willed! Tears glittered and fogged her glasses. For the first time my children and I shed tears together that didn't relate to my time in Kenja and their waiting and wondering. Mum said, 'I should have known. That tiny pizza wouldn't have fed Stefan, let alone the rest of us.' That night, she posed for photos in front of the pianola and the crystal cabinet, with this one and that one and, in fact, everyone.

At Mum's party, I met the man I would marry. His name is Darcisio Bianchi. I call him by his middle name, Vittorio. I had remembered him, the man with the extraordinary profile whom I had been introduced to when I came to Melbourne for Nina's wedding. Vittorio was striking. I think he still is, lithe and strong with an aquiline nose and easy, elegant walk. He remembered the weird woman in blue. Who could forget Glad's mad daughter?

On that very night he asked me out.

No way.

Nina, hands on hips, asked me if I really planned to spend my entire life cooped up in Nana's kitchen and, for heaven's sake, you don't have to sleep with him.

Good Lord, Nina, no sex for so long, I'm not starting now. And Italians are only interested in clothes and food, and sex!

Oh … maybe dinner.

Wearing a pair of slack, green trousers, a jumper Mum knitted some years ago, my old lecture shoes and no jewellery, I knew then that there was something about this man; he didn't seem to care. Seated at a table opposite elegant women in a room full of manicured ones, I sunk into my chair and beamed until my teeth ached. On the dance floor my shuffling erratically expanded to a hip-wriggling celebration.

The youngest of five children, Vittorio remembers the German army in his hometown, Corridonia, in Marche, central Italy. As a child he played with his friends as warplanes rushed overhead. If they could hear the whine they stayed and played; however, if there was silence, they ran from the bombs as fast as they could. In the post war years he and his family starved. He was ten when he began full-time work. During the war his father, a soldier, had disappeared for five years and never spoke of that time, and years after his death was posthumously awarded an Italian knighthood.

One of many young Italian men who arrived on an assisted passage, virtually penniless, Vittorio carried all he owned in a suitcase tied together with string. For extras on the voyage, like a glass of wine, he did what Italians have long been known for – he sang. Disembarking in Melbourne, he went to work picking asparagus and built an independent life for himself. He is a carpenter. When we met Vittorio was 60, with five adult children.

Nina immediately liked him. Stefan's every movement said, you had better do the right thing by Mum. Having no doubt about his intentions, my mother would speak her mind and protect her daughter. Our pleasure put paid to her fears.

Vittorio is a strong man. My track record with men of strong-will was appalling; I often found myself grudgingly agreeing to his wishes. I knew that I must, somehow, learn to stand up for myself. If not, I just might run away and that would be awful for us both. It took a little while but one day I took courage in both hands. Over a triviality, I yelled and shrieked, went crimson in the face, fell over my words, made absolutely no sense and was unstoppable. I raged at Vittorio for every man and his control that I could harness to mind and something strange happened. I averted my face to hide a smirk. It blossomed into the most joyous laughter. That was a start.

When we married in 1996, four years after I had left Kenja, we invited absolutely everyone to our wedding on the basis that with our backgrounds – his three previous marriages and my eternal deficiency – we needed all the good luck we could get; and it has worked.

Vittorio's sole dream, as a child, was to have a shirt for each day of the week instead of the one his mother washed each night. He had no concept of a life outside of his own and although my daydreaming is sometimes difficult for him we agree my abundance of fantasising has more than made up for his lack. No one else can bring me back to earth so softly as he. Once, standing in the water on an Italian beach I waxed lyrical about the joys of the here and now.

'Oh ... Oh ... and, oh my God ... I just can't believe I'm standing here, with my feet in the Adriatic Sea.'

'That's because you're not!'

'Oh ... but ...'

'You're standing in the Tyrrhenian Sea.'

One day, some months after I had left Kenja, Stefan and I stood on Mum's front porch, wisteria dormant; I was crying. He said he understood how hard it had been for me but he had gone by the time I mobilised my thought: I was crying for him, not myself.

Hobbled by guilt, I watched my children. Each time I tried to look at something hurtful it slipped to another place. Learn about cults, I implored them. I blamed myself, got lost in dead ends, and forgot to remember.

People speak of memory changing and distorting reality. I didn't care. I wanted to recall more than snippets and Ken's wretched data. I didn't mind if a careless word became a wail or a wink became rejection. I wanted the blanks filled in, the empty spaces gone.

It would take many years to reconcile this absence of memory.

I had left my children. If no other memory ever came forth, this one should. I tried to remember the day and the week before I left. I imagined myself crying, packing my bags, lamenting and looking forward to a brief trip, but I understood the difference between memory and imagination. Recovered memory for me is a shard, a flash. And imagination, well ... I can beautify anything, give me a stone and I will create a butterfly.

My family is gathered together, to celebrate a birthday, in a hotel dining room. After the presents, hellos, seating arrangements and drinks, I corner Nina and Stefan.

'What happened, how did I leave?'

Nina tries. 'It started slowly, at first you went to Kenja every few weeks ...'

'Yes, I know that but I don't remember leaving you both ...'

Stefan takes up the slack. 'Mum, you ...'

I turn to more immediate things. 'What a shocking outlook this place has – of a defunct railway line.'

Twice I left my family for Kenja. I wanted to at least do my children the courtesy of remembering that and, while I was at it, put an end to constant unease with their own questions, hundreds of them, about their lives.

'Did I have chicken pox or measles?'

'Think so.'

'Was I born in the day or the night?'

'Oh, one or the other.'

'Do you remember the time we went to Rosebud?'

'Did we?'

I remember only one holiday with them yet we went away every year. That time our tent got washed out and on our return home a frog jumped out of the suitcase to the kid's running, tumbling and laughing. I remember none of their teachers nor attending parent-teacher interviews and am assured I went to every one. I remember their kindergarten. I remember Stefan being ill with bronchitis and being told he would grow out of it, and Nina with convulsions.

Nina and Stefan eventually gave up on their forgotten lives and made allowances for my fenestrated and felicitous mind.

But I couldn't, wouldn't, give up on one memory; leaving my family.

From the depths came the rumblings, skitterings and dead ends. Out of these came the realisation that I have my memory of leaving my children that first time, but not of the second. Cracked and wafting as it is, it has always been with me. I went to Sydney sitting in a bus. On a seat of air I travelled through a void in a cloud of grey. In that hollow I sobbed and my heart ached. This *is* my memory. There may never be more. Recognition of my pain, this heart of grief long trapped in a teardrop, hurt.

I wanted to make amends and thought about setting up a business. I registered the name 'Get Sweet', then 'Corporate Cheek'. The first promised to be the best chocolate and flower delivery business in Melbourne and the second wanted to put corporate logos on underwear. The latter got no further than a business name.

Out came the chocolate paraphernalia. Mum's kitchen utensils were pushed aside; moulds slid everywhere. Poor Mum listened to my daydreams of impending success and patiently waited to prepare lunch.

Skimming past shop entrances, I was torn between reminders of Kenja and wanting to relieve the financial burden I had become. At the end of the day, Mum surreptitiously (ha!) peeped at the still full basket and put the kettle on.

The problem was resolved by the state of her kitchen. It fell short of the officially required stainless steel glimmering.

Nina and Stefan breathed a sigh of relief; their mother, hopefully, had realised that she had options other than 'Kenja' ones. I was grateful for the excuse and Mum, with the smallest shake of her head, reclaimed her kitchen.

❧

Mum and I continued our weekly modest escapes. In a polished and aging car parked close to the sea, Mum sat with a take-away coffee holder firmly on her knees. I walked, picturesquely framed by candy-striped bathing boxes, mumbling to myself about how the sea has such wonderful healing qualities and this is really doing me the world of good. Into the rubbish bin angled in the sand, I deposited the coffee cups and returned to the car reiterating the obvious virtues of sand and sea, and in tune with the tides.

Mum's head shook; she never was subtle.

On braver days we drove the length of the peninsula and Mum sat, back ramrod straight. In my childhood we had often driven to green destinations, eaten a picnic lunch and returned home. Here we were re-enacting our ritual – albeit with her truncated family of one in a green jellybean car.

In our disgruntled way, we found love. It had always been there, the love I had so questioned. As I delved into the meaning of our past there was Mum. She copped the lot, my indignation, confusion, tears, self-righteousness and my disjointed stories. Mum walked to the bathroom, I padded behind her intent on finishing this story or that.

Then one day the past arrived, gloriously, unexpectedly.

'Mum can you answer the phone?'

'You know me, I'm not good at talking to people I don't know.'

'How do you know you don't know them.' I retorted, exasperation rising while the phone clanged.

Britt-Louise opened the conversation by suggesting quietly that I may not know of this, it may come as a great surprise, but she is Josef's granddaughter. Long ago, in our Elwood bedroom, my husband had told of a child for whom he had acknowledged a paternity claim, denying to me that he was, in fact, the father. The subject never arose again and years later, when I met Britt-Louise's mother, Britt-Inger and her husband Bosse, in her features I recognised her father, Josef. My children have a half-sister.

Britt-Inger was born, and lives, half an hour out of Goteborg, Sweden, where her mother and father, Josef, had met. Britt-Inger had grown up wondering about him. All she knew was that he wasn't with her in Sweden. One of her three children, Britt-Louise, undertook to unravel this mystery.

She and her partner Fredrik travelled to Sydney, searching in one government department after another, ringing up every same surname in the telephone book. They nearly gave up.

At the eleventh hour they obtained information that led them to that sad-thought-filled flat in Elwood. No one of that name lived there; the occupants heard Josef had died. A neighbour remembered him, confirmed his death and the existence of a family now dispersed. Still they tried. Days before they were due to depart, through Josef's death certificate and the hospital where he died, they obtained Mum's phone number.

We met amid shyness and tears and talked, smiled, remembered, tried to understand and, squeezed together on a couch, took photographs.

Inspired to undertake private pilgrimages Nina, Stefan and I separately revisited the flat in Elwood. No one seemed to care for it anymore – oh, if it were mine I would renovate those beautiful large rooms with double doors and let the air in.

Stepping off the escalator in a shopping complex, shopping bags clunking against legs, I found myself right in front of a familiar face. Farida's! Our words were simultaneous: 'Let's have coffee!' She had reconnected with her family; by then, Vittorio and I had married. Two hours later, my diminutive friend and I were still talking.

With Farida, I could talk about Kenja. Friends were shocked at the state I was in but our relationships had been built on the past and to continue had to return to it – and I couldn't. In my absence, and their emotional sinking and flapping, some thought that when I joined Kenja, it seemed the logical continuation of my strange floating behavior. Many felt guilty because they had not rescued me. Others thought Kenja was something I somehow had to do. My experience was sometimes met with rejection. There were times I sensed jealousy; in the 'terrible experiences stakes' I had one-upped others. Our difficulties weren't always them; I often wanted to talk about myself and not listen to others. And sometimes I was unintelligible.

The single most frustrating attitude to deal with was: it wouldn't happen to me, I would never join a cult. The frequency of this comment struck me. Those believing it wouldn't happen to them considered themselves to be brighter, with more nous than me. I grant some of them that, but being bright is dodgy protection against induction into a cult. Education is best and, even then, knowing the hallmarks of a cult does not guarantee against meeting one that successfully masks these.

Some believed my entrapment in Kenja had empowered my children, made them strong, and I cried at the memory of Nina and Stefan, their fears and hopes and profound wounding. Things, for them, could have gone an irretrievable either way. I hope that, somewhere along the line before I left, I did something that contributed to their capacity to deal with those aching years.

Mum was unable to relate her experience of the Exclusive Brethren to mine in Kenja; that meant acknowledging pain too hard to address. Josef had lost hope that we might reconcile, without understanding why. Nina and Stefan swerved between despair, betrayal and hope. Without understanding what they were dealing with, the help they tried to give me was doomed and inadequate. This made them all unnecessarily guilty. In my absence, the optimism and resilience of youth was on the children's side. And they had their nana. Mum's unyielding love was always there for my children, through rains and storms and those dusty, crusty days.

∽

Riffling through the phone book, I rang every number that might point me towards a health professional with an understanding of cults. Nothing remotely resembled the heading, 'help for ex-cult members'.

One transforming day I read an article reviewing a book by the psychologist Louise Samways, *Your Mind Body Energy*. The reviewer referred to a chapter in the book on cults and mind-control techniques. I devoured its pages. Louise explains how tuning into our body's energy field and inner mind can help you change and grow.

In her mentioning of the yoga energy centres, or chakras, I recognised Ken's energy centres. I had abandoned all belief that he was original, but her book did more than debunk Ken. It enabled me to be kind to myself.

In one chapter Louise explains the psychological techniques that can be used to manipulate belief systems. I realised that she understood healing and cults. Her clinic was a few miles down the coast at the midway point on Mum's and my scenic drives. I hugged Mum, Allie the dog, and went to my first appointment.

The first thing I noticed was that I wasn't locked in her room.

Louise's technique, incorporating the natural ability of self-hypnosis, was the opposite of Kenjan processing. I was in control; she respected my instinct to protect my privacy and integrity.

She explained that I suffered from post-traumatic stress and was a victim of a sophisticated psychological process used without my informed consent. Leaving her rooms, I asked myself the question: was I? What if Ken was right when he said that being a victim means you give volition to someone else, that they hold the key? Ignorance I could lay claim to; I was afraid 'victim' might become a permanent label.

I was to see Louise several times but no one rang me every second day with urgent pleas to return. I made an appointment with her when

I needed to. After each appointment I had as much time as I needed to feel, think and let things settle.

In Louise I found an ethical counsellor who understood that hypnosis could bring to light incidents when one is not ready, and the dangers of that. She never pushed me beyond what I could deal with and helped keep me safe while I reconciled the damage of Kenja with my grieving for it.

Ken, Steven and Louise, had, unknown to them, swashbuckling battles in my mind. Ironically, all three agreed on one thing: it is important to find the positives from my involvement with Kenja.

I racked my brain, surveyed the havoc wreaked on my family. They had to be kidding.

chapter 14

Exposure

Ken's dictum, the spiritual universe will help you if you are playing a creative game, came to pass.

Instead of fading away, my 'if only's' escalated. If only I could woo Kenjans away ... expose the organisation that had trapped them ... help alleviate the pain my involvement had caused Nina and Stefan; I had not wandered carelessly off, and even their hapless mother could do something worthwhile.

I had fired off letters to the New South Wales Psychologists Registration Board and the Victorian Psychological Council. However, Kenja was outside their jurisdiction. I wrote to the Taxation Department. I doubt they understood a word.

In writing about the misuse of powerful psychological techniques, my psychologist, Louise Samways, had hit a nerve. *Your Mind Body Energy* provoked media interest. *The Sydney Morning Herald* journalist, Sheila Browne, separately interviewed the author and myself. The article, 'Own Your Own Life' was published on 12 August 1992. Focused on 'seminar junkies' hooked on expensive self-development groups, it critiqued the potential psychological damage of the techniques employed by group leaders and the growth industry these organisations were fast becoming. Sheila wanted to talk to an ex-participant of Landmark Education, Money and You or The Hoffman Process, but ended up with me from the virtually unknown Kenja.

The section in the article relating to Kenja outlines briefly my background and time in Kenja, records Kenja's denials and Ken's rejection of the use of covert hypnosis – 'a direct lie – and against our published code of ethics' – and he cites 'supportive testimonials of professional people who support the group'.

I wanted to see an organisation similar to the American Cult Awareness Network, CAN, established in Australia. There were limited resources available that related specifically to cults; when I needed them I could not find them. I even rang the American CAN. They didn't do long-distance counselling. Sheila Browne suggested I give my mailing address so people who had read the article could contact me; if not for that, Kenja might have sunk like a stone.

I believe I am the first ex-Kenjan to publicly condemn Ken, Jan and processing. I am by no means the first to have understood and passed on the message. Each previous exposure had its 15 minutes and faded away. Going public seemed the safest option, as threats to me would put Kenja under suspicion, even if they did not originate from there.

❧

The letters I received as a result of the article fell into three groups: those about cults in general, ex-Kenjans and from parents of then-active Kenjans. Some assumed I had established a cult watchdog. The response was unexpected and, not knowing what to do, I was overwhelmed, stashed their letters or wrote stilted replies. With parents of Kenjans, and ex-Kenjans, it was easier.

Ex-Kenjans wrote of their experience of betrayal, suffering and confusion. Several warned of the dangers of exposing Ken. They had been involved for various lengths of time and some had been and gone before my involvement. The degree of damage to people is not dependent on their length of time in Kenja, and those vulnerable to mental illness are especially prey.

Each had given their very best to Kenja, their personal and career-related expertise, and every one had given the sparkle in their eyes. With one exception, all said they had been maimed by Kenja's betrayal. One ex-Kenjan, by then a Uniting Church minister, spoke of one who had never recovered, who had been living in half-way houses and in and out of institutions. He was trying his best to keep an eye on this young man trapped crossing mindworlds.

One talked to another, and another, and so the connecting of ex-Kenjans began.

Despite identifying the pain of their involvement, some still believed that Ken was wise; his knowledge of energy beyond compare. Most felt guilty at having been compromised by the things they had done as Kenjans. One man had sat naked in session opposite a young Vanessa, at Ken's behest, and remained deeply offended at this. Successful recruiters had to accept they had trapped people; remembering the man or woman, the real one, still trapped in Kenja was a frequently mentioned source of pain. I was not the only Kenjan to have left their children for Kenja. Parents who had, as Kenjans, encouraged their child's continuing involvement had, on leaving, to deal with the considerable pain of that, especially those whose children had expressed doubts about Kenja and whom the parents had ignored. Many understood why, but understanding sometimes needs time in order to alleviate the guilt and pain.

Being an ex-cult-member is not a social plus and managing their Kenja years, in a résumé, had been difficult. As well as post-Kenja trauma, many had to deal with the prior reasons for their vulnerability. Where issues preceding the cult had been with the family, some remained influenced by Kenja's denigration of families and were unable to return home, especially those minus a framework within which to evaluate Kenja. This resulted in some families being unaware that their child had left. Feeling unable to return home, the ex-member's priority was financial survival and building a new life. Without family, some did this from scratch; some put the pain of these years aside in order to retain emotional and mental equilibrium hoping that, one day, when they have recouped their professional and financial losses, they will find the space in which to heal their souls.

Some of us would meet up and talk but a structured support group never eventuated. Talking about Kenja with ex-Kenjans, my emotions often wound up beyond my level of tolerance and I ran away. I thought that I could only talk about Kenja in adverse terms; fond memories of my Kenjan friends and clowning classes should be hidden. If I did mention these, I felt the need to emphasise their negative aspects. I felt denied of, and ashamed of, my grieving for some aspects of Kenja.

The sole positive letter came from a woman who had a few sessions with me, attended as many classes and left. She had experienced Kenja as positive but she thought she had a right to question Ken (!), wanted a part-time involvement and considered it too expensive. When I did ask her to leave, I explained that this was for her benefit. Amid the hurt-soaked letters, this one flippantly asked if I had cut my hair.

There were letters from parents whose children I knew; the children and I had been together intimately enclosed in session. Without exception they wanted their family member out. Parents saw little choice: wait and hope for a cataclysmic upheaval, find an exit-counsellor if aware of them, or pray to their god. In exit-counselling, or interventions, the cult member is given the opportunity to evaluate information about their group from professional counsellors and ex-members, become aware of their family's concerns and make up their own minds. Counselling sessions are structured, disciplined, ethical and sensitive to the needs of all. Given the information they did not have at the time of their induction to the cult, most leave.

Some wanted Kenja closed. I naively wanted whatever it took to release my Kenjan friends from their cult involvement. I privately thought closure impossible. I knew Jan and Ken, their determination and Jan's passion for their game; however, I was resolved to expose them. In time I appreciated that closure might devastate members. Cult members they may be but they are also human beings who have, despite their denials, been conned. The likelihood of forced closure with sufficient resources available for members to recover is slim. Closure could also send them underground, outwardly restructured, renamed and hard to keep tabs on. I wanted to see processing investigated and Kenja classified as a cult and monitored; any advertising, as in web pages, should include that classification. Informed consent is paramount.

Parents believed their loved ones could only suffer more through continued involvement. It is not unusual for parents to equate the loss of their child to Kenja with death. Options are limited, barring a miracle – and they do happen. It is not unheard of for a cult to disband through disillusion. Hassan cites as an example the Democratic Worker's Party of California, a former extreme left-wing political cult.

Perhaps the most difficult concept for parents to understand was that of internalisation. The comment, 'Ken forced my child' is accurate in so far as he has manipulated their minds. Some wanted to believe that Ken made all the decisions and then coerced Kenjans into attacking detractors, including parents. He certainly did, but not always. If Ken did his job well, members would do his thinking for him and volunteer and offer suggestions.

Hassan advises parents to maintain an open, non-committal communication. To inform a committed Kenjan that Ken is a crock of rubbish and Kenja sheer nonsense usually backfires. I am aware of only one set of parents who had successfully intervened by themselves and released their Kenjan daughter from her bonds. Parents do need to get on with their lives. Many find this difficult and do so after years of despair when there is not much left to do *but* get on with one's life.

The *Herald* article had been pinned on Kenja's notice board and one mother memorised my post office box number. Her son and I had looked into each other's eyes in sessions. She had picked up her phone several times before eventually contacting me, frightened that Ken might read her mind, or worse, that her son, with whom she maintained contact, might miraculously walk in on our conversation and with dire consequences. She gripped the feeble relationship hoping the most important thing was to maintain the connection with her child because one day her son might leave and return to the mother he has so distanced himself from.

Writing a testimonial stating her high opinion of Kenja, this mother kept that fine placental line in place by pleasing her son, stating that she had never seen him happier or more fulfilled. When he chose sessions over food she fed him, and when he begged to attend a seminar she gave him money.

She considered an intervention but the publicity grew and her son responded with a strident defence of Kenja, and withdrew some degrees from his mother. Unfortunately, the time to act had passed. Futility and regret mingled with fear. What would happen to their relationship when she could no longer feed her son's involvement in Kenja? What would happen to her son?

'I admire your going public' she said to me 'but it stopped me from getting my son back.'

The article caused a furore within Kenja's energy-logged walls. Attack tends to strengthen resolve. Ken neutralised the impact of the article with his version of events and shored up internal support. He never took anything lightly; any threat to his game deserved a game in return.

Ken and Jan dealt with members' doubts, in part, by systematically ticking off the criteria that define a cult, an easy verbal twist and shove. How dare anyone suggest Kenjans are not free when they know, for a fact, that they possess the most valuable freedom of all, that of the mind.

The danger of the publicity was not only the potential loss of membership, it might affect recruitment and inform members' families. Armed with sufficient knowledge they might discover the most appropriate ways to communicate with their offspring, or worse, find an exit-counsellor.

Within the parameters of their small world, Kenjans were hurt and angry. The version of Kenja that I described did not, to them, exist and I was seen as a hate-fueled liar. The question, why publicly deny the things members privately laud about Kenja, most likely never arose and, if so, was swept aside and bundled into the cliché: no one understands us. Their fear of leaving Kenja was vindicated – look at Annette now. The spiritual universe will take its revenge, and God help me then.

In the meantime, a more earthly and immediate response was required. The Kenjan game was, always had been, played with smoke and mirrors. Someone knew where the real game was, and hoped he had it covered.

ᕲᕲ

While Kenja roared and reacted, I found Alex. He had written to me.

'That fellow from Sydney is on the phone again,' Mum would knowingly say. Alex, the doctor whose status would defend Kenja, had left hurt and in despair, wondering if he would ever replace the life he had left in Melbourne all those years ago.

He still believed implicitly in sessions; that which had lured him remained bright despite his betrayal and collapsing ramparts. At an appointment with Louise Samways, I asked her why Alex didn't recognise hypnosis. She explained that hypnosis is a two-year course and many who have not been trained fail to recognise it.

We agreed on the misfortune of our involvement but not on our assessment of sessions.

'Alex, they don't bloody work!'

I reminded him of sessions on creepy crawlies in which our flesh crawled as spiders crept greedily into every orifice.

'And look, Alex, I saw a huntsman spider on my shoulder the other day and landed on my back in a squealing panic!'

I recalled the three sessions that I had with Nadine, in which I followed the tragedy of an unfamiliar planet and the fate of its last alien. In these sessions I had tried to communicate to myself, an unconscious attempt to comprehend the reality of my plight in Kenja. I was the sole disconnected alien. Some cult-members dream these unconscious attempts to understanding their situation.

Ken taught that an angry man might initially blame his anger on the imminent demise of the world. Ask the same question again and he will find a lesser reason; and if one continues probing he will, with the same emotional force, complain of trifles. In processing, the arousal of emotion was important and inducing pain and tears was a speciality of Ken. The mind did its best to ascribe reasons for these powerful traumatic emotions, latching onto Ken's confident explanations. One linked, sometimes frivolous, words to the emotion and the emotion gave credibility to the words. It is a terrible vulnerability to play on.

I responded to the power of suggestion but managed, at times, to retain a distance. In one session, I had imagined my father's bathing of me when I was a baby but, despite my attempts to animate this image into sexual abuse, I couldn't. In sessions that regressed to early childhood I found nothing, including the incident that so haunted Mum – her turmoil when I had merrily plastered poo as far as my two-year-old hands could reach. I never retrieved my birth, nor did I process on the pain associated with the loss of my family to the Exclusive Brethren. These never arose despite Ken's frequent reminders to purge the pain of our pasts. The internalisation of my cult persona had gone deep, but it had never been total.

For a brief time after I had that session with Matt long ago, when I saw myself being raped as a child, it seemed so real. No matter how hard

I tried I could not retrieve this image with its emotional impact, and soon enough it settled into the deep – as if the session hadn't happened.

Still, I cried passionately in session and ignorantly blamed my tears on regurgitated incidents that I remembered. I did Mum and my stubborn despotism to death. I had been open to processing because I hoped to uncover the reasons and history of my perceived calamitous mothering. On this subject I found an endless, intense well of hurt but few actual examples.

In the end, all I could say to Alex about processing was, 'Look at me, Alex, and tell me if you really think processing has delivered on its promise!'

In a brown-brick building, squat against the footpath, his almost tidy room featured a piano. Touched by the survival in Alex of something good from Kenja, we overloaded our human resources. Talking about Kenja at that early stage, dragged us into internal conflict; we were still crossing mindworlds, lurching between the known, lingering Kenjan and the unknown new. Sometimes it was 'cult Alex' and 'cult Annette' doing the Kenjan unforgiveable: complaining bitterly about Ken. In between my visits to Sydney he faxed me copies of newspaper articles relating to Kenja. They have symbolically faded to illegibility.

We had one late-night vigil hoping to read an article about Kenja. We sat on a bench in Kings Cross, challenging our pasts on a balmy night within cooee of the fountain. The article was not printed in that edition. We stayed up all night watching Kings Cross nightlife wrap itself in morning, magnanimously embracing the drunks and hookers our Kenja selves had rejected, and laughed off feeling like naughty children in a place that mummy Jan and daddy Ken disapproved of.

Alex had been through his own hell trying to understand Ken's betrayal. Had Ken and Jan gone home each night and calmly decided who to haul over the coals and who to eject from professionalism or from Kenja? Alex had, to a degree, succeeded. By then, he understood that Ken was a 'true believer' yet, at the same time, sufficiently detached from Kenja to protect it. Alex was concerned the publicity might see him face to face with his former master, as well it might, so he refused to go public.

Nor did Alex have to go public. Ex-member's families, careers, recovery and futures are their priorities. Not everyone can go home to Mum, like I did.

Then the surveillance of Alex began. The first time he saw a Kenjan outside his flat he tried to dismiss it. Then he rang one day saying that *they* were opposite his flat, standing and staring, and he was very, very uneasy.

ᗢ

Jill's letter grabbed my attention. Supported by her husband Ian, she had refused to supply a testimonial. She would not lie and say nice things about Kenja when she saw none.

Their daughter, Helena, was my wake-up call and cab partner when we both lived in Jan and Ken's Double Bay unit. I had no idea how alike she and her mother were. As both move, their hair sways; Helena moved and swayed and rose quickly through the ranks. Helena's older sister had died in a car accident – an opportunity not missed by Ken, who easily reduced her to tears over this. We went shopping together once, my sole 'girly' moment in Kenja, and Helena bought luxurious, even sexy, underwear for herself and a cup, an encouragement award, for me. In one Wednesday class Helena went down on her knees and begged Ken not to demote her. She was the first person I ever saw challenge a decision by Ken – mother and daughter *were* so alike.

On a balcony under an outrageously large tree, Jill and I sat opposite each other, two complicit women. One was hungry for information the other was desperate to talk.

When I needed a break Jill sent me over the road to the beach. I wandered past pools, stared across the invisible boundary separating private from public land; toes wet, I spied homes nestled in foliage and the ferry carrying windswept passengers. To the left of this wistful scene, and visible, was Ken's cliff-top house.

Jill had written to parliament saying she had lost her daughter to a cult. How does one explain 'lost'? That her daughter's address is known but she has gone missing in a belief system?

Jill and Ian's position and the subsequent public feud with Helena proved distressing for them. Their attitude to Kenja was little different to that of other parents, but they did not hide it. They became enemies of Kenja. Anxious and dogged, they wanted the truth known and so set aside their fears that Kenja might retaliate.

Jill and Ian knew another member of the New South Wales parliament, Stephen Mutch, who had expressed concern about the threats cults posed and suggested I write to him. They had known him for some time and trusted him.

When I first met Stephen Mutch I was surprised; his looks were darkly cavalier but he was not. I found him amicable, sincere and too young to be a politician.

Whenever I had thought of my abandoned letter-writers, guilt stung. I stuffed them and their letters back in their envelopes. Now I had something to offer. I wrote to each of my patient scribes, including one I suspected was a Kenjan (what the hell, I thought), imploring them to write to Stephen Mutch.

They responded with a barrage of letters to him. To the best of my knowledge, every ex-Kenjan who had written to me wrote to him, as did those who were hurt by other cults.

On 24 November 1992, in the New South Wales parliament, Stephen warned of the dangers of Kenja.

Jill's daughter, Helena, came out fighting for her guru. When we bumped into each other once, on the way to our respective politicians, our hackles rose and our necks elongated with the rightness of our causes.

From Stephen's first speech came more anti-cult letters to him – and Kenja's response. They fired off letters to another politician, Ian McManus, the member for Bulli. Ian McManus passed the letters onto Stephen who tabled them in parliament. Most wrote two each. I could ghostwrite aspects of them. A warrior needs an appropriate foe and their past is, well, readily accessible. The saddest aspect is pride in their achievements because these qualifications were, overwhelmingly, gained prior to involvement in Kenja.

McManus and his wife visited Kenja, Sydney. He looked, listened and, at first, found nothing wrong with the organisation. What is seen, often enough, by outsiders is a group of genuinely nice people who say with sincerity how influential Ken and Jan are. Kenjans *are* nice people, slowly neutralised by shrouds and sackcloth, but in their desire to impress, the spirit looks on from its silent remove and the childish humans shine.

In his next speech, on 22 April 1993, Stephen began by referring to a previous (1977) move to set up a select committee to enquire into the Children of God, to make recommendations, if required, for controlling them and similar organisations. This had been defeated. Stephen pointed out that he believed attitudes had changed since then. This second speech was long, detailed and refers to a number of cults. He called again for the setting up of a new parliamentary select committee.

Ken entered Parliament House for this speech, leaning on a walking stick, taking one slow step after the other, wearing a sports jacket made popular by men like my father in the 1940s, and looking tragic. I recalled his boast: he was a better actor than Jan ever was. Later, standing outside the building, Ken thrust his walking stick aside and strode towards the hare-brained adoration of his Kenjans.

Ken made much of Stephen hiding behind parliamentary privilege. I blessed its very existence. Stephen gave the walking wounded a voice but fear of potential repercussions prevented many ex-cult members from giving him public support.

On Stephen's wedding day, uninvited Kenjans pitter-pattered and mingled with their wedding guests outside the service. Stephen was, apart from a slight puzzling, largely unaware of the presence of these strangers in odd clothes and big sunglasses; their quiet audacity. At least one person, who was mindful of them, took a photo and gave it to Stephen. This silent assault didn't appear to be Ken's form. Perhaps Jan had fallen back to her past in the theatre? A closer look at Kenjans might have revealed a nervous giggle, a glance seeking reassurance, a real-clown human hesitation. It shocked me because, for the first time, I sensed the extent of the corrupting of Kenja.

I could easily be dismissed. Jill and Ian could not and remained in Kenja's firing line. Stephen loomed large.

That it had come to this, tenacious grieving parents and a politician highlighting Kenja, was not only unexpected, for Kenja it was a disaster. Kenja drew their battle lines.

⁓

There are three ways a cult member leaves: those who leave voluntarily, usually as a result of disillusion; those who are counselled out, receiving information and support; those who are kicked out. The last have the worst outcomes.

Michael, who had been kicked out, came back into my life. His mother, Wendy, contacted me as a result of the *Herald* article. She had fair hair and the greenest of green eyes. As we spoke, her face dissolved to those brimming eyes.

After a trip to Bali, Wendy said, Michael had changed. Cult experts speak of mind control lying dormant until something activates it. Bali, to a Kenjan, was the most evil place in the world, harbouring a congregation of rogue entities strong enough to resist the power of Ken's processing. For a Kenjan to visit Bali was to invite a personal hell.

Michael had also travelled to Darwin, under an assumed name. This is particularly dangerous for an ex-Kenjan still believing Ken's words: in order to change one's life one must create a new identity. The Darwin hospital discovered Michael's identity, Wendy was contacted and he was returned to Sydney.

Michael was admitted to a psychiatric unit, diagnosed with schizophrenia and had attempted suicide. His family queried this diagnosis believing that his problems were specifically related to Michael's cult experience; he had no prior history of mental illness. The work of the hospital in treating Michael was not made easy. When he was first hospitalised, Michael still considered Ken, the man who wanted nothing more to do with him, as the greatest thing in his young life.

Wendy told the hospital staff about Kenja and lamented the dearth of understanding. Yes, they recognised the role of Michael's cult involvement but he was sent home, Wendy cried bitterly, with enough pills in his pocket to enable him to do a better job on his next suicide attempt.

Michael's voice sent shivers down my spine. Words fail as I write the reason he was willing to talk to me: I had been a professional in Kenja and was therefore to be trusted.

When I first saw Michael I froze in shock at the young man before me. His very soul seemed wasted. He wrestled with his thoughts and confusion. I did my best not to ram information down his throat, indoctrinated as he was to believe his betrayal of Ken brought untold pain. Coming to grips with Ken's betrayal of him saw him plummet into despair, veering between fear of, and anger at, Jan and Ken.

Mum baked her fruitcake in readiness for a weekend visit by Michael and Wendy. 'I hope they don't mind me hanging around.'

'No formality here,' Mum said, as we sat at her table, surrounded by cake crumbs, squashed between the wall and Mum's kitchen bench.

The green jellybean car shunted us to the Sorrento back beach where the wind sighed and skipped across waves. Scrambling from the car, Wendy and I grabbed jumpers and pulled them over our heads. *Brrr*, the shock of the cold. Ditching a car-bound Mum, we sat shivering on sand. Michael smiled in his own world and walked, a bear-cub of a man, in a crooked line between sand and sea to the rocks and returned still smiling softly.

Driving home via the scenic route, we stopped on impulse at the Arthur's Seat chairlift that slowly jerked down a steep cliff with the sea in magnificent view.

Mum stayed in the car. 'You won't get me on that thing.'

Wendy and I sat together, Michael behind us. Halfway down our ride Michael yelled.

'Mum! I lost my flip-flop.'

Wendy laughed, 'Oh, Michael,' and peered to a far distant ground seeking a solitary sandal. 'Maybe we could find it.'

'Maybe ...'

'You can't go barefoot for the rest of the weekend!'

Michael tried but could contain himself no longer. He produced his sandal from behind his back and looked at Wendy with a look that said, how gullible can you be.

That night, Mum fussed over dinner, the rifle club that practised in a tin shed in the park at the back of Mum's house erratically fired and Allie the dog barked at each bang.

Mum looked at Michael. 'You do whatever you want here Michael. Make yourself at home.'

All he wanted to do was sit on the couch, nurse a beer and talk about nothing in particular. He said he was having the best time since he had left Kenja.

We met up with a mixed bag of ex-members, their families and mental health specialists with an interest in cults, hoping that talking to others who had been children in Kenja was the best thing for Michael. It was a gentle, gentle day. The lingering sorrow ex-Kenjan adults embraced was put aside with respect for the young people present. In a suburban lounge room, on that day, hope saw beyond a raw edge. Wendy and other parents threaded together by fate, met and spoke together and sometimes the thread loosened and other times it snapped.

How long was it, or perhaps it was never, before the tremulous, hopeful, anticipation of that day returned to those present? Girls, who once upon a time had stood on Kenja's dais in front of us, were there; their secrets nearly filled to overflowing. For the first time Michael spoke with others who had been youngsters in Kenja. They spoke hopefully and encouraged each other to come to terms with their Kenjan pasts, to move ahead, not knowing they played with a blind and gnarled fate.

When Michael attempted suicide again, those of us who had come to love him were shocked. Perhaps talking to him about Kenja was triggering his turmoil? With us, he seemed like a child grateful for his mother's skirts. Alone, he found no soothing, no kind words or hope held out. God knows what kind of disorienting hell veiled Michael.

Jumpy and frightened, some thought we had a spy in our midst. We knew there wasn't but, in truth, we were all so frangible, like the newest, most tenuous of tentacles on that ivy-covered Brighton wall of my youth.

As Michael's father's second marriage neared, Michael was in hospital; however, he wanted to attend the wedding. His father pleaded with authorities for his son's release and Michael's face pleaded back. At the reception Michael was almost transparent, hanging on by a smile.

Michael applied for the army and was rejected … still he hoped to return to bricklaying … nothing got better.

The hospital saw no choice and, for a time, Michael was scheduled.

Recommended to a psychiatrist, he walked out of his first visit; running down the street, clumsy and crying, a vestige of hope remained so he returned. The psychiatrist encouraged Michael and Wendy, believing he could help.

Alex thought that walking along the beach with Michael and his dog would help. Mum offered to keep his Mornington bed made up. Wendy mourned her lost son and cooked for everyone who loved him. Jill sat him on her magical balcony, hoping that comparing his future with Helena's might cheer him. Stephen Mutch hoped the chance to talk at an official level would encourage him. I hoped that reading Hassan's book would help. His brothers hoped playing footy and hanging out together would reach him. His father hoped …

Michael was one of the few ex-Kenjans (myself included) who gave permission to Stephen to publicly use his name. 'If I can help just one person,' Michael said.

Wendy prayed. Please God make it Michael.

Michael threw himself off a cliff into a surging ocean. His car was found, and in it was a suicide note. In his note he said, '… Kenja is only partly to blame, they have exposed me to truths …' and gave his love to his family again and again and again.

Wendy waited, praying that, somehow, Michael had not jumped. I joined her. It was an unutterably poignant time. She ran the gamut of emotion, from the lost heart of grief, to despair, to guilt devoid of logic and an anguish that cried, how could he do this to us?

Several tormented days later his body was found and Wendy went to the morgue to identify her son.

Michael's body was bloated, his face the wrong colour. He was 20 years old.

At the funeral Wendy wore a new outfit and fanciful hat. As the minister said, 'ashes to ashes, dust to dust …' tears were shed, a splintered moan hung in the air waiting for gravediggers to trap the pungency of earth as we stood, as friable as the dirt that would cover his coffin.

Wendy, hat askew, walked to her mourning.

Michael's suicide note was never returned to Wendy. The authorities lost it. She was given a colour photocopy. She wants the real one, the one with the pain in it.

There is a place Wendy can visit, a monument to her son. It is a fence he built at a house on a cliff with a path that leads to water. The fence is large and Michael built it without payment, an act of love for the people he loved. For weeks to months on weekends, in his spare time he toiled and sweated and was never offered a glass of water by the lady of the house. Michael wondered why? He hid his doubts. I suppose they are too busy, he said to Wendy. The fence was Michael's pride and joy – and hid the founders of Kenja.

The New South Wales Coroner dispensed with holding an inquest into Michael's death after an examination of the evidence given by Michael's family, three police officers, a psychiatrist, the man who found Michael's body – and Jan Hamilton.

The exhibits were: Michael's suicide note, a copy of Kenja's Purpose and Ethics, nine Statutory Declarations and one letter, all ten from Kenjans, all taken by a Justice of the Peace, himself a committed Kenjan.

These letters sound considerate, apparently demonstrating concern for Michael, but they have a sting in the tail when read together; they add up to a portrait of Michael that is false. Michael was a nice young man with bad acne – until Kenja; a nice young man who drank too much – until Kenja; a nice young man who used illegal drugs – until Kenja: a nice young man with a warped mother; and a nice young man who visited a prostitute – nothing to do with Kenja.

This is not an indictment of the Coroner. Nor is it an indictment of the hospital that believed Michael when he said, at first, that Ken was great. I believe we all stand condemned by our ignorance. Kenja capitalised on it.

I did not instigate the setting up of CultAware but supported others already planning such an organisation. We had met up through those letters. Led by a dynamic couple, people ranged from parents affected by their children's past or present involvement in cults, psychologists, businessmen, academics and ex-cult members all with a common purpose: to help others, disseminate information for those affected, to provide a forum and a multi-faceted focus.

CultAware was independent, not associated with the American Cult Awareness network or with other Australian groups. It raised questions of abuse in cults, including Kenja, and reprinted relevant articles about cults in its newsletter, *CultWatch*. We were careful about naming a group a cult. Because a group had been referred to CultAware did not mean it fell within the parameters that define a cult. Believing in different ideas or lifestyles does not qualify a group as a cult, and some people, on understanding the characteristics of a cult, realised that a particular group was different but not dangerous.

CultAware spokespeople were threatened, stalked and hassled by cults. Despite being brave and determined, the business of running CultAware, handling queries, producing *Cultwatch*, providing support, and researching and giving information was a hard grind.

Everything that emanated from CultAware I endorsed. These ranged from meeting people, including exit-counsellors, to conferences, meetings, surveys and communicating with ex-members and, once, being part of a panel at a Sceptics Society lecture in Melbourne addressed by CultAware's dynamic leaders.

Approaching the Melbourne venue for the lecture, I passed a Kenjan with a walkie-talkie who ostentatiously contacted the next who whipped out another and whispered the news: she's here. I walked straight into Jill's daughter, Helena, who squinted icily in my direction. Not that I minded; I wanted Kenjans to notice me, the prodigious thorn in their side. Eye-clashing wreck, actually, but sometimes ignorance is, if not bliss, then handy.

Then ... all of a sudden in this crush there was Jess, who had attended Melbourne's very first seminar. With her short, straight, fringed dark hair, she reminded me of my childhood passion for Milly

Molly Mandy. Crossing the foyer, Jess saw me and, in that instant, spontaneously and wonderfully smiled at me. Her happiness is etched in my mind. It lasted a fraction of a second and was gone, replaced by the cult replica hiding the real and lovely daughter of a Melbourne poet who stumbled trying to find her own poetic voice.

For all my good intentions, involvement in CultAware was overloading me. Far too much of my waking life had become devoted to exposing Kenja. When I was interviewed by Channel Nine for the first time, about the dangers of hypnosis, I could barely answer the questions. The interviewer patiently repeated them until I made sense. Had they screened my bumbling, that would have demonstrated the risks. This, in turn, activated my phobia indoctrination. Jill found me shivering. I returned to Melbourne, still trembling. Mum hoped I wasn't coming down with something and fetched me cups of tea. The phobia that I would be on ice for a thousand years if I betrayed Ken was out in the open. When I wrote down the details of a processing session for someone to read, paranoia reared but, by then, I knew the confusion and tears routine and, forging on, another punching fist relaxed. My fear of insanity and of disobeying Ken caused pain and confusion as the exposure escalated, but pushed into the broad light of day, these fears would also fade.

My personal life was slowly and erratically moving ahead but meeting people hurt by cults was taking a toll. Women who had been involved in satanic cults told me stories of ritual satanic abuse, sacrifice and even murder. In turmoil, believing they had been accessories to crimes and fearful for those still trapped, these women with their perplexing stories were the most riven.

I would like to record my support of CultAware through a difficult time – it no longer exists – but I can't. CultAware personnel had backed me and I abandoned ship, and not respectfully and openly; I stopped contributing and deferred phone calls. The pain of ex-members plagued me. My desire to console parents had, in light of the evidence, fled.

Ironically, the only people to accord me a measure of the importance I initially yearned for were Kenjans. I am still referred to as the ex-participant who brought CultAware to Australia. Kenja remains direly oblivious of the facts.

❦

Another ex-Kenjan and I prowled around outside the Kenja Sydney Centre once, way past midnight, after Kenjans had gone home. Darkness compressed trees, the building and two hesitant people. Unnerved by the whiz of cars and roar of motorbikes, we pushed on, satisfying our great need to stand outside, and what? Shake windows and kick doors?

We sensed a watcher and fear clenched our toes.

Nicholas materialised in the dark, a caricature of his howling, raging master, and hustled us into a doorway. Taut and grey and haggard, his eyes were pinpricks. There were no formalities; no hello, how are you, long time no see. Steeped in anguish, out came the whole bloody lot. Nicholas had fallen in love and our Uncle Kenny didn't approve. He had been kicked out of Kenja. Nicholas had refused to break off his relationship and, in doing so, believed he had committed a sin, that of betraying Ken. You don't disobey Ken and stay in Kenja – especially Nicholas, the first of the drones to heal, who would set an example.

Nicholas merged with the dark and, in the half-light, hugged himself. His body was bent, eyes sunk to bone.

'Look at one guy still buying that the death of the child was his fault; the child had severe burns. Treatment was delayed so Ken could process the child and he later died. An inquest was held but Ken's name was kept out of it. Ask the Manly police, Annette. Ask Kathryn!'

'Do you know how much money was raised for a convention centre in Canberra? Do you know that the Brisbane Centre was closed to stop the Taxation Department from auditing it? Do you know about the lease of the new Sydney Centre – Brian courted the family of a council member for favours.'

'Jan told Paddy not to advertise his fatuous Saturday night functions in his idiotic restaurant. Poor old Paddy! He's got nothing! The silly man had, once upon a time, abandoned his own path as a guru and handed the lot over to Uncle Kenny. Kenjans should support each other's ventures – as long as they don't detract from Kenja's toxic, social nights.'

Jagged words spewed from a face in bits.

'Do you know how much property some people had when they joined Kenja and where is it now? I spent hours altering computer records. It was me who put the anti-Kenja posters on cars outside the Centre.'

'Did you know Miss Pure-as-Driven-Snow Jan had an affair with a Kenjan?'

I had wondered. If anyone knew about this it was Nicholas, who was closer than most to Jan and Ken. Unlike Nicholas, if Jan had fallen in love and had an affair, I couldn't condemn her for that.

'Do you know that Ken told me to go and fuck all the women of Kenja? Have fun, Nick! I had genital herpes. I gave it to some women and Ken knew I would.'

Nicholas caved to us. He had tears in his eyes.

I remembered the day in Noosa when Ken screamed at Nicholas for sleeping with a married woman; he was meant to stick with the single ones. In professional class Ken looked coldly at Nicholas who psychically washed and washed his young, strong body and withstood the heat.

'Ken keeps a loaded gun in his house. With a bit of luck, he'll shoot himself.'

His face stalled. He had crossed a line. He had wished Ken dead and if Ken was right, this *would* eventuate. Could kind, anguished Nicholas bear this?

Too late to stop now, he forged on.

'Have you ever wondered about Ken and all those young girls?'

There was no time to interject, to say that I couldn't bear to think about it and that I sliced these thoughts away. What can you confront?

'Kenja handled one taxation department investigation by getting all the pretty women in, and as the auditors went through the books they were swamped with women smiling sweetly saying, 'Oh really, oh, you mean this is not how it's done?'

'Do you know how many houses Ken has?'

'I'm using heroin again.'

I could only stand, and stare, and silently yelp.

'If not for my fiancé ...'

'And look at Nadine. Imagine trusting your life to *her*!'

Instinctively, I wanted to defend her but Nicholas was right, and not only with Nadine – us too.

'I've got copies of the *Sydney Morning Herald* article …'

And now he sought understanding and maybe even forgiveness.

As I reached to Nicholas he leaned back to an old and stricken corner.

Eyes locked together in the lull, we could have been processing.

'When I wrote to Stephen Mutch I used a pseudonym. I'm ashamed of that but despite knowing the truth about Kenja, I'm afraid that Ken might still be right … I'm writing a book.'

Nicholas scribbled his phone number on a scrap of paper in this half-lit windy place then turned back to the shadows.

Nicholas threw himself in front of a train and left a suicide note. I am told it implicates Kenja. I have not seen it but trust the source of this information.

One legacy of Nicholas stands in contrast: the articles he wrote in faith and misplaced hope; his love and humanity are in his words. So is the futility of his years with the master. And perhaps his death lies hidden there too.

Nicholas said he was tormented most of all by one single thought: perhaps Ken was right and, in some kind of spiritual judgment, the value of his desire to expose Ken will be found wanting by the power of Ken's spiritual quest.

In the saddest footnote, Nicholas, in his letters to Stephen Mutch, used the Christian name of Ken's son and Ken's middle name, Emmanuel, as his *nom de plume*.

chapter 15

On Justice

Bev had attended Vittorio's and my wedding, and laughed and toasted us. She was an early letter writer. I hadn't known that she was a nurse or that she had kept a diary of her time in Kenja. Nor did I know, after our dalliance with proper frocks, that she loved nothing more than to toss her shoes and go barefoot. I did know to never underestimate an ex-Kenjan. Bev was one of the few who went public, and whom Stephen had quoted in his second parliamentary speech. Kenja does not deal gently with its critics and declared that she had stolen from Kenja.

Channel Nine took up the exposure of Kenja. Bev and I were interviewed for *A Current Affair*. During the taping Jan and Ken, and Bev and I, were interviewed by Michael Willessee in separate studios.

The editing process deleted most of the confrontation. Jan queried my comments regarding my financial state in Kenja by asking what happened to the $12,000 dollars I received from the sale of my Brunswick house? How did they know that? I hadn't told anyone.

By the time the subject of taxation arose, Jan and Ken had taken over the interview. I responded defiantly to their comment that I cheated the Taxman. Indeed I had, and I had informed the Taxation Department.

Jan claimed they had asked me to leave because they could not help me. Not true, but as for not helping me ...

When Jan informed me that Nina had benefited wonderfully from their session together, my fear crumbled. Not according to Nina!

At that moment I knew freedom.

I listened to them, so smug and self-righteous and, without thinking, coldly spat out the words: I was naked in sessions and Ken had masturbated me in one.

Women had made allegations of sexual abuse by Ken to me. The stories were the same. In the name of our Excalibur, they went like this: Ken asked women having private sessions with him about sex; perhaps they had problems? The way through was to experience whatever obstructed one's pleasure. So suck his dick. For your benefit, said our man with the bruised eyes.

Bev had witnessed his sexually aggressive behaviour and said so. Ken tried to find a place in her mind he still occupied by demanding answers to his questions; however, Bev fought back and maintained her integrity.

Pandora's box had opened.

The program that was aired featured sexual abuse. I was indignant. Of all the allegations against Ken, they had to pick on that. Why didn't they highlight the mind control agenda, because that allowed for everything else.

⌒৹

Several women contacted Channel Nine and another program was aired in which these women, heavily disguised, related their experience of sexual abuse by Ken. They were offended and had been hurt by their experience. The response to Ken's sexual activity is not black and white. Some accepted it on the basis of being a consenting adult. Not all women saw it as a betrayal of trust. I heard of ex-Kenjan women who found it hard to believe; Ken had never sexually approached them.

Some ex-Kenjan girls watched this program. They confided to their mothers that Ken had sexually abused them. The mothers never doubted it, as they understood Ken could. They believed Ken had.

When the girls revealed their abuse to their families, the parents allowed them to make up their own minds. If they made their accusations public, they needed the courage of their convictions. A meeting was arranged for them with Stephen Mutch at Parliament House, Melbourne. The interview was openly tape-recorded. Stephen interviewed them and I observed. From the top of Parliament House steps as they approached us, the girls looked tiny. They walked to us in a manner I recognised; wagging it would have been better.

They had sat that day with Michael planning future happiness; it seemed touchable, a tiny reach away, when the mutilated teenagers of Kenja were brought together in hope. The sexual abuse of children in Kenja had not been raised that day. Sometimes one needs permission to speak and, in talking publicly about their abuse, these ex-Kenjan women had given that permission. I believed these younger women to be telling the shocking truth, the appalling, sad accounts of their sessions with the black magician of Kenja.

The two girls told their own stories. There was no bravado or one-upmanship. Each individual story was given equal respect. Their muted sadness, their vulnerability, their awkward laughter and pulsing hurt as the girls talked distressed me, and their openness and courage in coming forward moved me. These girls know everything, Ken and his corrupting smile had said. He had asked them in class if this is so, and they had raised their hands.

After the meeting with Stephen Mutch, the girls and I went to a solicitor. I was asked if I wanted to charge Ken. I did not. I took the view that I was a consenting adult. If I had had sex with Ken in that long-ago session – and on the balance of probability I most likely had – then I had consented. They were children at the time and, in comparison, my experience hardly mattered. After much thought, the girls had decided to go ahead in the belief that through the justice system, truth will prevail.

I could not help remembering the haunting image of another naked young woman and an old man; the look on his face and the look on hers. The man, switched on and unscrupulous, controlled a slender girl; she exhibited the same lack of conscience, and with a pride that was moving.

Ken Dyers was charged with 11 sexual offences against four girls, aged between eight and 15 at the time of the alleged offences. I heard that he ran to the local newsagents and bought up papers carrying the offending articles. (Oh, Annette, this is gossip). I thought, 'Ken, you wanted your name in lights and Kenja on the front page, and the spiritual universe has upped and helped you'.

Kenjans responded with genuine shock and disbelief. They would defend their leader. Thirty supporters stood outside the police station for two hours, as Ken was interviewed, waiting in a display of loyalty. They wrote earnest letters to editors of newspapers and magazines and placed whole-page, heartfelt, aggrieved and quite expensive advertisements in newspapers.

Kenja's enemies deserved no mercy. Others had left and some, like Bev, were declared to have stolen from Kenja and of behaving unethically. As a professional I had been praised for my love and honesty; despite ongoing sessions, my behavior had supposedly deteriorated to 'unethical'.

Ken assured his followers: 'The untrue communication about Kenja that is being bandied about will have an interesting effect on the parties involved when the honest truth about Kenja is finally revealed.' Apparently innocuous, these words have a powerful meaning to Kenjans: spiritual retribution. The enemy should be very, very afraid.

Jan expressed her feelings. She praised Kenja and expressed her absolute trust in Ken and in the path she had dedicated her life to. She referred to her opponents as: 'ravening hordes of ignorance, illiteracy, lies, hypocrisy, ego, power and corruption join in a sort of huddled little mob to spew their bile over hope and joy'. Not only that, 'the dogs of dirt' and 'the ignorant sing their stilted songs in their little black corners with eyes that droop and hide the light'.

I fumed at Jan's invective.

The Canberra directors, Marilyn and Natalie, spoke for Kenjans: '... Ken, we have seen you handle the most outrageous dishonest allegations and stand tall, still not hating or resenting your attackers, but never doubting – you inspire people not as a person on a pedestal but as a fellow traveller who displays friendship to all people as we all should to each other.'

These lovely soft words were, in themselves, not enough. Kenja vigilantly monitored criticism, their responses quick. *The Age* had to print an apology – they had abbreviated a Kenjan letter of response to criticism. A Channel Nine reporter mysteriously disappeared from the screen. Personally, I thought his foot-in-the-door technique appropriate under the circumstances. Sometimes one has to fight fire with fire.

Apparently, Ken considered taking me to court but decided against it. The sad-sack dud of a Kenjan, Annette, was now an unknown quantity.

Some of Kenja's assertions, in their defence, bordered on the whimsical. Who are the positively influenced Kenjan thousands? The nonplussed families who sat through shows? The strangers who attended Ken's lectures, never to be seen again?

A press statement by Ken in late 1993, denying guilt, claims a long campaign of vilification against his reputation and life's work by individuals – notably Stephen, Jill and me – motivated by spite and malice and in league with a criminal US organisation he likened to the Ku Klux Klan, namely the American Cult Awareness Network. He is a World War II combat veteran who had served his country and still does. Both he and his wife had experienced distress and he remained confident of his acquittal.

I confess: I was captivated by the reference to him and his wife. Are Jan and Ken married? When? Formal? Did she wear white? Did the thousands so positively influenced get an invite? I do acknowledge Jan as Ken's wife. It's just that I don't know if they *officially* tied the knot. (They didn't.)

It was many years later, when war records were released to the public, that Ken's war service details became known. Ken was in the army. His record notes, in part, that he was absent without leave, fined for leaving his sentry post and again for misconduct. The army noted he was mentally unstable; Ken's degree of disability was ten percent. I cannot harshly judge a man's response to the brutality of war. His misrepresentation of his service is another matter.

A fighting fund was established and Kenjans donated money for Ken's defence; one man contributed several hundred thousand dollars – a good guru dips sparingly into his own pocket and a good member wouldn't have it any other way. Presumably, having achieved their goal of one united Kenjan mind helped.

The old enemies – drink, drugs, imperfect pasts, miserable families and fear of a dismal future without Kenja – were propelled into the service of the new enemy: CultAware and interventions.

Families have long sought ways to extricate loved ones from cults. In some attempts, the cult member was grabbed, dragged to an anonymous venue, like a hotel room, and deprogramming attempted. Fuelled by some returning members who cried foul play, cults found the excuse to call these attempts at rescue 'kidnappings'. The divide between Kenjans and their families intensified; it is families who utilise 'kidnappers'.

Kenja found a new accord with at least one other cult, the maligned shoulder to shoulder with the maligned, and when the Children of God was subject to media scrutiny, some Kenjans wrote letters to editors in support of them. Ken even acknowledged that his 'original' data had been filched, claiming that he simply made the words of others his. This was a deft way of stilling the doubts of supporters while retaining the image of a man in charge.

Ken sold some of his real estate. I pored over these official documents, confused between the wording of lot numbers and the names of addresses I knew. I noted that some property Ken called his was jointly owned and the exclusion of his and Jan's first names in favour of their middle names, Emmanuel and Rita, were on one transaction.

Selected members were taken under Jan and Ken's wing to assist in his defence. Those not directly involved with Ken's protection also ardently defended him. Kenja was not on trial, Ken Dyers was, but in the minds of members it, and they, were.

Ken had turned the tables. Kenja is not a cult; CultAware is. He doesn't lie; his opponents, currently dramatically referred to as witch-hunters, inquisitors and fanatical religious extremists, do.

When a Kenja woman attempted to convict Stephen Mutch of sexual abuse, claiming to be 16 at the time of the alleged offence, it was shortly before an election. When asked to do this by Ken, I am told she resisted, but she did it. Her mistakes were easily caught out and the case never made it to trial. I wonder if the real pre-Kenja woman was unconsciously at work here, sabotaging her own efforts? Stephen won his pre-selection afterwards. However, the allegations impacted deeply on him. I did not doubt Stephen. Both have been damaged by this incident. If the woman, who has since left Kenja and clawed her way back to a tenuous emotional equilibrium and new life, speaks out she believes she risks her career. He has since completed a doctoral thesis on cults, was for a time patron of CIFS, Cult Information and Family Support (CIFS is not, as Kenja insists, the reincarnation of CultAware) and continued to call for an enquiry into cults.

∽

The mothers of the four girls alleging sexual abuse by Ken, and I, decided not to meet or speak – as that could be misconstrued or used against us and interfere with the court case – as did Stephen and I. I fell back into a degree of loneliness except for the quiet presence of Mum.

She was always there: knitting, pottering, chirping into a few shaky musical notes before clearing her throat. When the police interviewed me at home in Mornington out came Mum's cups of tea. As we sat in her kitchen, she clattered her dishes and, aiming at discretion said, 'Don't mind me.' Mum would have attended court with me had her body allowed. 'If I wasn't so old and have to look after the animals.'

A subpoena arrived from Ken's solicitors requesting a list of items. All I had to do was say that nothing existed. I couldn't. I wrote to the court saying I couldn't hand over my diary. In the end I did surrender it as Ken's legal team assured me that any statements in my diary couldn't be used or disclosed for purposes other than the defence of their client. Ken's last remaining hidden command had bitten deeply: be honest and good in the service of Kenja. I don't regret my diary, but I am sorry I gave Ken access to CultAware personnel.

I learnt later that Louise Samways successfully challenged a subpoena demanding she produce records with details of my counselling sessions with her. In one, I had spoken of my guilt at liking those long ago 'games' with Brian. She had protected my privacy. Details of my other appointments with her would have demonstrated my damaged state.

I write here of my experience of the committal hearing and trials, not the long, intricate procedures. For most of the time I was not involved. I was essentially a bystander and definitely not, as Kenja proclaimed, a feature witness.

Approaching the Sydney courthouse, I was rendered incredulous. Not you, I thought, as I glimpsed an ex-Melbourne Kenjan grasping his walkie-talkie. I had hoped he had left Kenja but there he was, callously eyeing me and diligently reporting on my progress. The next walkie-talkie aficionado was geared up and waiting. I farcically progressed up the stairs and into the foyer. I sought refuge in a café and there they were, Kenjans en masse. I refused to budge so we all sat there, sipping and nibbling, eyes right.

Although the courtroom was crowded, it was strangely quiet. Ken's defence was outlined: Stephen and I were bitter, malicious liars who had connived, fabricated evidence and encouraged the girls to lie. The whole thing was a vicious plot and a waste of taxpayer's money. Ken was committed to trial.

My memory was tested, and found wanting. In my diary I had written the words 'new tactics' minus the context, in the belief that I would easily recall it. They were pounced on in court and I couldn't explain them. Later, I recalled the context. They referred to a concerted attack on CultAware by Scientology, and new tactics were needed to counter this.

Another diary extract Ken's solicitors targeted was: 'Me to be careful – so not accused of eliciting confessions from kids'. It would be many years before I discovered that they had omitted my words that immediately followed. 'Kids to only tell truth, what they remember.'

At one stage, as I stood in the witness stand, seated Kenjans looked unblinking at me as in processing sessions. It was intimidation, designed to return me to my Kenjan mindset and reactivate my Kenjan allegiance. I complained; their behaviour stopped. I was followed wherever I went, including to my hotel, and twice registered a complaint to the police. The monitoring continued. I was advised not to complain again; continued objection might be interpreted as 'out to get' Kenja and strengthen Ken's defence of 'victim'.

I hoped that those involved in the defence of Ken might, under pressure, blurt out the truth. They didn't. They did do Ken proud, displaying a memory many might envy. One Kenjan woman insisted that she was with one girl at the time of an alleged offence. The prosecution gave proof that this was impossible. The building she claimed to be in at the time had long before been demolished. She simply insisted and I had to admire her faith; a spirit, as everyone knows, can be anywhere, at any time – with or without the building.

Ken sat in court, scornful and unrepentant; his absence of remorse and his lack of interest in proceedings was remarkable. It was noted. During the lunchbreak in a wide, crowded city street Ken and I passed each other. He noticed me and weaved away to the far side of the footpath. No scorn, no whirling, howling dancer, just an old man, his face averted. When proceedings resumed, that brief image was nowhere to be found.

It had taken three long years before the case was heard. Ken was found not guilty of three of the 11 charges, with the Crown having to decide whether to prosecute on the remaining eight charges. Ken's solicitors insisted they would ask the prosecution to drop the matter. Ken remained on $50,000 bail, preventing him from being alone with children.

New trials took place. This time the cases were heard separately. Processing was described, by a Kenjan, as Buddhist eye-gazing, whereby emotions gently effervesced and came up. This explanation was no relation at all to the aggressive nature of sessions I, and this convert, had experienced.

That Ken had supporters in the general community was noted, as was his clean record. When I was a member, Ken had frequently referred to 'friends of Kenja'. Some of these 'friends' took classes attended by and limited to Kenjans, such as dancing and gymnastics, and thought highly of Ken. There was also some former Kenjans with respected positions in the community who had been cultivated as 'friends of Kenja'. I did slyly wonder how hard it might be to find 'friends' when necessary. And perhaps Ken really did have friends outside of Kenja?

By the time I was called to Sydney to give evidence, Ken had been found guilty of one charge but had not been sentenced. Since then a new judge had been appointed. Informed, by the prosecution of subject matter I could not mention in court, I stood dumbfounded. Any evidence I had hoped to give was restricted due to legal reasoning that I didn't understand. As far as I was concerned, I was left with saying what a charming fellow Ken is.

I waited, seated, outside the courtroom, deliberately doing crosswords next to assembled Kenjans. Ken looked at me through the open doors of the courtroom and, shortly after, the prosecutor informed me I would not be called.

Ken was sentenced to 12 months imprisonment for the one charge he had been found guilty of – assault, an act of indecency – with a non-parole period of four months. Ken had touched the girl's breasts while she was semi-naked in session with him, he had kissed her, pulled her towards him, and asked her to take off the rest of her clothing; she refused to. He spent six days in jail. It was not the end, an appeal failed and a High Court Appeal, based on a technicality, followed.

In 2002, approximately nine years after he was first charged, the High Court delivered its verdict on Ken Dyers. Three of the five High Court judges upheld the appeal. They set aside the order of the Criminal Court of New South Wales made on 25 August 2000 and 'in lieu thereof' ordered that the appeal be allowed and the conviction be quashed. A new trial was to be had; however, no new trial eventuated.

Ken always maintained that he would be found innocent. He claimed exoneration. He pushed the envelope but I have to give it to him: his methods worked for him. His means justified his ends.

Kenja continued to maintain the indignant stance that Ken was found guilty of kissing a girl.

⁓

Ex-Kenjans had clung together for so long but the trial saw us falling away from each other. We needed to find that which we had sought, and in fact lost, in Kenja, that Ken had initially promised us: time, space and energy.

The last time Alex and I had spoken his voice was ragged and I had no need to see his face. He had seen Jan outside his flat. This man with the wispy smile, untethered between mindworlds, would soon leave Sydney. When he did, I received a letter saying goodbye. I never saw nor heard from Alex again.

Bev and I had talked, timidly sipped wine together, guffawed at Jan's description of Ken's penis as a golden shaft, shared our painful healing and yet, the time to let go neared.

Marcia and I met up. Our conversations unsettled me; my head clamped tight. She held fears for the wellbeing of some then-current Kenja girls and other girls who had left were also mentioned. Guilt enveloped me; I seemed unable to cope emotionally with the alleged sexual abuse of Kenja's children. In the face of their heartbreak, I had come to feel nothing. After one afternoon spent together I went home; that laden conversation was our last. It was Marcia who told me that Nicholas had committed suicide. For weeks I left telephone messages for Marcia and went to her place. She had disappeared. I glimpsed her in a shopping centre, years later, and was confused. Was it her? While I hesitated, she moved away.

In the end our experience provided few bonds. Perhaps what had united us was so painful it painted all else? It reflects the reality of our time in Kenja; unity was an illusion. Ken said that we travelled in the same direction like a train, but on separate tracks. This resulted in a lot of individuals who have difficulty working as a team. In finding ourselves again, there were few links to grasp. There was little to talk about other than the Kenja we wanted to leave behind.

Wendy and I stayed in touch, as did Jill, Ian and I. Even though Jill and Ian had pursued a gentler path, refused public involvement and, every birthday and Christmas, sent Helena a card, they eventually faced the glaring fact that Helena seemed further from them than ever. When Ian died, Helena attended her father's funeral flanked by two Kenjans; contact between Helena and Jill minimal. Helena's younger sister married and had children and neither birth nor death, landmarks in our ordinary lives, penetrated that blurred trace, the missing Helena. Helena's sister lived in a cream house with a disused barn, where a child's giggle ran across the grass. Here, Jill and her other daughter put Helena aside, accepted a living death and waited. When Helena passed the age of childbearing, Jill lamented her abandoned fertility. Helena, who grieved so abjectly for her older sister, remained impervious to her younger sister's mourning for her.

Helena stayed in her manacled world guided by the cryptic dreams of an aging man. Would Helena leave, and what would it take? Something emotionally cataclysmic, or perhaps a thing so light, an unnoticed presence that, in her sequestered mind, would gather strength and pour out like milk?

⁓

One, who left Kenja after the trials, came forward and admitted to lying in court. I asked a woman involved in the prosecution case if the authenticity of Ken's diaries had been verified. Perhaps they could have sought a handwriting expert, she said. I asked if Ken's war record had been checked. The answer was no.

On reclaiming my own documents from the courts, I found some were missing. They included my diary. They were located, still in the possession of Ken's solicitor. These were returned along with four photocopied, black appointment diaries I recognised as Ken's. Phony and fake, they screamed to my untrained mind. Blank pages, or at least blank on one side as the markings on the flip side were clearly visible, appeared to be photocopied and re-used. This was all too late and wouldn't have helped, I was told. They were given to the police. Returning them to Ken hardly seemed a good idea.

And as for my diary ... there were my words, 'Kids to only tell truth, what they remember,' the missing part of that ill-used quote. I didn't know whether to laugh or to cry.

⁓

Marilyn's Canberra co-director, Natalie, has since left. Kenja's cook, Lillian's, status is uncertain. She is no longer a signatory to Kenja's continuing full-page newspaper advertisements. Jill's daughter, Helena, has left. Nadine, Kathryn, Brian, Claudia and Evan (2010) still carry the burdens imposed by the organisation.

The last time I saw once familiar Kenjans was outside the Sydney courtroom; when my testimony had been judged needless.

As I did the crosswords, small groups hurried past me to Jan waiting nearby. They sat and stood and huddled and roamed, their demeanours rising to smiley when approached, and falling to crestfallen for the rest of time. My eyes strayed to the group clumped together, some wearing dark colours – even black. State publicly that many have short hair and don't wear black; you can bet they will be seen with long hair and in black.

In the earlier trial, the young and lovely Kenjans gathered adoringly around Ken. This time, middle-aged women with pinched, obsessed bodies and quick steps cast furtive glances in my direction. I sat torn between anger, sadness and frustration.

Why don't you all miss a session and buy a hat instead? A Melbourne Cup hat with layers of tulle and massed satin ribbons or, maybe, Jan, a feather boa wound seductively round your head.

Sometime, somewhere, in the brief annals of Kenja, a wave had been made. A long and wide wave of assorted blue fabric stitched together that became grubby and frayed over the years. It was large enough to cover an entire stage and was held by black-clad stagehands hiding in the wings, flapping and billowing away, while a makeshift drum beat the crack of a thunderstorm. In our tableaux the nymphets stood centred in the storm. The black-clad stagehands wringing and shaking were men and older women.

When I first became involved in Kenja I was one of the very few older women – at 40 years of age. By the time I left, there was a troop of them. They remind me of the wombat in Ivan Smith and Clifton Pugh's book, *The Death of a Wombat*. Fleeing from the fire, kangaroos leap, snakes slither and birds rise high but the wombat can only 'waddle and crump'.

Nadine was not in court that day. I never saw her again, except in a photo taken at a Kenja function; she wears a satin gown, her body has swelled and lumped but, in her smile, hope incongruously survives.

Outside the courtroom, Kathryn studiously avoided me. She had the same slim body and quick movements of a grasshopper. She seemed to have osmosed only Ken's limitations. Her life's time is passing, she had sketches of grey in her curly hair and apparently still lives in deference to that long ago quickie.

I want the real Nadine and Kathryn to rise from the ashes like the fabled phoenix. I caught myself uselessly thinking, 'Oh, come on, look at logic will you? Leave!' Their minds are masked in serge and tied with the brightest, prettiest, satin bows.

Vanessa was there … or at least the grown-up body of Vanessa was. I stared in alarm at a bizarrely buckled shape hidden between two women who seemed to be half-carrying her. I saw a caricature, a travesty of a young woman. Hair styled in a rigid version of the perfect little girl, circa 1950, wearing an old-fashioned skirt and practical shoes, her eyes never left the floor and her lips never stopped moving.

Vanessa remains a Kenjan and would strenuously deny the fears I have about her relationship with Ken. She would be thanking Ken as her source of all wisdom.

☙

I still see the young girls of Kenja, the many junior and teenage professionals – those who, as adults, remain committed Kenjans and those who have left – trying their hardest, proud of being eulogised by Ken and acclaimed by the converted.

I believed I had failed the girls whose allegations had led to the trials and should have advised them against taking Ken on, warned them that justice is not easily upheld against those with no respect for it. The Kenjan battle cry was 'what can you confront?' They had so courageously confronted him.

I recall the stories of their alleged sexual abuse by Ken, and his justification, to them, for his actions: he was helping them.

I also recall the words of an ex-Kenjan:

'Remember Shelley?' she asked me. 'And her daughter who had loved Ken and Kenja?'

Shelley and the child who was her fair-haired double jumped to my mind.

'Her daughter drew pictures of men on top of children and had taken to defecating in the corner. I told them that that sounded like the behaviour of a sexually abused child. Maybe it was someone else she drew the pictures of … oh no.'

I cannot forget my deep dread, a response that Kenjan Annette ruthlessly suppressed, watching Vanessa naked with Ken, and I remember the little girl Vanessa who first stood on the dais in Kenja, christened the love goddess. I want to go back in time and acknowledge that cry for release, the creased dress I insisted she iron.

Those at the top, Ken said, paid the highest price.

⌒⌒

The trial was also the last time I saw Jan. She wanted the 'ja' in Kenja and now lives with all that entails. Jan stood behind Ken, loving him, believing in him and fighting for him. Without her, I suspect he could not have set up Kenja. I believe that his flaunted independence was, at times, unstable and that he hid his fear of dependence behind rip-roaring anger. Jan gave Ken the balls he needed to maintain his control over Kenja, and the control he had over her.

Despite my difficulties in relating to Jan when I was a Kenjan, since leaving I have grown to feel for the woman whose mission it was to lead her Kenjans towards a new world order; that if she can do it, then anyone can. Since meeting Ken, she has wholeheartedly devoted her life to pursuing and upholding Kenja's ideals. I describe her now in sorrow, not anger.

Because concerts have been so important in my life, I cannot attend one without recalling Jan and her her spiralling enthusiasm and luckless striving. She determined we match that *tour de force*, a disciplined orchestra. She reminds me of a little drummer girl blowing party whistles that, with each puff, furl and unfurl with a long and ardent squawk.

I wish Gladys, Jan's scaredy-cat, blue-belted karate clown, had climbed Kenja's impossible mountain instead of Jan. Gladys would have failed at the first hurdle and we'd all have a cup of tea instead.

Jan wanted relevance; she has not achieved it nor can she lay claim to notoriety. She is largely overlooked. There will not be a world based on the vision of Gladys the clown, with her aspiring and second-hand clothes – or even that of Jan. She lived in a world of ambition, duplicity and ignorant transmuting faith seen through an imprecise prism of love, faith and hope, for a time kept in check by her karate-kicking clown.

Jan's catch-cry was 'what can you confront?' The flawed sidekick, whose dream of being a star, found a limited truth. She can stand against the hordes waving her banner – the heroine in her own spectacular.

She can confront, on her own terms, that she can mess things up.

She cannot confront that she was a victim, swept off her feet in love, beguiled by the prospect of power, unable to question the chance of a scam or to sift through the fluff and dazzle Ken offered and realistically assess the really, really slim chance Kenja stood of achieving celebrity status. Instead, when the ideals decomposed and the shit hit the fan, Jan splashed second-hand scent.

In a way her betrayal beats that of Ken. He was openly a bastard. Jan smiled and said she was one of us.

Ken said if you can't stand the heat then stay out of the kitchen. Degree by degree, little by little it got hotter and hotter, and she lived up to her word and stood in the fire.

chapter 16

Bliss and Ignorance

Kenja faded from cognition; weeks and months went by without my giving it a single thought. The years passed. Life became my husband, children, grandchildren, our closeness, sharing Melbourne's café culture with friends and my neighbourhood walks along tree-lined streets.

Then one day there they were, looming large, and associated with another tragedy. Cornelia Rau was an ex-Kenjan who had been kicked out. In 2005, her detention by the Australian Government in the Baxter Detention Centre as an apparently illegal immigrant made media headlines. Claims of her deterioration in Kenja were raised as contributing to the incidents that led to her situation. Cornelia's story is not for my telling, nor is that of Richard Leape, a young man who disappeared after leaving Kenja. His sister found him rambling out loud outside Kenja's offices; Richard agreed to accompany her but fled from her car when she reached to touch him and he has not been seen since. My knowledge of these stories comes from the media.

No sooner had the dust settled when, once again, there was Kenja, upfront and uncomfortable. In late 2005, Ken was charged with the sexual assault of another two ex-Kenjan girls who were 12 at the time of the alleged offences. He was committed for trial. Publicity flared, mostly in Kenja's home state of New South Wales. This time, a smaller group of followers prepared to defend him. Ken's solicitors got vocal and Ken was granted a temporary stay of proceedings for 12 months on the grounds of his mental health. He claimed a continuing witch-hunt and protested his innocence.

My interest waned; there is, after all, life after Kenja. I drew a large black line under the year 2005.

I had watched a charged-up, kohl-eyed predator ascendant and had, for a time, been engrossed. The Ken I knew was a complex man. Although my experience of him was problematic, I recall times when he showed real compassion for me, as in that traumatic session with Paddy. Hindsight has not altered this perception.

Ken had told us to ride our own tigers. He lived with the hidden tail of his tiger: his followers. Which of his caged souls would understand their entrapment and leave Kenja? What would they do next? The story of Kenja continues, as do the stories of Kenja's survivors. If not for other ex-Kenjans, Kenja might have had its prayers answered by the spiritual universe and the exposure collapsed with the conclusion of the earlier trials.

Protected by his Kenjans, and I believe, dependent on the internalisation of his justifications for his actions, this man with his ravenous, rampaging psyche fought on.

His Kenjan warriors rose to climb another mountain, another level, and to knock off another nemesis. Then Ken and Jan sensed a reprieve in the making: their participation in the documentary, *Beyond Our Ken*, by Luke Walker and Melissa McLean. Luke had been involved in Kenja Melbourne for six months. Jan and Ken gave them considerable access to enable the 'honest truth about Kenja to be revealed'.

The filmmakers made a powerful documentary. They went to some lengths to give Kenja's side of the story, alongside that of ex-members, myself included, the independent cult expert and Uniting Church minister David Millikan, and the psychologist Louise Samways. Two scenes, towards the end of the documentary, grabbed the public's attention. In one, Ken is filmed eyeing a young Kenjan woman up and down. This image of a sleazy Ken shocked. While bound in Ken's attention the young woman, a long-term member, accepts and understands his lasciviousness: it is for demonstration purposes only. But as she glances at the camera, confusion is evident. Her confusion is the line between what is her life and the norms of society. With her considerable experience of mind control she has the least ability to understand it, but other standards can and do reach and affect her. She is quite lovely. She is compromised. She is the trapped future of Kenja.

Ken is shown, in the final scenes, to explode. The violent outburst was so familiar that it no longer shocked. But it disturbed me; I couldn't work out why. At first I thought it might reinforce the stereotype of idiot members who can't see through him.

Ken talked about the difference between awareness and consciousness and I think, now, I understand what he meant. Imagine a television set. It is switched on. Without warning it is switched off but the power source is still on. The television is switched back on and normal programming resumes. In this switched-off state that I have experienced, post-Kenja, and have no conscious control over, I am aware of nothing, not my body or its breathing, but I am aware of the silent passing of time. I interpret this as a level of dissociation and can relate this to being aware of being aware: to Ken's difference between awareness and consciousness.

In his switching off and rambling in class, his experience of separating from his body, his fear of having Alzheimer's, his capacity to be in the here and now to the exclusion of all else ... and I wonder if the dots do connect, that on one level he and I are alike? Dissociated.

That was it: there but for the grace of God ...

Melissa and Luke had initially been ambivalent and could see merit in Kenja, but that changed. Ken knew it. His explosion was beyond rage; it was a kind of grief. In practically every lecture I heard Ken give he spoke of a small boy overwhelmed by his father's anger. I sometimes speculated if he was that little boy. In his regret at what he had committed to film, he tried to explain it; he seems detached from the driven cult leader he became. I sense the boy, the humanity he had no longer any conscious means of communicating with.

Nothing takes away from the immense damage Ken wreaked in the lives of others, his betrayal of individuals hopes and dreams, his verbal and emotional manipulation of Kenjans, the allegations of his sexual abuse of women and children and his lack of respect and compassion for the human mind; that his personal understanding was superior to that of others devoted to recognised scientific endeavour. Nor does his apparent lack of empathy justify his attitudes and actions. He knew to hide them.

Ken's Kenjans all dived with him into the abyss of personal responsibility for the failure of Kenja to rise to its potential, and protested against the world outside that does not understand. Ken, and not the world at large, failed Kenja. In their blindness, his Kenjans were doomed to also fail Ken.

I had sometimes tried to elicit the positives from my experience, and I finally have. I think it is called compassion.

❧

In July 2007, 25 years after I met Ken, he committed suicide. He was 85 years old. He shot himself in the head. The latest allegations of sexual abuse would remain unresolved. Ken had been informed that yet another young woman had come forward alleging sexual abuse when she was a Kenjan. The following day he was dead. He did not live to see the screening of the documentary, which notes the latest allegations. His suicide provided it with a dramatic footnote. It is widely interpreted as an admission of guilt. If it was also anything else, we will never know. I recalled Ken's bitter words to Michael's brother, Max: that he would commit suicide rather than go to jail.

Jan assigned his death to the witch-hunt Ken endured, leaving him too weak to handle yet another continuing and ferocious attack on him.

His supporters, depleted in numbers but ardently loyal, placed rows of death notices in obituary columns, an indication, surely, of his influence and, yes, it surely is. A press statement defended him with their personalised version of the facts, and whole-page advertisements reiterated them. The ads featured a photo of him and I could see it in the photo, like the portrait of Dorian Grey, Ken's deeds had to go somewhere and they were all over him.

Kenja's web site invited accolades and the same taut, compacted people filled pages and further homage was encouraged. A disclaimer warned that only nice comments would be printed – they had, at least, a toehold on reality.

I didn't attend his funeral, or watch from a distance. Kenja displayed photographs of Ken's funeral and tributes to him on their web pages.

In a marquee in a Sydney park, they met to celebrate his life. People gathered together, those from Kenja festooned with aqua and orange shawls, in that rambling, otherwise almost empty park. They listened to the call of bagpipes, watched a performance of the Maori Haka, paid homage to his still-vaunted wartime exploits, represented by medals positioned perkily on a pillow. Doves were released to a brilliant blue sky, that same sky was adorned by the surreally fluffing and dissipating words, 'Ken'. Ken's coffin sat draped in the Australian flag; reverence nurtured grief. At night a tribute in mammoth illuminated letters strung along the harbour, glimmered and reflected across the water.

For 25 years Kenjans had clustered together for this or that event that could be interpreted, within its ranks, as momentous. It was, for them, the final act of their leader, the man who once proclaimed that, on his death, a thousand lights would illuminate the night sky.

Jan, the surviving enlightened spirit of Kenja, would later call passionately for the media or the police, or someone, to study the reality of Kenja. And I, who should know better, wondered where has she been all this time? Now, as Jan Dyers, she continues her involvement with Kenja and to glorify Ken.

Days after Ken committed suicide, Michael's brother Max stood in a funeral parlour. He transported bodies and had been assigned to this job. He wondered if it was Ken? It was. He stood looking at the body of an old man whose matted face defied description. Standing there his emotion ebbed to a depth of sadness, a cry for the whole sorry saga of Kenja.

He went home to his family to wonder at the turns of fate; the paths of his brother, Michael, his surviving brother who had grieved with him, and his green-eyed mother Wendy.

Ken was cremated at the same cemetery as Michael and, following the gala celebrations, was remembered in the same chapel. Wendy had put aside her fears, that lingering mixed bag, and on the day of Ken's funeral visited Michael's grave. With heart full of Michael she walked across the open space of the park and, at a quiet distance, sat looking at Kenja's memorial marquee. She turned to see Ken's hearse slowly mowing its way through the grass directly approaching her and sat, bemused, amazed, unable and unwilling to move.

Not that I was totally alone, mused Wendy later: an ex-Kenjan wandered over, the furtiveness of the past long gone, taking this last opportunity to dally and linger near the remnants of our collective and dissipating past. 'Have you come to pay your respects?'

'Disrespects!' said Wendy, and went home.

༄

Kenja's stoic warriors have had no time for hiding, no reprieve, no new beginning and, perhaps, no time for their grieving. They are trapped on Kenja's mythical mountain in a never-ending blizzard. They continue to wave flags, rally to the cause, galvanise their hearts and minds, and are willing to chop off arms and shed blood.

They must be terribly tired by now.

༄

One quiet night I awoke from the following dream:

The timber walls of my grandmother's house were limpid and shrouded, rows of purple tessellated roof tiles, glimmered through fog. My mother inherited that house and refused to enter it but each week she watered the garden and mowed the grass. When my mother died the house became mine. Terror dwelt behind that door and I dreaded opening it. Visions of rats and an unspeakable stench hid behind transparent, swaying images and my hand hesitated before opening that once familiar door. It opened lightly and easily. Light filtered through that haunting hallway and my dead grandmother's life lay covered in dust.

༄

This prompted me to write to my long-dead nana:

My dearest floral Nana,

Here we are, Nan, so many years later.

In your last letter to Mum, you hoped I might find Him. I did. Nan, you would have recognised him as a false prophet and definitely ungodly.

In one of the photos that Mum gave me, you are old and I am not yet two; we are in your front garden and you hold me, leaning back slightly, showing me off. I look at it often. Who was to know what a bond we would have?

We did the worst, didn't we, we left our children – don't gods say something about forsaking others? In the absence of memory, my guilt was so profound it distorted the facts to the extent that I came to think that I had left when Stefan was 11 and Nina 13 and had been away for the entire ten years, and it took me years to look past my feelings, confusion and memory loss, at the facts. Guilt can twist. Unlike you, I never thought of death. My time in Kenja had, after all, been all about life.

And my children now … they are indeed amazing. You should read the letters that Nina and Stefan wrote to Stephen Mutch. Nina said that if she had known I was in a cult, she would have tried to get me out. Stefan wrote that I had been a wonderful mother, until I met Ken. Stefan's wild-haired Jacqui was angry at the impact Kenja had on him and his family and Mum's short note was right to the point. I didn't re-read mine for years and, when I did, it concerned me. I had written that I had been raped. Why? I had to concede that, for a time, I must have given it some credence. And then Nan, guess what, I forgot all about it.

Stefan has long been content with Jacqui, who came from New Zealand to study and found love in a fast-food outlet, and with her sons from a previous relationship they have grown together. It took Nina longer for another Kiwi to bob up in front of her when she least expected it. I am so proud of them. They are decent, responsible, caring and plain nice people.

I desperately wanted to show Nina and Stefan how much I loved them and one day I knew how; I would make them quilts. Each has hundreds of hand-stitched diamonds and hexagons. They were shown in the annual Loch quilt show in which quilts flapped in the breeze in Loch's tiny main street. Nina, Jacqui, my grandchildren and Farida and I ate a picnic lunch and bobbed up and down between the quilts. How lovely is that.

Making quilts is not unlike creating minds, Nan, the possibilities are many and harmony is paramount.

Do I need to tell you about Mum? I think of you as having x-ray vision or second sight, and you know how our saga has unfolded. Many times I told you to switch your hearing aid on so you could hear me. Of all the people I talk to in my mind, deafness aside, you are my best listener.

Mum became a symbol of hope to some parents whose children were in Kenja. She was the mother who had loved and waited and her wait had been rewarded. She had a humbleness that was truly touching. Mum always thought she was one of the lucky people in life. We never did stop our bickering and bantering. As Allie, Mum's dog, and I circled the park once, she yelled to Allie.

'Here, girl.'

Allie kept romping along after me.

When we met up Mum said disconsolately, 'The dog prefers you.'

'The dog is going deaf.'

Mum looked at me and I shut up.

Her spirit remained indomitable; her body was failing. Watching her struggle to control her bowels in the car was heartrending.

My life expanded; Mum's contracted.

'I wish I could see Nina settled ... you home from Italy ... Jacqui and Stefan married ...'

Jacqui and Stefan wed in a rotunda on a grey day with bitter wind that has always, to me, augured well. In one wedding photo we stand, my small family and I, in a straight line on the beach. Jacqui, proudly pregnant, Nina, Mum and I with our high heels that have sunk in sand, stand wind-whipped, our toes pointed up like elves.

When Mum learnt Jacqui and Stefan were expecting a second child, she determined to greet this baby. She was 87, with barely three months to love this tiny boy. With this birth, reasons for living failed.

The last time Mum sat at our table she held our new baby on her knee. She was afraid and held him tentatively. Her heart, body and mind smiled at the last of her progeny, one of the last sighs of memory handed on.

Mum had cancer. I moved back into my Mornington bedroom and we enjoyed some weeks of my exclamations and her headshaking. She was frightened. I pleaded with her to swallow her medication. Mum shut her mouth tight and shrank. A few days before she died she went to her bed. She wrestled against the indignity of losing control and Vittorio carried her to the toilet. I cried for this pride, the integrity of her body. Then Mum lay in her bed on her side, one hand between her legs, snuggling to death.

We were all there, her once fragmented family. One great-grandchild lay next to her overnight as she had often done, the other played on the bed. 'Is that alright?' an anxious Jacqui asked. A wave of Mum's hand indicated to change nothing.

In time it was Mum and I, as it had been when we were one. In these last hours the unfolding of love continued. I told her that I wished I had been a better daughter, how I had always loved her; she asked me to hold her hand. It was the first time Mum had ever asked. Her hand was still and soft, unlike her draining body that was always stiff when hugged.

I sang to Mum, and for as long as she could, she responded, until all that was left was a hint of a smile, then silence and a frail line of breath. Suspended in time, we lay together. Before she died she uttered a small cry; or maybe, for Mum, it was a very big one.

In a photo of you, Millie and Mum, you stand between your daughters, one of your arms circles Mum's waist, the other circles Millie's. Their arms enclose you and perhaps they touch behind your back. You all wear floral dresses.

In my absence, Mum had scoured the phone book ringing every entry listed under her sister, Millie's, surname. A stranger always answered. Their meetings would have been taboo. And yet, just once …

My return was almost too late for Mum. It was years after her death that I learnt of her sequel: news of Millie.

It is news of the crying kind.

I met a couple whose daughter, would you believe, was a Kenjan. They considered an intervention and had been given my name. I refused to be involved. If at some crucial point I went blank and couldn't find the required argument or information, then poof to their chances. Although I could explain the belief system, the manipulation and background of Jan and Ken, I could not tell them who their daughter was living and eating with, and that is what they needed, a face and a name – facts for the heart.

We got chatting; that's when their involvement with the Exclusive Brethren (they had left) arose. The lady remembered a lovely childhood and terrifying breakdown when she and her family were kicked out. I asked if they remembered you and Grandpa. They didn't. I asked about Millie and Dan. They were in contact with one of their daughters who had left the Brethren.

It is Lexie. I remembered only three children and was reminded that Millie and Dan had six. Lexie is the fifth and, wait for it, a grandmother too. When informed that a relative wanted to see her, she thought only of her father's family. Our side didn't exist. No Gladys or John or Annette to consider; we were hidden in the family bible and out of sight, out of mind – consigned to the idolaters, murderers and etceteras.

Lexie has your long narrow face, slim legs and Millie's dark hair. You should see her sewing; she can make anything. Perfectly. Remind you of Glad-arse and Happy-bum, your dear daughter?

Do you know how many children Millie's six had? Thirty-nine. Nan, that's almost as many as there were chickens!

Oh, my dearest Nana, can you bear this, where your faith led your family?

Dan, whose unswerving belief in the Exclusive Brethren felled us all, said in frustration in his later years, that there are better

Christians outside of the Exclusive Brethren than in. Did you know he broke their rules? You did. He loved playing the drums and refused to stop. Not then. Not ever. He gave up everything but not his music. Oh, Nan, that's why he was so guarded in his shed! He kept his drums in there. His peers may not have known of his secret sin but surely the rest of the neighbourhood, to say nothing of the chickens, did.

Lexie was destined to be a wife and mother and rear children continually from the age of sixteen. At the time she was kicked out, she had never written out a cheque or used a petrol pump. She told of one woman who had given birth to eight thalidomide children because termination is banned by the Brethren. Her ninth pregnancy was borne through tears and worrying that the child would be normal, and it was.

After Lexie had been put out of the Exclusive Brethren her bonds with her far-flung siblings stayed strong. One nearby sister detoured to secret lunches with her. Until recently. The Brethren were highlighted with unwanted publicity due to their active interest in political influence, despite the fact that they do not vote. They tightened up. Lexie's sister could no longer find excuses to explain her absences and the furtive and excited lunches ceased.

We visited that old Springvale house. The walls looked as thin as the canvas they had replaced. If houses have hearts, this one must smile at fate; it now forms part of a religious complex.

Lexie remembered playing hide and seek with Noah. The pine trees survive, rammed against concrete due to road-widening, and she reminisced about climbing them, of running in and out the back door to a quietness long gone. We stood, transfixed by the past, aware of the marring of the moment as we shouted to each other over the thundering of trucks.

Lexie taught me to recognise Exclusive Brethren women. While shopping one day we spied two with a pram inside a baby's shop. We tiptoed in, pretend-sampling bonnets and booties. I cast snooty glances at what now passes for head covering – a flower, a ribbon – until Lexie told me that head covering represents a token for angels. I imagined chubby seraphim whispering to God, pointing at women signposted by ribbons. Then Lexie realised they had recognised her. Out we darted and walked slap bang into another Brethren woman. Oh, Lexie worried, now they will go and tell everyone I wear lipstick.

She hears news of the Exclusive Brethren: that alcohol abuse is widespread, as is sex before marriage; her shock at them running around with mobiles stuck to their ears makes me smile.

The ties that bind go deep; it took years for her to understand and find her own path, and she has. We are both a bit of you, Nan: nice, and as stubborn as mules.

Noah makes me cry.

Lexie tells me he disapproves of his community that is reduced to a brittle containment that mocks its own rules. His life has held great personal tragedy. He cannot contemplate leaving. Noah decided to set an example to his peers and be the upright, God-fearing and respectful man he was brought up to be.

One day, on a rare excursion from his diminished community, Noah found himself face to face with Lexie, who was patently not of the dogs and whoremongers. Noah was shocked; his sister untainted. Lexie had grown quiet and proud.

Noah and I are nearly the same age; his memory is failing yet his recall of the Bible remains prodigious. It is his harmonic mindset, his sanity and it has been well guarded. Noah will, in all probability, never make the journey across mindworlds. If he does, his son who has escaped and Lexie, her children and grandchildren will hold his hand.

When Lexie left the Exclusive Brethren, Millie and Dan were still alive. On learning of Millie's ill health, Lexie put aside her fears and visited. It was dusk as Millie opened her front door to see, through the old wire door, the daughter she could have no contact with. Years of submission to a doctrine had squashed her pain tight and seared her heart, not to exclude love but to hold it. Lexie whispered. Millie responded by pretending she spoke to a salesman. After hurried words Millie shouted a loud thank you, and to Lexie mouthed the words: I love you.

I feel for you, for your sad, sad letters, for your pain and that you never had the chance to understand. I want you to know, in case you still ache, that you never offended beyond love or beyond forgiveness or, ultimately, beyond understanding and I know how much you loved Mum and me.

You have been far more than my role model. We have, in a sense, been one. I became you. I, unconsciously, protected myself against being hurt in the future and so I adopted the personality of someone who was too nice to attract violence: you. But sweet and kind can so limit and it is time to let go. Letting go has been hard and I have clung to remnants of you: your crochet bedspread and tablecloth and those many doilies and dressing-table sets and lace-edged serviettes and handkerchiefs and ... There is something I must do without you.

My helix had unwound.

In 1993, I was hypnotised by a psychologist who believed he could help me. He used a traditional technique, staring at a spot on a wall. In the first session I remembered sex with Ken in that confusing, long-ago Kenja session that ended with him semi-naked.

The second session with this man was painful.

In this session, as my eyes lost concentration, grey eddying mush washed through the air around me then cleared. That night I wrote:

He asked me to go back to when I was ten years old.

My voice sounded lighter.

'Where are you?' he asked.

'I'm in my living room with my mummy and daddy. I'm sitting in a chair opposite the fire. There's someone else in the room.'

'Who?'

'A friend of my daddy.'

'Who is the friend, is it a stranger?'

'No, it's a friend of my daddy.'

The thought tries to slip through, gathering shape and substance.

'It's a friend of my daddy.'

'Now you are 11 years old'

I am hysterical. My voice has the lightness of a child.

'No. No. No.'

'What's happening?'

I cannot talk. I see the picture. He has black hair, moustache and wears a bright blue jumper. I wear my cowgirl outfit. I am on the ground in my pearly, gloomy secret place and he is on top of me.

Someone help me please.

'Soon I will count backwards from twenty. When I reach five you will open your eyes, you will not be fully awake until I finish. You will feel alert. You will not remember anything. When I tell you, you will remember.'

The psychologist believed I had been raped. I remembered that session with Matt. Did I really believe? Did I want to? I didn't know. I had my unconscious solution; I returned memory to its cryptic grave. I rejected this session, and never went back.

༄

That I had something specific to accept remained incomprehensible and, if not for Jane, might have stayed that way. Jane is my doctor. She is amazing. Everything about her is compact and pensive, especially her thoughts. Her voice is soft and I listen intently to her. I had no idea, when she became my GP, that she had a special interest in dissociation.

Before I met Jane, I happened to catch a radio program in which Attention Deficit Disorder was being discussed. For most of the time, the speaker described hyper-active children then added that there are children at the other end of the spectrum suffering the disorder who are intelligent, very quiet and often overlooked. That is me! For the first time, I thought my strange state might be knowable. When I sought information, I found a lot on hyperactivity but nothing that I could relate to, and after a while I gave up.

Apart from the word, dissociated, Jane has never burdened me with labels and states of order and disorder. At first I was label-happy and slotted myself into every recognised dissociative disorder, and others – depression and bi-polar – until I realised that it was not the labels that I craved but the understanding and especially the knowledge that I was not alone. Others experienced this too.

The advantage, for me, of not being diagnosed as a child is that I was forced to reach to my concept of normality, I never had a fall-back position; there were no excuses to be found within my disadvantages. I am grateful that my memory was never pushed. I believe I was so much safer for that. Yes, the understanding that I have now would have helped Mum, Dad and me but, in 1954, this knowledge was 55 years in the future. I had the greatest advantage of all; my parent's love and constancy.

When I first tried to enlighten Nina and Stefan, they must have despaired at my excellent bewildering definition of dissociation. I had the basics right, a separation of consciousness. Now, I can do without the definitions. I'd rather be me and, on increasingly rare occasions, away with the birds.

I recalled my confusion long ago, after the second workshop in Melbourne when, in the dark of night, I heard Ken shout '42 people'. On the day that 42 people attended a workshop, I thought his prophecy had materialised. Now I understand this experience as a foiled flashback. Unable to flashback to actual hidden experience, my mind had latched onto equivalents: a dominating man and, in the case of my fear of Uncle Dan, a mistakenly scary one. I was trying to help myself. I also came to understand that the blackness that surrounded me for the first year of processing in Kenja was the journey through to my deeply hidden experience. I had waited until it was safe. Ken's son, Matt, was safe. Ken Dyers and his saturated kitchen had very slippery floors and I had instinctively heeded the warning bells.

Like my tears after Kenja, you don't want to know the ins and outs of the years it took to find understanding; nor do I remember, or want to remember, them all.

Jane understood the time was right and stepped back, with her arms open – just in case.

In one moody conversation, I astounded myself by announcing that I couldn't attribute my poor memory entirely to Kenja. Memory was not to be trusted because I remembered, in a session, being raped as a child and I hadn't been.

Jane said that regarding repressed memory there is usually something to it and the possibility exists that I have been dissociated all my life.

I rushed for information. Sentences trembled and shattered. Maybe I have been like this all my life? Maybe I have been like this since Mum 'nearly shook the living daylights' out of me in a room imbued with poo? I never took that seriously and prayed that Mum did not, although … oh, I hope not.

Flinging blankets off the bed one night, trying to lie still, sluggish movement rumbled through my head, interspersed with grotesque shudders; revulsion gripped my face contorting to sleep. I woke tense. The possibility of childhood sexual abuse was on the loose.

I remembered a penis in my mouth. This picture slipped to consciousness like a tiny, shiny, darting fish. It lasted a fraction of a second. My mind grabbed this flash of memory and took up the slack. I imagined a rape, a neat sequence of events, but this I knew to be my imagination and a waste of time except … maybe I had woken something and stirring the pot might help.

This new picture didn't slip to its place. It stuck to my forehead and I, with some levity, conceded the possibility of the man in the blue jumper raping me. Weighted, emotion like sludge, I yearned for release. Tears were abundant and alleviated nothing.

Months later, I wrote the following:

Oh … let's ramble, roam around a bit, flitter here and flutter there, what the fuck, after so many years of memory loss and confusion does a couple of pages mean? When I first left Kenja I wrote pages and pages saying I hate and I hurt. Now I have pages and pages of grief and no words, not even repetition of the same word to fill them up with … I am covered with sticky flypaper. Fine roll-your-own cigarette paper, pasted, built up, pasted, built up, little unstuck bits flapping. White paper, soiled paper, now papier-mache and, lucky me, I have one jagged fingernail. Keep smiling. Keep picking. Lucky no one can hear you.

'No one can hear you!' I knew, irretrievably, that with those words I had found my point of entry to memory. The man in the blue jumper told me that no one could hear me.

That night, Nina had dinner with Vittorio and me. After the meal I was unaccountably hostile and snapped at her, 'Well you always reject anything I have to say.' Nina retreated to a book and I to tears.

Leaving, she said, 'Mum, I really do appreciate everything you do for me.'

'No you don't!'

Fuming, I picked up my patchwork and stabbed the needle through fabric. I'd tried to inform Vittorio about my childhood dilemma. He didn't appear to notice. I picked on him – snide, out-of-line comments – and he said in frustration, 'I don't know what you are trying to tell me.'

I replied sarcastically, 'I'll put it in a language, dear, you will understand. I was raped. I was eleven.'

Little holes like those running down stockings broke through and water seemed to pour from all. He held me. Pain overtook crumbling reserve. Tears rushed to the light. Vittorio took me in his arms and would have held me past the end of time.

I found the answer to two questions: two men.

The next day, crying and light-headed, acknowledgement undulated through my mind. Realisations rose, I savoured, rattled and waved them and endlessly repeated them.

Jane tells me that men of dangerous intent sometimes befriend families to gain access to the child; that men abuse children of the same emotional age as themselves.

Desperate for proof, I fantasised about visiting the Heidelberg Police Station where serious police would flick through dusty files and one old policeman would remember and give me a copy of a confession.

Fractured memories popped in and I made an effort to retain them. I had always remembered the events before and after; the photos, returning home behind our milk bar with my cowgirl outfit unclean.

Mum had reason to be upset with me when I was a child; my state of vagueness, the detachment behind my smile must have hurt her immensely. My cat's cradle teen years engulfed a wealth of anti-Mum stories. I had wafted this way and that with the influence of others.

I wondered if Mum would like to know why, so we had an imaginary chat:

'You remember the man over the road?'

'Oh, him, he just disappeared, never came over again, not a word as to why.'

'Well do you remember the doctor saying I had no hymen?'

'Do you remember the day I came home and my cowgirl outfit was filthy?'

Better the words are strangled. Mum braces. Her stillness hides the turbulence she can barely suffer. I am more than glad she knew not.

In the end I hope my vagueness became endearing to Mum and Dad. What would they have done? Dwelt in a quagmire of pain? They might have felt duty bound to go to the police. The nice man would call us liars, his family rise to his defence, neighbours doubt the accusation; after all, they had known him for years. And I would have been no help whatsoever.

That should have been the end, but the black days continued, and if not for my scattered notes I might have forgotten them. I wrote of isolated incidents like the feeling that I was being grabbed from behind (a flashback) and of my startled response.

My fragmented memory had opened itself up and closed up again. No nice narrative to appease, only scraps.

So I went and visited the past.

'Get out of the car,' Jane said.

In Heidelberg our old shop still stands. The backyard no longer exists, no length of fence to rattle a stick along. The theatre has been extended to form a reception centre and people celebrate on a vanished and little celebrated, garden.

I had forgotten the side door opposite the stairs leading to the private section and had a fleeting memory of a neat young man coming to escort me to a concert long ago. The other side door that theatre patrons once rushed through, had lost its knob and was covered in cobwebs.

Six men in overalls sat under the shop veranda, burly men in soft chairs at wonky plastic tables; big men, legs spread, gathered round, taking up the footpath like my parents' friends had once hogged the fire. I kept walking.

It's still dark, the place of a man and his blue jumper. Trees have been cut down for a car park but they still tower and surround it. Again, I was there where no one could hear me. I didn't stay. I walked back past the shop that was once home and saw through the upstairs window to the window at the back of my bedroom that shadows had chased themselves in, and I was immeasurably sad for the little girl who said that nothing happened.

Jane was right, you need to put your feet on the ground and walk it. Walking shakes the mind like light illuminating silk in a box full of holes.

cᴑ

When I returned again to Heidelberg the pain had eased … maybe one day it will, like raw eggs, slide away.

Memory, in its entirety, has not returned.

On the balance of probability – my fragmented flashes of memory, my broken hymen and behavioural change – he called my name, offered me lollies, grabbed me from behind, forced oral sex, broke my hymen with his fingers and then raped me, took me to his house and washed me, and then sent me home to our milk bar opposite the station.

❧

Another childhood place continued to haunt. It has tall eucalypts, peppercorns and conifers. Agapanthus, strong-rooted and passive, line the paths. Earth reeks, water flows, and grass eternally smells. It is not the glowing and beckoning place. This is where my dog Terry and I used to run, the park where I vowed to be brave in the face of danger.

I had always known that a child had been murdered there. I found myself often thinking about this dead child. I see her. She lies on the ground in a hollow like an upturned palm. Her clothes have fused with flesh. In winter she lies cold but in autumn leaves caress her, in summer branches protect her and, on windy days, grass strokes her. She lies on her back. One leg stretches in front of her, the other twists to one side. One arm is beside her body. The other reaches to her genitals. I see her so clearly.

In an instant I knew why I can. I was there. I am her.

Awareness quietly slipped to mind like a child talking to another small child and gently dancing.

On my 11th birthday, wearing my black and red cowgirl outfit I had tried to fight off a man whose penis first choked and whose body then suffocated me. I believed I was being murdered, the same as Shirley Collins. Part of me took flight and a new girl took my place on a changed course, a good little girl, just like my nana, whom no one would ever hurt.

In a beautiful and quiet place away from where I was attacked, I had created in my mind, a cenotaph, a marker for memory, an image and memory of a dead little girl. Something that would be there for me to grasp when I was ready. It had taken 50 years.

Although we are one, we remain separate. I still call her 'she'. Perhaps one day we will be one again. In the meantime I miss her so. She holds the secrets and the rage. We share the pain and I protect her; that's the least I can do for her.

My flatness lifted. I visited my memorial. My dog Terry yaps at my heels, so real ... I remember a ten-year-old child who pushed her bike to the top of the hill and free-wheeled down, crossing roads, legs spread out in front, alive with the sheer heart-stopping thrill of it all. I am finding her.

resources

Cult Information and Family Support (CIFS)

In The *Good Little Girl*, Annette Stephens brilliantly takes us on a journey engaging us with her openness and honesty. She combines and shares early childhood and family memories of her life growing up as an only child with an in-depth look at the personal experience of her journey and life within a group called Kenja.

It is captivating reading that allows the reader to understand about cults and learn how ordinary, intelligent, good people can come under the coercive influences of manipulation and psychological techniques known as 'mind control' or 'thought reform'; techniques that can result in people giving up their freedom, family and sometimes even their lives.

Cult Information and Family Support (CIFS) is a non profit organisation that began in New South Wales in 1996 to help and support families and those leaving and recovering from cult involvement. It started with a few people who had experienced the loss of family members into a cult. CIFS is run by volunteers who understand the devastating effect cults have on individuals, families and society.

The organisation has grown and along with New South Wales there are CIFS support groups in Queensland and Victoria, and support networks in other states. We keep in close contact with other groups around the world who also work in this area to support, educate, help and inform society about the many thousands of cults that exist and cause immeasurable harm to individuals families and ultimately societies.

Our web site offers help and information: www.cifs.org.au

Ros Hodgkins

President

CIFS (NSW)

Books

Combatting Cult Mind Control, The # 1 Best-selling Guide to Protection, Rescue and Recovery from Destructive Cults, Steven Hassan, Park Street Press, 1990

Freedom of Mind: Helping Loved Ones Leave Controlling People, Cults and Beliefs, Steve Hassan, Freedom of Mind Press, 2000, www.freedomofmind.com

Your Mind Body Energy, How to Access Your Hidden Energies and Take Control of Your Life, Louise Samways, Viking O'Neil/Penguin, 1992

Dangerous Persuaders, An expose of gurus, personal development courses and cults and how they operate, Louise Samways, 1994, Penguin, updated to e-book in 2007

about the author

Annette Stephens

Now retired and living happily in Melbourne with her husband, Annette has a Diploma of Teaching (Primary) and a Graduate Diploma of Media Studies.

Annette has spoken about her experience at a cult awareness conference attended by leading international anti-cult activist Stephen Hassan, and been interviewed for the documentary *Beyond Our Ken*. Annette is keen to finally share the story that has been 20 years in the telling, hoping it will in some way help others who find themselves dealing with similar issues.